W9-CMK-598

THE POETRY OF VACHEL LINDSAY

volume 2

DENNIS CAMP, editor

The Poetry of

Vachel Lindsay

complete & with Lindsay's drawings

newly edited by

DENNIS CAMP

volume 2

SPOON RIVER POETRY PRESS
PEORIA, ILLINOIS

MAY · 1986

ELMHURST COLLEGE LIBRARY

first edition

The Poetry of Vachel Lindsay, edited by Dennis Camp, copyright © 1985 by Spoon River Poetry Press. All rights reserved. No portion of this book may be reproduced without written permission, except for quotations embodied in reviews or scholarly articles and books.

Published by Spoon River Poetry Press; P. O. Box 1443; Peoria, Illinois 61655.

Typesetting by Tom Guttormsson, Minneota (MN) *Mascot*.

Cover design by David R. Pichaske.

Printing by D J Graphics, Peoria, and M & D Printing, Henry, Illinois.

ISBN 0-933180-67-5

This book is published in part with funds provided by The Illinois Arts Council, a state organization, and by the National Endowment for the Arts. Our many thanks.

Many of the poems and drawings in this book are reprinted from *The Tramp's Excuse and Other Poems; The Sangamon County Peace Advocate; The Spring Harbinger; Rhymes to Be Traded for Bread; General William Booth Enters into Heaven; The Congo and Other Poems; Adventures while Preaching the Gospel of Beauty; The Chinese Nightingale and Other Poems; The Golden Whales of California and Other Rhymes in the American Language;* and *Johnny Appleseed and Other Poems,* copyright 1914, 1916, 1917, 1920, 1923, 1925, 1928, 1929 by Macmillan Publishing Company, Inc.; renewed 1942, 1944, 1945, 1948, 1951, 1953 by Elizabeth C. Lindsay, and renewed 1956, 1957 by Nicholas C. Lindsay and Susan L. Russell (The Viscountess Amberly). Reprinted with permission of Macmillan. Other poems and drawings are printed with the permission of Nicholas Cave Lindsay, executor of the Lindsay estate.

Acknowledgments are due and gratefully made to the University of Virginia Library, Barrett Library, for permission to publish the reproduction of the Lindsay watercolor frontispiece and the following manuscript poems: "Come," "I Turned My Head Away," "The Massacre," "Going to the Sun. Waterfalls, Remembered Long After," "Now Comes a Cartoon Letter," "Avanel Boone Flies from the Hearthfire," "The Peacock's Daughter," "The Stars for Chandeliers," "My Bitter Rivals," "I Am Travelling Too Fast to Vote," "Young Daughter of the Ancient Sun," "Before the Oration," "Today There Is a Market for Pink Bubbles," "New Fashions," "In Praise of Wit," "Remarks by the Captain of a Tramp Steamer," "My New Singer, Sacajawea," and "Time Gives Me Strength Each Hour." The following poems were published in *Western Illinois Regional Studies* (Spring, 1979): "My Middle Name," "The Goodly, Strange Lanterns," "The Woman-Voter Comes," "Saturday Night in the Park," "The Anglo-Saxon Language," "St. Francis," "The Maggot, the Hyena and the Jackal," "Buddha Was a Prince," "The Girl with the Red Shawl," "The Christmas Ship," "What the Burro Said," "What the Sailor Said," "What the Court Jester Sang," and "What the Clock-Maker Said." "The Tree of Laughing Bells" frontispiece for volume one of this edition is a four-color reproduction of the original which is presently at the Lindsay home, 603 South Fifth Street in Springfield.

For Trula . . .

of the Palace of Eve

TABLE OF CONTENTS

See ''The Five Dragons'' (page 797).

The Poetry of

Vachel Lindsay

From THE VILLAGE MAGAZINE

Second Edition

June 1920

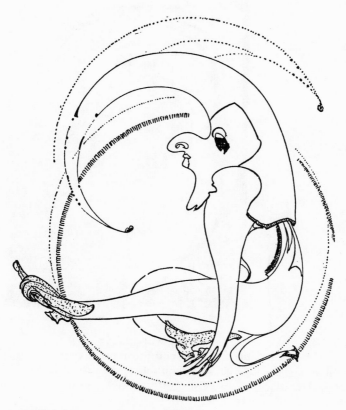

THE MOON IS A DEVIL–JESTER

VACHEL LINDSAY 1922

THE TRAVELLER

The Moon's a devil-jester
  Who makes himself too free.
The rascal is not always
  Where he appears to be:—
Sometimes he is in my heart—
  Sometimes in the sea.
Then tides are in my heart,
  And tides are in the sea.
O traveller! abiding not
  Where he pretends to be!

1920

A SONG IN JULY

A little bird has told me that today will appear
The lost land of Atlantis, so drowned for many a year.
With blue harbors for you, and mountain peaks for me,
Atlantis, Atlantis, the lost land of Atlantis,
Rising again from the sea!   5

There storms of raining attar drench
And drug the isle with calm.
And dawn will bring us cloud cups heaped
With lightning, spice and balm.
There we will rest from all old things,   10
From hot and long endeavor,
Two sages lost in glorious thought
And ocean dreams forever.
Come sail, O Sinbad, we shall tame
The waves between, in Allah's name.   15
Coral palaces for you,
Fog chalices for me,
Mohammed's girls for you
And Mab's girls for me,
Soft shore winds for you,   20
And mountain streams for me,
In Atlantis, Atlantis, the lost land of Atlantis,
Rising again from the sea!

       1910?

A PAGE OF OWLS

Old Judge Hoot Owl sits by his inkwell
Writing wills for the wealthy and swell.
He knows something he won't tell.
Three little house flies, drowned in his inkwell.
Three little scandals in a peanut shell.

There's a house in Carmi haunted by the ghosts of a
    thousand owls,
The wisdoms that died early in the family of the Sprowls.
They lived a hundred years, — to rob and sow and reap,
But never, since the town was built, thought a thought
    that's deep.
And so the owls keep hooting, and nip them in their sleep.

1920

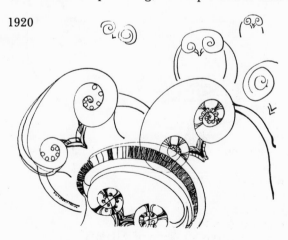

THE LAND HORSE AND THE SEA HORSE

The Land Horse
Everybody rides,
Until his eyes are dim.

The Sea Horse!
Every wave he rides.
  And nobody
Rides him.

1920

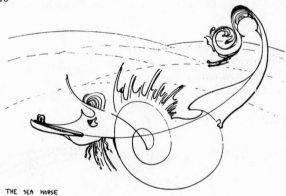

THE SEA HORSE

A PAGE OF DANGEROUS BEASTS

"I'm the bat from the Salt desert
I suck the clouds on high.
Until they turn to ashes
    And all the sky is dry."

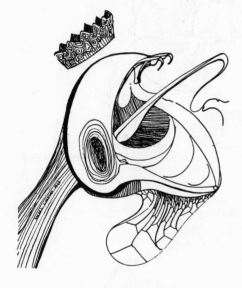

The King of the Chameleons
  Has a lying tongue.
Whoever trusts the king
    Is stung.

A big eared rat once heard a cat
  A mile away or more.
Alas the rat was eaten
  By a cat next door.

1920

THE BIG EARED RAT

GIRLS WE ALL KNOW

"Who is inferior to who?"
  Asked the snob when she came to the city.
"I want to know people to kick.
  I want to know people to pity."

A duck within the harem of a drake who ran for president
Swam in his parade, and made it an event.
She carried a big card of his footprints and she said: —
"He waddles like an arrow, straight ahead."

    1920

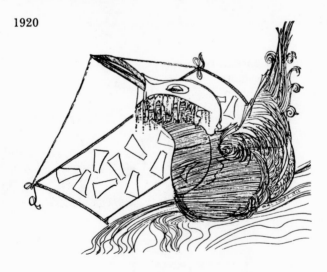

A NATURE STUDY PAGE

A cat with nine tails
Climbed from out the lagoon,
Escaped from the stone
They had tied to his middle:
And . . . .
      played . . . .
"Hey diddle diddle,"
Upon his old fiddle,
Till the cow once again
Jumped over the moon.

A meditative little deer
Watched a buzzard hatch her eggs;
And said to her:—
"I'd hate to have
Dirty wings and dirty legs,
And sit there hatching dirty
    little plagues."

1920

AN
IMAGIST

A FRANK CONTRIBUTION TO
CURRENT DISCUSSION

Did you ever see an imagist?
    I wonder what they are?
I'd rather see an imagist
    Than own a motor car.

    1920

FANTASY OF THE GOLDEN BOOK
AND ITS ESCORT

Tricking us, making our hearts their prey
The dreams of the dreams
With books of the dreams
Haunt the homes of the town this day;
The visions of the visions   5
With rhymes of the visions
Haunt the yards of the town this day;
The fairies of the fairies
With the flowers of the fairies
Haunt the factories of the town this day;   10
And we throw them kisses, and they fly away.

Tricking us, making our hearts their prey
The angels of the angels
With the flags of the angels
Haunt the clouds above the town this day: —   15
And we throw them kisses, and they fly away.

1920

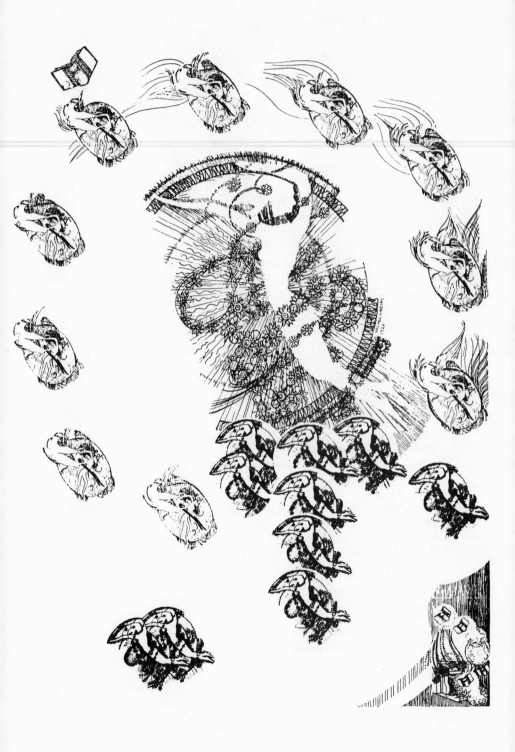

From COLLECTED POEMS

First Edition

Spring, 1923

I KNOW ALL THIS WHEN GIPSY FIDDLES CRY

Oh, gipsies, proud and stiff-necked and perverse,
Saying: "We tell the fortunes of the nations,
And revel in the deep palm of the world.
The head-line is the road we choose for trade.
The love-line is the lane wherein we camp.   5
The life-line is the road we wander on.
Mount Venus, Jupiter, and all the rest
Are finger-tips of ranges clasping round
And holding up the Romany's wide sky."
Oh, gipsies, proud and stiff-necked and perverse,   10
Saying: "We will swap horses till the doom,
And mend the pots and kettles of mankind,
And lend our sons to big-time vaudeville,
Or to the race-track, or the learned world.
But India's Brahma waits within their breasts.   15
They will return to us with gipsy grins,
And chatter Romany, and shake their curls
And hug the dirtiest babies in the camp.
They will return to the moving pillar of smoke,
The whitest toothed, the merriest laughers known,   20
The blackest haired of all the tribes of men.
What trap can hold such cats? The Romany
Has crossed such delicate palms with lead or gold,
Wheedling in sun and rain, through perilous years,
All coins now look alike. The palm is all.   25
Our greasy pack of cards is still the book
Most read of men. The heart's librarians,
We tell all lovers what they want to know.
So, out of the famed Chicago Library,
Out of the great Chicago orchestras,   30
Out of the skyscraper, the Fine Arts Building,
Our sons will come with fiddles and with loot,
Dressed, as of old, like turkey-cocks and zebras,
Like tiger-lilies and chameleons,
Go west with us to California,   35
Telling the fortunes of the bleeding world,
And kiss the sunset, ere their day is done."
Oh, gipsies, proud and stiff-necked and perverse
Picking the brains and pockets of mankind,
You will go westward for one-half hour yet.   40
You will turn eastward in a little while.
You will go back, as men turn to Kentucky,
Land of their fathers, dark and bloody ground.

When all the Jews go home to Syria,
When Chinese cooks go back to Canton, China,   45
When Japanese photographers return
With their black cameras to Tokio,
And Irish patriots to Donegal,
And Scotch accountants back to Edinburgh,
You will go back to India, whence you came.   50
When you have reached the borders of your quest,
Homesick at last, by many a devious way,
Winding the wonderlands circuitous,
By foot and horse will trace the long way back!
Fiddling for ocean liners, while the dance   55
Sweeps through the decks, your brown tribes all will go!
Those east-bound ships will hear your long farewell
On fiddle, piccolo, and flute and timbrel.
I know all this, when gipsy fiddles cry.

That hour of their homesickness, I myself   60
Will turn, will say farewell to Illinois,
To old Kentucky and Virginia,
And go with them to India, whence they came.
For they have heard a singing from the Ganges,
And cries of orioles, — from the temple caves, —   65
And Bengal's oldest, humblest villages.
They smell the supper smokes of Amritsar.
Green monkeys cry in Sanskrit to their souls
From lofty bamboo trees of hot Madras.
They think of towns to ease their feverish eyes,   70
And make them stand and meditate forever,
Domes of astonishment, to heal the mind.
I know all this, when gipsy fiddles cry.

What music will be blended with the wind
When gipsy fiddlers, nearing that old land,   75
Bring tunes from all the world to Brahma's house?
Passing the Indus, winding poisonous forests,
Blowing soft flutes at scandalous temple girls,
Filling the highways with their magpie loot,
What brass from my Chicago will they heap,   80
What gems from Walla Walla, Omaha,
Will they pile near the Bodhi Tree, and laugh?
They will dance near such temples as best suit them,
Though they will not quite enter, or adore,
Looking on roofs, as poets look on lilies,   85
Looking at towers, as boys at forest vines,

That leap to tree-tops through the dizzy air.
I know all this, when gipsy fiddles cry.

And with the gipsies there will be a king
And a thousand desperadoes just his style,   90
With all their rags dyed in the blood of roses,
Splashed with the blood of angels, and of demons.
And he will boss them with an awful voice.
And with a red whip he will beat his wife.
He will be wicked on that sacred shore,   95
And rattle cruel spurs against the rocks,
And shake Calcutta's walls with circus bugles.
He will kill Brahmins there, in Kali's name.
And please the thugs, and blood-drunk of the earth.
I know all this, when gipsy fiddles cry.   100

Oh, sweating thieves, and hard-boiled scalawags,
That still will boast your pride until the doom,
Smashing every caste rule of the world,
Reaching at last your Hindu goal to smash
The caste rules of old India, and shout: 105
"Down with the Brahmins, let the Romany reign."

When gipsy girls look deep within my hand
They always speak so tenderly and say
That I am one of those star-crossed to wed
A princess in a forest fairy-tale.   110
So there will be a tender gipsy princess,
My Juliet, shining through this clan.
And I would sing you of her beauty now.
And I will fight with knives the gipsy man
Who tries to steal her wild young heart away.   115
And I will kiss her in the waterfalls,
And at the rainbow's end, and in the incense
That curls about the feet of sleeping gods,
And sing with her in canebrakes and in rice fields,
In Romany, eternal Romany.   120
We will sow secret herbs, and plant old roses,
And fumble through dark, snaky palaces,
Stable our ponies in the Taj Mahal,
And sleep outdoors ourselves.
In her strange fairy mill-wheel eyes will wait   125
All windings and unwindings of the highways,
From India, across America,—
All windings and unwindings of my fancy,

All windings and unwindings of all souls,
All windings and unwindings of the heavens.   130
I know all this, when gipsy fiddles cry.

We gipsies, proud and stiff-necked and perverse,
Standing upon the white Himalayas,
Will think of far divine Yosemite.
We will heal Hindu hermits there with oil   135
Brought from California's tall sequoias.
And we will be like gods that heap the thunders,
And start young redwood trees on Time's own mountains,
We will swap horses with the rising moon,
And mend that funny skillet called Orion,   140
Color the stars like San Francisco's street-lights,
And paint our sign and signature on high
In planets like a bed of crimson pansies;
While a million fiddles shake all listening hearts,
Crying good fortune to the Universe,   145
Whispering adventure to the Ganges waves,
And to the spirits, and all winds and gods.
Till mighty Brahma puts his golden palm
Within the gipsy king's great striped tent,
And asks his fortune told by that great love-line   150
That winds across his palm in splendid flame.

Only the hearthstone of old India
Will end the endless march of gipsy feet.
I will go back to India with them
When they go back to India whence they came.   155
I know all this, when gipsy fiddles cry.

        Winter, 1920-1921

HAMLET

    (Remembering how Walker Whiteside played Hamlet in
Chatterton's Old Opera House, thirty years ago.)

Horatio took me to the cliff
Upon the edge of things
And said: "Behold a cataract
Of the thrones of old dream kings."
And I saw the thrones falling   5
From the high stars to the deep:
Red thrones, green thrones,

To everlasting sleep.
I saw crowns falling
From the zenith to the pit: 10
Crowns of man's mighty moods
And whims of little wit.
And all the birds of Elsinore
Flew round Horatio's head
And crying said: —   15
"Though all the crowns go down,
Hamlet, Hamlet, will never lose his crown."

Oh, monarchs muddled, stabbed and lost,
Who have no more to say:
Gone with Caesar, with the Czar,   20
And the Kaiser on his way!
But now I see a student-prince
More real than all such kings,
Hamlet, home from Wittenberg,
And every bird sings: —   25
"Though all the crowns go down,
Hamlet, Hamlet, will never lose his crown."

Some of the dreams we saw dethroned
Were merely hopes of mine: —
One that a child might love me,   30
And give one leaf for a sign;
One dream I had in babyhood
That my rag-doll was alive;
One that I had in boyhood
That a sparrow, caged, would thrive.   35
One that I had for years and years
That my church held no disgrace.
One that I had but yesterday: —
Faith in Wisdom's face.

Oh, royal crowns, falling fast   40
From the days of boy's delight,
The frost-bright time when first I made
A giant snow-man white.
And the time of my first Christmas tree,
My first Thanksgiving Day,   45
My first loud Independence dawn
When the cannon blazed away. . . .
Oh, high fantastic hours
That died like dog and clown,
Into the awful pit   50
We saw their crowns go down,

But Hamlet, Hamlet, will never lose his crown.

As sages walk with sages
On the proud Socratic way,
Hamlet struts with players   55
Till the world's last day.
With seeming shameless strollers
He swaggers his black cloak,
With a prince's glittering eye.
He spoils the townsmen's joke.   60
As I watch him and attend him
He compels them to give room,
And makes Fifth Street out battlement
Against the shades of doom.
With poetry, authority,   65
With every known pride,
Hamlet stands with drawn sword,
His Gypsies at his side.

And all the gardens of the town
Are but Ophelia's flowers,   70
And all the shades of Elsinore
Fly round our Springfield towers;
And Hamlet kneels by all the hearts
That truly bleed or bloom,
As saints do stations of the cross   75
To Christ's white tomb.
And all the birds keep singing
To my heart bowed down:
"Hamlet, Hamlet, will never lose his crown."

        1920

IN PRAISE OF JOHNNY APPLESEED*
(Born 1775; died 1847)

        I. *Over the Appalachian Barricade*

In the days of President Washington,
The glory of the nations,
Dust and ashes,
Snow and sleet,
And hay and oats and wheat,
Blew west,

*To be read like
old leaves on
the elm tree of
Time, Sifting
soft winds with
sentence and rhyme.*
                                                         5

*The best account of John Chapman's career, under the
name "Johnny Appleseed," is to be found in *Harper's
Monthly Magazine*, November, 1871.

Crossed the Appalachians,
Found the glades of rotting leaves, the soft
    deer-pastures,
The farms of the far-off future
In the forest.   10
Colts jumped the fence,
Snorting, ramping, snapping, sniffing,
With gastronomic calculations,
Crossed the Appalachians,
The east walls of our citadel,   15
And turned to gold-horned unicorns,
Feasting in the dim, volunteer farms of the
    forest.
Stripedest, kickingest kittens escaped,
Caterwauling "Yankee Doodle Dandy,"
Renounced their poor relations,   20
Crossed the Appalachians,
And turned to tiny tigers
In the humorous forest.
Chickens escaped
From farmyard congregations,   25
Crossed the Appalachians,
And turned to amber trumpets
On the ramparts of our Hoosiers' nest and citadel,
Millennial heralds
Of the foggy mazy forest.   30
Pigs broke loose, scrambled west,
Scorned their loathsome stations,
Crossed the Appalachians,
Turned to roaming, foaming wild boars
Of the forest.   35
The smallest, blindest puppies toddled west
While their eyes were coming open,
And, with misty observations,
Crossed the Appalachians,
Barked, barked, barked   40
At the glow-worms and the marsh lights and the
    lightning-bugs
And turned to ravening wolves
Of the forest.
Crazy parrots and canaries flew west,
Drunk on May-time revelations,   45
Crossed the Appalachians,
And turned to delirious, flower-dressed fairies
Of the lazy forest.
Haughtiest swans and peacocks swept west,
And, despite soft derivations,   50

Crossed the Appalachians,
And turned to blazing warrior souls
Of the forest,
Singing the ways
Of the Ancient of Days.   55
And the "Old Continentals
In their ragged regimentals,"
With bard's imaginations,
Crossed the Appalachians.
And   60
A boy
Blew west,
And with prayers and incantations,
And with "Yankee Doodle Dandy,"
Crossed the Appalachians,   65
And was "young John Chapman,"
Then
"Johnny Appleseed, Johnny Appleseed,"
Chief of the fastnesses, dappled and vast,
In a pack on his back,   70
In a deer-hide sack,
The beautiful orchards of the past,
The ghosts of all the forests and the groves—
In that pack on his back,
In that talisman sack,   75
Tomorrow's peaches, pears, and cherries,
Tomorrow's grapes and red raspberries,
Seeds and tree-souls, precious things,
Feathered with microscopic wings,
All the outdoors the child heart knows,   80
And the apple, green, red, and white,
Sun of his day and his night—
The apple allied to the thorn,
Child of the rose.
Porches untrod of forest houses   85
All before him, all day long,
"Yankee Doodle" his marching song;
And the evening breeze
Joined his psalms of praise
As he sang the ways   90
Of the Ancient of Days.
Leaving behind august Virginia,
Proud Massachusetts, and proud Maine,
Planting the trees that would march and train
On, in his name to the great Pacific,   95
Like Birnam wood to Dunsinane,
Johnny Appleseed swept on,

Every shackle gone,
Loving every sloshy brake,
Loving every skunk and snake,   100
Loving every leathery weed,
Johnny Appleseed, Johnny Appleseed,
Master and ruler of the unicorn-ramping forest,
The tiger-mewing forest,
The rooster-trumpeting, boar-foaming,
    wolf-ravening forest,   105
The spirit-haunted forest, fairy-enchanted,
Stupendous and endless,
Searching its perilous ways
In the name of the Ancient of Days.

    II. *The Indians Worship Him, But He Hurries On*

Painted kings in the midst of the clearing   110
Heard him asking his friends the eagles
To guard each planted seed and seedling.
Then he was a god, to the red man's dreaming;
Then the chiefs brought treasures grotesque
    and fair, —
Magical trinkets and pipes and guns,   115
Beads and furs from their medicĭne-lair, —
Stuck holy feathers in his hair.
Hailed him with austere delight.
The orchard god was their guest through the night.

While the late snow blew from bleak Lake Erie,   120
Scourging rock and river reed,
All night long they made great medicine
For Jonathan Chapman,
Johnny Appleseed,
Johnny Appleseed;   125
And as though his heart were a wind-blown
    wheat-sheaf,
As though his heart were a new built nest,
As though their heaven house were his breast,
In swept the snowbirds singing glory.
And I hear his bird heart beat its story,   130
Hear yet how the ghost of the forest shivers,
Hear yet the cry of the gray, old orchards,
Dim and decaying by the rivers,
And the timid wings of the bird-ghosts
    beating,
And the ghosts of the tom-toms beating,
    beating.   135

But he left their wigwams and their love.
By the hour of dawn he was proud and stark,
Kissed the Indian babes with a sigh,
Went forth to live on roots and bark,
Sleep in the trees, while the years howled by.
Calling the catamounts by name,
And buffalo bulls no hand could tame.
Slaying never a living creature,
Joining the birds in every game,
With the gorgeous turkey gobblers mocking,
With the lean-necked eagles boxing and
    shouting;
Sticking their feathers in his hair, —
Turkey feathers,
Eagle feathers,
Trading hearts with all beasts and weathers
He swept on, winged and wonder-crested,
Bare-armed, barefooted, and bare-breasted.
The maples, shedding their spinning seeds,
Called to his appleseeds in the ground,
Vast chestnut-trees, with their butterfly nations,
Called to his seeds without a sound.
And the chipmunk turned a "summerset."
And the foxes danced the Virginia reel;
Hawthorn and crab-thorn bent, rain-wet,
And dropped their flowers in his night-black
    hair;
And the soft fawns stopped for his perorations
And his black eyes shone through the forest-
    gleam,
And he plunged young hands into new-turned
    earth,
And prayed dear orchard boughs into birth;
And he ran with the rabbit and slept with the
    stream,
And he ran with the rabbit and slept with the
    stream,
And he ran with the rabbit and slept with the
    stream.
And so for us he made great medicine,
And so for us he made great medicine,
And so for us he made great medicine,
In the days of President Washington.

*While you read,
hear the hoof-
beats of deer
in the snow.
And see, by
their track,
bleeding foot-
prints we know.*

145

150

*While you read
see conventions
of deer go by.
The bucks toss
their horns, the
fuzzy fawns fly.*

160

165

170

III. *Johnny Appleseed's Old Age*

Long, long after,
When settlers put up beam and rafter,
They asked of the birds: "Who gave this
   fruit?
Who watched this fence till the seeds took
   root?
Who gave these boughs?" They asked the
   sky,
And there was no reply.
But the robin might have said,
"To the farthest West he has followed the
   sun,
His life and his empire just begun."
Self-scourged, like a monk, with a throne for
   wages,
Stripped, like the iron-souled Hindu sages,
Draped like a statue, in strings like a scare-
   crow,
His helmet-hat an old tin pan,
But worn in the love of the heart of man,
More sane than the helm of Tamerlane!
Hairy Ainu, wild man of Borneo, Robinson
   Crusoe—Johnny Appleseed!
And the robin might have said,
"Sowing, he goes to the far, new West,
With the apple, the sun of his burning
   breast—
The apple allied to the thorn,
Child of the rose."

Washington buried in Virginia,
Jackson buried in Tennessee,
Young Lincoln, brooding in Illinois,
And Johnny Appleseed, priestly and free,
Knotted and gnarled, past seventy years,
Still planted on in the woods alone.
Ohio and young Indiana—
These were his wide altar-stone,
Where still he burnt out flesh and bone.
Twenty days ahead of the Indian, twenty years ahead of
   the white man,
At last the Indian overtook him, at last the Indian
   hurried past him;
At last the white man overtook him, at last the white
   man hurried past him;

175
*To be read like
faint hoof-beats
of fawns long
gone From re-
spectable
pasture, and
park and lawn,
And heart-beats
of fawns that
are coming again
When the forest
once more, is
the master of men.*
185

190

195

200

At last his own trees overtook him, at last his own trees
   hurried past him.   205
Many cats were tame again,
Many ponies tame again,
Many pigs were tame again,
Many canaries tame again;
And the real frontier was his sunburnt breast.   210
From the fiery core of that apple, the earth,
Sprang apple-amaranths divine.
Love's orchards climbed to the heavens of the West.
And snowed the earthly sod with flowers.
Farm hands from the terraces of the blest   215
Danced on the mists with their ladies fine;
And Johnny Appleseed laughed with his dreams,
And swam once more the ice-cold streams.
And the doves of the spirit swept through the hours,
With doom-calls, love-calls, death-calls, dream-calls;   220
And Johnny Appleseed, all that year,
Lifted his hands to the farm-filled sky,
To the apple-harvesters busy on high;
And so once more his youth began,
And so for us he made great medicine—   225
Johnny Appleseed, medicine-man.
Then
The sun was his turned-up broken barrel,
Out of which his juicy apples rolled,
Down the repeated terraces,   230
Thumping across the gold,
An angel in each apple that touched the forest mold,
A ballot-box in each apple,
A state capital in each apple,
Great high schools, great colleges,   235
All America in each apple,
Each red, rich, round, and bouncing moon
That touched the forest mold.
Like scrolls and rolled-up flags of silk,
He saw the fruits unfold,   240
And all our expectations in one wild-flower written dream.
Confusion, and death-sweetness, and a thicket of
   crab-thorns!
Heart of a hundred midnights, heart of the merciful
   morns.
Heaven's boughs bent down with their alchemy,
Perfumed airs, and thoughts of wonder.   245
And the dew on the grass and his own cold tears
Were one in brooding mystery,

Though death's loud thunder came upon him,
Though death's loud thunder struck him down—
The boughs and the proud thoughts swept through the
    thunder, 250
Till he saw our wide nation, each State a flower,
Each petal a park for holy feet,
With wild fawns merry on every street,
With wild fawns merry on every street,
The vista of ten thousand years, flower-lighted
    and complete. 255

And there stood by his side, as he died:
Buddha, St. Francis; no others could praise him.
They were there, in the name of the Ancient of Days.

Hear the lazy weeds murmuring, bays and rivers
    whispering,
From Michigan to Texas, California to Maine; 260
Listen to the eagles screaming, calling,
"Johnny Appleseed, Johnny Appleseed,"
There by the doors of old Fort Wayne.
In the four-poster bed Johnny Appleseed built,
Autumn rains were the curtains, autumn leaves were
    the quilt. 265
He laid him down sweetly, and slept through the night,
Like a stone washed white,
There by the doors of old Fort Wayne.

    1920-1921

LITANY OF THE HEROES

    Being a chant about many historical characters in chrono-
logical order, but with Woodrow Wilson and Socrates as the
ultimate and final heroes of the song.

Would that young Amenophis Fourth returned,   *Egypt and*
Prince Hamlet and the Poet Keats in one;   *Israel in*
He mocked at fraud, even his own crown;   *History.*
He loved all classic beauty in the town;
He rode abroad to build his lotos tomb,   5
Praising one god, and that one god, the sun.
The idol-worshippers chipped out his name
From wall and obelisk, to end his fame.

Still let that brave, flower-loving King of Time
Be throned in your deep hearts, to raise for you   10
The hopes the prince and his mother Thi, well knew,
Filling these barren days with Mystery,
With Life, and Death, and Immortality,
The devouring ages, the triumphant Sun.
God keep us brooding on eternal things,   15
God make us wizard-kings.

Then let us raise that Egypt-nurtured youth,
Son of a Hebrew, with the dauntless scorn
And hate for bleating gods Egyptian-born,
Showing with signs to stubborn Mizraim   20
"God is one God, the God of Abraham,"
He who in the beginning *made* the Sun.
God send us Moses from his hidden grave,
God help us to be brave.

Would we were scholars of Confucius' time   25
Watching the feudal China crumbling down,   *The Soul of*
Frightening our master, shaking many a crown,   *China in*
Until he makes more firm the father sages,   *History.*
Restoring custom from the earliest ages
With prudent sayings, golden as the sun.   30
Lord, show us safe, august, established ways,
Fill us with yesterdays.

Would that by Hindu magic we became
Dark monks of jewelled India long ago,
Sitting at Prince Siddhartha's feet to know   35
The foolishness of gold and love and station,   *The Soul of*
The gospel of the Great Renunciation,   *India in*
The ragged cloak, the staff, the rain and sun,   *History.*
The beggar's life, with far Nirvana gleaming:
Lord, make us Buddhas, dreaming.   40

Would that the joy of living came today,
Even as sculptured on Athena's shrine   *The Classic*
In sunny conclave of serene design,   *Spirit.*
Maidens and men, procession, flute and feast,
By Phidias, the ivory-hearted priest   45
Of beauty absolute, whose eyes the sun
Showed goodlier forms than our desires can guess
And more of happiness.

Would I might waken in you Alexander,
Murdering the nations wickedly,   50
Flooding his time with blood remorselessly,
Sowing new Empires, where the Athenian light,
Knowledge and music, slay the Asian night,
And men behold Apollo in the sun.
God make us splendid, though by grievous wrong.   55
God make us fierce and strong.

Would I might rouse the Caesar in you all
(That which men hail as king, and bow them down),
Till you are crowned, or you refuse the crown.
Would I might wake the valor and the pride,   60
The eagle soul with which he soared and died,
Entering grandly then the fearful grave.
God help us build the world, like master-men,
God help us to be brave.

Behold the Pharisees, proud, rich, and damned,   65
Boasting themselves in lost Jerusalem,
Gathered a weeping woman to condemn,   *Religion in*
Then watching curiously, without a sound,   *History.*
The God of Mercy, writing on the ground.
How looked his sunburned face beneath the sun   70
Flushed with his Father's mighty angel-wine?
God make us all divine.

Would I might free St. Paul, singing in chains
In your deep hearts. New heavenly love shall fight
And slay the subtle gods of Greek delight   75
And dreadful Roman gods, and light the world
With words of flame, till those false powers are hurled
Burning to ashes in the avenging grave.
"St. Paul" our battle-cry, and faith our shield,
God help us to be brave.   80

Yea, give the world no peace, till all men kneel,
Seeking with tears the grace of Christ our God.
Make us like Augustine beneath Thy rod.
Give us no other joy but Thy repentance,
Thunder our just, hereditary sentence   85
Till shame and fear of Hell blot out the sun.
Christ help us hold Thy blood-redemption dear.
Christ, give us holy fear.

Nay, let us have the marble peace of Rome,
Recorded in the Code Justinian,   90
Till Pagan Justice shelters man from man.
Fanatics snarl like mongrel dogs; the code   *The Secular*
Will build each custom like a Roman Road,   *Spirit in*
Direct as daylight, clear-eyed as the sun.   *History.*
God grant all crazy world-disturbers cease.   95
God give us honest peace.

Would that on horses swifter than desire   *The World-*
We rode behind Mohammed round the zones   *Spirit of*
With swords unceasing, sowing fields of bones,   *Islam.*
Till New America, ancient Mizraim,   100
Cry: "Allah is the God of Abraham."
God make our host relentless as the sun,
Each soul your spear, your banner and your slave,
God help us to be brave.

Would I might wake St. Francis in you all,   105
Brother of birds and trees, God's Troubadour,   *The Medieval*
Blinded with weeping for the sad and poor;   *Spirit in*
Our wealth undone, all strict Franciscan men,   *History.*
Come, let us chant the canticle again
Of mother earth and the enduring sun.   110
God make each soul the lonely leper's slave;
God make us saints, and brave.

Would we were lean and grim, and shaken with hate
Like Dante, fugitive, o'er-wrought with cares,
And climbing bitterly the stranger's stairs,   115
Yet Love, Love, Love, divining: finding still
Beyond dark Hell the penitential hill,
And blessed Beatrice beyond the grave.
Jehovah lead us through the wilderness;
God make our wandering brave.   120

Would that we had the fortunes of Columbus.
Sailing his caravels a trackless way,
He found a Universe—he sought Cathay.
God give such dawns as when, his venture o'er,
The Sailor looked upon San Salvador.   125
God lead us past the setting of the sun
To wizard islands, of august surprise;
God make our blunders wise.

Would that such hills and cities round us sang,
Such vistas of the actual earth and man   130
As kindled Titian when his life began;
Would that this latter Greek could put his gold,   *Great Art*
Wisdom and splendor in our brushes bold   *and Letters*
Till Greece and Venice, children of the sun,   *in History.*
Become our everyday, and we aspire   135
To colors fairer far, and glories higher.

Would I might wake in you the whirlwind soul
Of Michelangelo, who hewed the stone
And Night and Day revealed, whose arm alone
Could draw the face of God, the titan high   140
Whose genius smote like lightning from the sky—
And shall he mold like dead leaves in the grave?
Nay, he is in us! Let us dare and dare.
God help us to be brave.

Would that in body and spirit Shakespeare came   145
Visible emperor of the deeds of Time,
With Justice still the genius of his rhyme,
Giving each man his due, each passion grace,
Impartial as the rain from Heaven's face
Or sunshine from the Heaven-enthroned sun.   150
Sweet Swan of Avon, come to us again.
Teach us to write, and writing, to be men.

Would that the lying rulers of the world
Were brought to block for tyrannies abhorred.
Would that the sword of Cromwell and the Lord,   155
The sword of Joshua and Gideon,   *The Ironside*
Hewed hip and thigh the hosts of Midian.   *Ideal in*
God send that ironside ere tomorrow's sun;   *History.*
Let Gabriel and Michael with him ride.
God send the Regicide.   160

Would we were blind with Milton, and we sang
With him of uttermost Heaven in a new song,
That men might see again the angel-throng,
And newborn hopes, true to this age, would rise,
Pictures to make men weep for paradise,   165
All glorious things beyond the defeated grave.
God smite us blind, and give us bolder wings;
God help us to be brave.

Would that the cold adventurous Corsican
Woke with new hope of glory, strong from sleep   170
Instructed how to conquer and to keep   *The Napoleonic*
More justly, having dreamed awhile, yea crowned   *Ideal in*
With shining flowers, God-given; while the sound   *History.*
Of singing continents, following the sun,
Calls freeborn men to guard Napoleon's throne,   175
Who makes the eternal hopes of man his own.

                                                        The Eye of
Would that the dry hot wind called Science came,   *Science in*
Forerunner of a higher mystic day,   *History.*
Though vile machine-made commerce clear the way—
Though nature losing shame should lose her veil,   180
And ghosts of buried angel-warriors wail
The fall of Heaven, and the relentless Sun
Smile on, as Abraham's God forever dies—
Lord, give us Darwin's eyes!

Would I might rouse the Lincoln in you all,   185
That which is gendered in the wilderness   *The American*
From lonely prairies and God's tenderness.   *Spirit in*
Imperial soul, star of a weedy stream,   *History.*
Born where the ghosts of buffaloes still gleam,
Whose spirit hoof-beats storm above his grave,   190
Above that breast of earth and prairie-fire—
Fire that freed the slave.

Then let us seek out shining Emerson,
Teacher of Whitman, and better priest of man,
The self-reliant granite American.   195
Give us his Heaven-sent right to strike and spare,
Give us the wools and hair-shirts prophets wear,
Then Adam's freedom in the Eden-sun.
God help us make each state an Eden-flower,
And blaze long trails to power.   200

These were the spacious days of Roosevelt.
Would that among you chiefs like him arose
To win the wrath of our united foes,
To chain King Mammon in the donjon-keep,
To rouse our godly citizens that sleep   205
Till, as one soul, we shout up to the sun
The battle-yell of freedom and the right—
"Lord, let good men unite."

Nay, I would have you lonely and despised.
Statesmen whom only statesmen understand,   210
Artists whom only artists can command,
Sages whom all but sages scorn, whose fame
Dies down in lies, in synonyms for shame
With the best populace beneath the sun.
God give us tasks that martyrs can revere,   215
Still too much hated to be whispered here.

Yea, I would have you like stern Woodrow Wilson,   *The Conclusion*
Drinking his cup, as such proud men have done   *and the*
Since Amenophis Fourth addressed the sun,   *Ultimate and*
Staking his last strength and his final fight   *Final Heroes*
That cost him all, to set the old world right.   *of this Song:*
The League of Nations' course is yet to run.   *Wilson and*
The Idol-worshippers would end its fame,   *Socrates.*
And cut from every wall its builder's name.

Would we might drink, with knowledge high and kind,   225
The hemlock cup of Socrates the king,
Knowing right well we know not anything,
With full life done, bowing before the law,
Binding young thinkers' hearts with loyal awe,
And fealty fixed as the ever-enduring sun —   230
God let us live, seeking the highest light:
God help us die aright.

Nay, I would have you grand, and still forgotten,
Hid like the stars at noon, as he who set
The Egyptian magic of man's alphabet;   235
Or that Egyptian, first to dream in pain
That dauntless souls cannot by death be slain—
Conquering for all men then the fearful grave.
God keep us hid, yet vaster far than death.
God help us to be brave.   240

        1907-1908

WHAT THE CLOWN SAID

"The moon's a paper jumping hoop,"
    Went on the circus clown,
"A film of gilded nonesense
    For the games of Angel-town.

"If I could break those horses   5
   That gallop through my sleep,
I'd reach that aggravating hoop
   And make my finest leap.

"I climb upon their backs, and ride,
   But always slip too soon . . .   10
And fall and wake, when just one mile
   Remains to reach the moon."

        Summer, 1912

BEING THE DEDICATION OF A MORNING
   To Hilda Conkling, Poet

Eyes of the eagle are yours, eyes of the dove are yours,
Heart of the robin is yours, heart of the woods is yours.
The long hair of Mab is yours. The long hair of Eve is
    yours.
And you are a cool clear river at play,
A river of light, that sweeps through the breast: —   5
Of healing and power,
That surely cures.
And I am young as Hilda today,
And all heavy years are hurried away,
And only the light and fire endures.   10

I am a trout in this river of light,
A cataract,
Or a pool,
A wave, or a thought, that curls and whirls,
Because of these magical silly reasons: —   15
You are all our birds, and all our seasons,
And all our hopes, and all little girls,
In one little lady, very polite,
The doll and the darling and boy of the forest,
The fern that is tallest, the dawn the heart fears,   20
All the stars of the morning in my sight.
Eyes of the eagle are yours. Eyes of the dove are yours,
Oh Hilda, singer, America bringer,
The prophets have told us ten thousand years—
Only the light of life endures   25
So I here deny sorrow,
And here denounce tears,
Only the light of life endures.

        1923

TO A GOLDEN-HAIRED GIRL IN A LOUISIANA TOWN

You are a sunrise,
If a star should rise instead of the sun.
You are a moonrise,
If a star should come, in the place of the moon.
You are the Spring,   5
If a face should bloom,
Instead of an apple-bough.
You are my love
If your heart is as kind
As your young eyes now.   10

    March 1920

GOING-TO-THE-SUN

Fall, 1923

WE START WEST FOR THE WATERFALLS

Tricking us, making our hearts their prey,
The dreams of the dreams, with books of the
    dreams,
Haunt the homes of the town this day;
The visions of rivers, with rhymes of the waterfalls,
Haunt the yards of the town this day;   5
The fairies of the fairies, with the flowers of the
    fairies,
Haunt the factories of the town this day;
And we throw them kisses, and they fly away.

Tricking us, making our hearts their prey,
The angels of the angels, with the flags of the
    angels,   10
Haunt the clouds above the town this day,
And we throw them kisses and they fly away.
And they call us west to the glacial mountains,
To the mines that are books, to the natural
    fountains.

1920

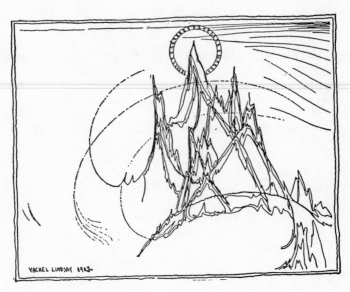

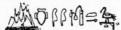

GOING-TO-THE-SUN

The mountain peak called "Going-To-The-Sun,"
In Glacier Park,
Is the most gorgeous one,
And when the sun comes down to it, it glows
With emerald and rose.

1921-1922

THE MYSTIC ROOSTER OF THE MONTANA SUNRISE

On the mountain peak, called ''Going-To-The-Sun,''
I saw the rooster that no storm can tame,
The center of the sun was but his eye,
His comb was but the sun rays and the flame.
·There in the Glacier Park, above white glaciers,   5

There, above Montana and the west,
He crowed and called his boast around the world,
Emotion shook his red embroidered vest.
There is humor in the very biggest rooster,
But even more magnificence than fun.   10
I laugh because he acted like a rooster,
I am solemn, for he was the biggest one.
I like a rooster or a turkey gobbler,
I like their forthright impudence at times.
They are neither larks, nor trilling nightingales,   15
And yet they always sing in splendid rhymes.
When I heard the vast bird of the sunrise crying,
The world held not one inch of silly prose.
Any rooster is a flowerlike fowl,
And this one was a crimson Yankee rose.   20

        1921-1922

THE BIRD CALLED "CURIOSITY"

Round the mountain peak called "Going-To-The-Sun,"
In Glacier Park, a steep and soaring one,
Circled a curious bird with pointed nose
Who led us on to every cave, and rose
And swept through every cloud, then brought us berries,   5
And all the acid gifts the mountain carries,
And let us guess which ones were good to eat.
And even when we slept his sharp wings beat
The weary fire, or shook the tree-top cones,
Or rattled dead twigs like a fairy's bones.   10
The vulgar bird, "Curiosity"! When we
Were tired, and lean, and shaking at the knee,
We put this bird in harness. He was strong
As any ostrich, pulled our packs along,
Helped us up over the next annoying wall,   15
And dragged us to the chalet, and the tourists' resting hall.

And when once more we were young, well-fed men,
He beat the door to call us forth again.

        1921-1922

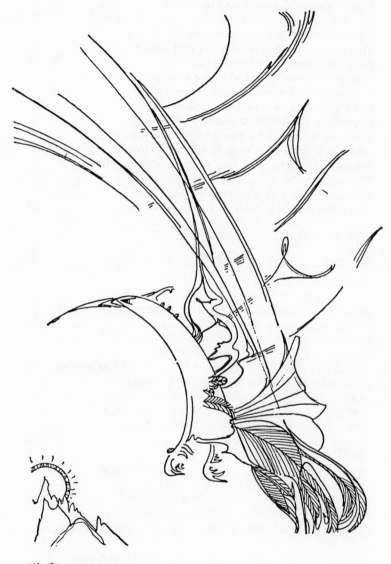

VACHEL LINDSAY 1922

THE THISTLEVINE

The Thistlevine saw the butterflies
Disappear through the morning skies.

1921-1922

AND THEY LAUGHED

By the mountain peak, called "Going-To-The-Sun,"
A dizzy mountain, where paths twist round and round
And nothing in sober order can be found—
I asked the poppies: "What fairies do you see?"
And they shook their long stems, and they laughed at me.

1921-1922

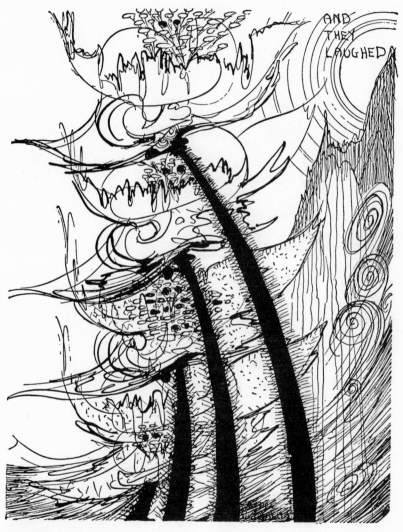

THE FAIRY CIRCUS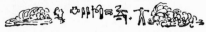

A fairy ran a circus
  With a pigeon puffed and proud,
A humble bullfrog
  And a rather solid cloud.

She wore her underwear,   5
  The rest wore what they had,
The frog wore a blue coat
  Just like his dad.

The pigeon wore his feathers
  And spread himself—O My!   10
The cloud wore sunshine
  He gathered in the sky.

    1921-1922

THE BATTLE-AX OF THE SUN

On the mountain peak I reached the drift
And I took it for a Christmas gift,
And I made ten soldiers out of snow.

But the battle-ax of my fairy foe
Cut to the ground my men of snow.   5

And who was he, my fairy foe,
Who brought my snowy army low?

The mountain sun was my fairy foe.

1921-1922

THE CHRISTMAS TREES

On the high slope of Going-To-The-Sun
Is a stormy Christmas, all year round,
And snow-filled Christmas trees abound.

1921-1922

THE PHEASANT SPEAKS OF HIS BIRTHDAYS

Up the good slope of Going-To-The-Sun,
I saw the Pheasant-Of-The-Sunrise fly.
Jewels in his feathers, mixed with dew.
Dew and jewels made his jeweled eye.
He paused to make a sonnet, which he sang,   5
Though nowhere else are pheasants sonneteers.
He emphasized with swooping and with skipping,
With winkings and intoxicated leers.
And how the bushes twinkled as he caroled:

"Each morning is another birthday, friend.   10
And I have lived so many happy birthdays!
There are gifts with all the suns that here ascend!
Each bush, you see, has an unextinguished candle

And angel-food, and icing, and candy flowers,
And this long vine that climbs from earth to heaven   15
Gives me thoughts, and most erratic powers.
I eat its scarlet berries and its frosting.
If I choose, it is my present every day.
Then I can fly straight up to heaven's doorstep
Following the green line all the way.   20

"And then I tumble like a limber leaf
To my nest here, and another year is done
Or another thousand years, what does it matter
On the mountain peak called 'Going-To-The-Sun'?"

1921-1922

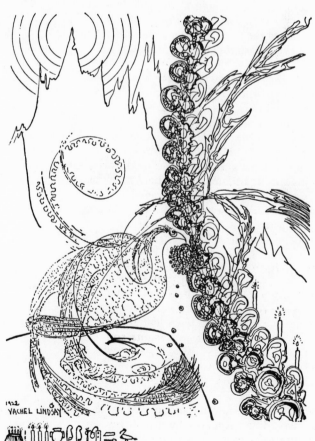

THE MYSTIC UNICORN OF THE MONTANA SUNSET

On the mountain peak, called "Going-To-The-Sun,"
I saw the Unicorn-No-Storm-Can-Tame.
The center of the sun was but his eye,
His mane was but the sun rays and the flame.
There in that Glacier Park, above green pastures,   5
There above Stephen's campfire in the rocks,
He foamed and pawed and whinnied round the world,
His feathered sides and plumes and bristling locks
Seemed but the banners of a great announcement
That unicorns were spry as heretofore,   10
That not a campfire of the world was dead,
That dragons lived in them, and thousands more
Camp-born, were clawing at the clouds of Asia,
Were rising with tomorrow's dawn for men,
Campfire dragons, with the ancient unicorn   15
Bringing the Rosicrucian days again.
Any unicorn can drive away
Any thoughts the grown-up race has spoiled.
When I heard the Unicorn-of-Sunset ramping
New fancies in my veins bubbled and boiled.   20
Any unicorn is worth his oats,
And so we fed him bacon, and we made
An extra cup of tea, which he drank.
Then he curled up coltwise, and in slumber sank.
Dragons sprang up, next day, where he had stayed.   25
They were in Fujiyama silks arrayed,
Or spoke of Everest to Stephen. Then began
Discussing the strange peak in Darien
That poets climb to see the Pacific well.
How Stephen climbed it later, I will let him tell.   30
Following the Unicorn-No-Storm-Can-Tame
Alone, in tropic woods, is a great game.

1921-1922

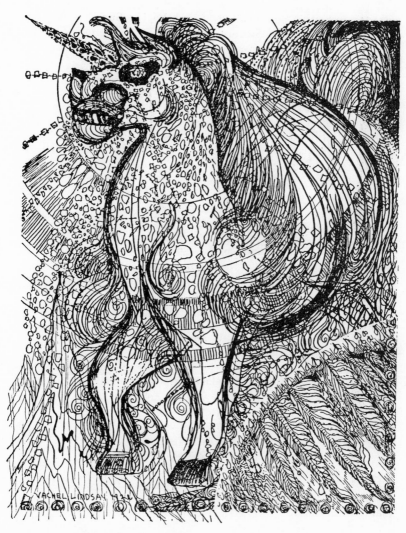

JOHNNY APPLESEED STILL FURTHER WEST

On the mountain peak, called "Going-To-The-Sun,"
I saw old Johnny Appleseed once more.
He ate an apple, threw away the core.
Then turned and smiled and slackly watched it fall
Into a crevice of the mountain wall.   5
In an instant there was an apple tree,
The roots split up the rocks beneath our feet,
And apples rolled down the green mountainside
And fairies popped from them, flying and free!

And   10
Fairies
Came from them.

      1921-1922

THE APPLE-BARREL OF JOHNNY APPLESEED

On the mountain peak, called "Going-To-The-Sun,"
I saw gray Johnny Appleseed at prayer
Just as the sunset made the old earth fair.
Then darkness came; in an instant, like great smoke,
The sun fell down as though its great hoops broke   5
And dark rich apples, poured from the dim flame
Where the sun set, came rolling toward the peak,
A storm of fruit, a mighty cider-reek,
The perfume of the orchards of the world,
From apple-shadows: red and russet domes   10
That turned to clouds of glory and strange homes
Above the mountain tops for cloud-born souls: —
Reproofs for men who build the world like moles,
Models for men, if they would build the world
As Johnny Appleseed would have it done —   15
Praying, and reading the books of Swedenborg
On the mountain top called "Going-To-The-Sun."

    1921-1922

VACHEL LINDSAY 1922-

THE COMET OF GOING-TO-THE-SUN

On the mountain peak, called "Going-To-The-Sun,"
A comet stopped to drink from a cool spring
And like a spirit-harp began to sing
To us, then hurried on to reach the sun.
We called him "Homer's soul," and "Milton's wing."   5
The harp-sound stayed, though he went up and on.
It turned to thunder, when he had quite gone—
And yet was like a soft voice of the sea,
And every whispering root and every blade of grass
And every tree   10
In the whole world, and brought thoughts of old songs
That blind men sang ten thousand years ago,
And all the springtime hearts of every nation know.

    1921-1922

THE BOAT WITH THE KITE STRING AND THE
CELESTIAL EYES

On the mountain peak, called "Going-To-The-Sun,"
I sat alone; while Stephen explored higher,
I dragged in sticks and logs and kept our fire.

On soft-winged sails of meditation
My boat of spiral shells and flowers,   5
And fluffy clouds and twinkling hours,
My thought-boat went with the sun all day
Over the glaciers, far away.
I sat alone, but the chipmunks knew
My boat was high, and plain to view.   10

I flew my ship like a kite. The thread
Was a cobweb silk, fine and thin,
That came from out the palm of my hand.
There I saw the ship begin.
From the gypsy's life line thence it came   15

A feather of mist that flew to the dawn,
And I felt the spool in my wrist unwind,
And I saw the feather on heaven's lawn,
Now a glimmering ship like a lark awake.
And the kite string sang, but did not break.   20

It stretched like the string of a violin
Played by invisible tides and waves.
It sang of Springfield yet to be.
It sang of the dead hours in their graves.

And of the United States to be,   25
And of all the map stretched out below.
And my kite had pansy eyes in its wings,
And I saw the states in their bloom and glow
Yet a child's block-map, and nothing more,
Flat patterns on a playroom floor.   30

Texas the fort, by the river to the south,
Michigan a pheasant with a leaf in its mouth,
Illinois an ear of corn, in the shock,
Maine a moose-horn, gray as a rock.
California a whale, in gilded mail,   35
Montana, a ranch of alfalfa and clover,

Montana with its mountain called "Going-To-The-Sun,"
An outdoor temple for the singer and the rover,
Wyoming a range for a summer lark,
With sparkling trails, and its Yellowstone Park,   40
Colorado an Indian tent for the world,
Where the smokes of care-free camps are curled,
Arizona a mission in the desert for all time,
Where the nerves find peace, and thoughts find rhyme,
New Mexico a clay pueblo full of dreams,   45
Eldorado in its valleys, ghosts by its streams.
Utah a throne for a grandeur unknown,
For haughty hearts, with ways of their own.
Nevada the cabin of Mark Twain in his youth,
Where he mined in the cañons, where he dug for the
      truth.   50
Washington a western soldier's tent,
Idaho a chair for a president,
North and South Dakota, one buffalo hide,
Oregon a lumber mill on a mountain side,
Nebraska, Oklahoma, cowboy pistols pointing west   55
Kansas a wheat field where I, once, was a guest,
Iowa a corn pone sizzling hot,
Minnesota a farmer's coffee-pot.
Arkansas a steamboat at Mark Twain's door,
Missouri Mark Twain's raft on the shore.   60
Louisiana a cavalier's boot, just the thing
When we wade toward the mouth of the delta in the spring.
Mississippi a cotton scales,
Alabama many cotton bales,
Georgia a peach-basket red,   65
Florida a wild turkey's head,
North Carolina a crane, flying through a cloud,
South Carolina a soldier, with head unbowed,
West Virginia, the raccoon, shrewd and slow,
Tennessee Bob Taylor's fiddle and bow,   70
Virginia Thomas Jefferson's mountain and shroud,
Kentucky the log cradle of the proud.
Maryland a plow, Delaware a pruning hook,
Indiana Riley's Hoosier book,
Wisconsin a caldron, cool it who can,   75
Ohio Johnny Appleseed's park for man.
Vermont a poet's house, with waterfall and fern,
Where Frost writes songs that the world will learn.

New Jersey the doorstep of the nation,
Pennsylvania the front room of the nation,   80
Where once Penn welcomed all creation
And let them sleep on the grassy floor
And let them eat the wild berries and explore.
Rhode Island, Roger Williams' holy place,
Connecticut, an arbor of innocence and grace   85
Filled with flowers, and souls like lace,
Especially one little girl six years young
Who tells me stories in the fairy tongue.

New Hampshire the mast of the Mayflower,
Massachusetts the prow of the Mayflower,   90
Most famous ark forevermore.

The whole map a temple, if we patiently read,
With the statue of Liberty in majesty to plead
For Arcady to come once more,
And with New York on guard,   95
New York a sentinel,
New York a lion by the door.

By my campfire I grew older,
There were chipmunks on my shoulder,
While I saw the world,   100
With the eyes of my boat,
As one land,
With Asia and Alaska by the ice bound as one,
The Aurora Borealis was a cross bright as the sun.
I seemed to live through myriad days.   105
My eyes looked down like searching rays.
I took my flight over many races,
I saw, in my thought, all human faces.
And my spirit had its fill.
And the thread in my wrist wound in again   110
The cobweb shortened, strand on strand,
And my little ship came back to land
And was only a feather in my hand.

       1921-1922

SO MUCH THE WORSE FOR BOSTON

I read the aspens like a book, and every leaf
was signed,
And I climbed above the aspen-grove to read
what I could find

*Some words about singing
this song,
Are written this border
along.*

On Mount Clinton, Colorado, I met a mountain-
cat.
I will call him "Andrew Jackson," and I mean
no harm by that.
He was growling, and devouring a terrific moun-
tain-rat.   5
But when the feast was ended, the mountain-cat
was kind,
And showed a pretty smile, and spoke his mind.
"I am dreaming of old Boston," he said, and
wiped his jaws.

THE BIG EARED RAT OF BOSTON

"I have often HEARD of Boston," and he folded
in his paws,
"Boston, Massachusetts, a mountain bold and
great.   10
I will tell you all about it, if you care to curl
and wait.

"In the Boston of my beauty-sleep, when storm-
flowers are in bloom,
When storm-lilies and storm-thistles and storm-
roses are in bloom,

The faithful cats go creeping through the
   catnip-ferns,
And rainbows, *and* sunshine, *and* gloom,   15
And pounce upon the Boston Mice, that tremble
   underneath the flowers,
And pounce upon the big-eared rats, and drag
   them to the tomb.
For we are Tom-policemen, vigilant and sure.
We keep the Back Bay ditches and potato cellars
   pure.
Apples are not bitten into, cheese is let alone.

*If I cannot sing in the
aspens' tongue,
If I know not what they say
Then I have never gone to
school,
And have wasted all my da*

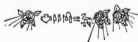

THE BOSTON MOUSE WAITS IN TERROR OF THE
MOUNTAIN-CAT, UNDER THE SHADOW
OF THE STORM-ROSE

Sweet corn is left upon the cob, and the beef left
    on the bone.
Every Sunday morning, the Pilgrims give us cod-
    fish balls,
Because we keep the poisonous rats from the
    Boston halls.''
And then I contradicted him, in a manner firm
    and flat.
''I have never seen, in the famous Hub,
    suppression of the rat.''
''So much the worse for Boston,'' said the whiskery
    mountain-cat.

And the cat continued his great dream, closing one
    shrewd eye:
''The Tower-of-Babel Cactus blazes above the sky.
Fangs and sabers guard the buds and crimson fruits
    on high.

*Come, let us whisper of men
and beasts
And joke as the aspens do,
And yet be solemn in their
way,
And tell our thoughts
All summer through,
In the morning,
In the frost,
And in the midnight dew.*

VACHEL LINDSAY 1922

THE TOWER-OF-BABEL CACTUS
BLAZES ABOVE THE SKY

Yet cactus-eating eagles and black hawks hum through
 the air.　　　　　　　　　30
When the pigeons weep in Copley Square, look up,
 those wings are there,
Proud Yankee birds of prey, overshadowing the
 land,
Screaming to younger Yankees of the self-same
 brand,
Whose talk is like the American flag, snapping
 on the summit-pole,
Sky-rocket and star-spangled words, round sun-
 flower words, they use them whole.
There are no tailors in command, men seem
 like trees in honest leaves.
Their clothes are but their bark and hide,
 and sod and binding for their sheaves.
Men are as the shocks of corn, as natural as
 alfalfa fields.
And no one yields to purse or badge; only to
 sweating manhood yields,
To natural authority, to wisdom straight
 from the new sun.
Who is the bull-god of the herd? the strongest
 and the shaggiest one.
Or if they preen at all, they preen with Walter
 Raleigh's gracious pride: —
The forest-ranger! One grand show! with gun
 and spade slung at his side!
Up on the dizzy timber-line, arbiter of life
 and fate,
Where sacred frost shines all the year, and
 freezing bee and moss-flower mate.

"Boston is tough country, and the ranger
 rides with death,
Plunges to stop the forest fire against
 the black smoke's breath,
Buries the cattle killed by eating larkspur
 lush and blue,
Shoots the calf-thieves, lumber-thieves, and
 gets train-robbers too.
Governor and Sheriff obey his ordering hand,
Following his ostrich plume across the amber sand.

*The mountain-cat seems vio-
lent,
And of no good intent.
Yet read his words so gently
No bird will leave its tree,
No child will hate the sim-
per or the noise
And hurry away from you
and me.
Read like a meditative, cat-
like willow-tree.*

*Some words about singing
this song,
Are scattered this border
along.*
40

*Read like the Mariposa
with the stately stem,
With green jade leaves
like ripples and like waves,
And white jade petals,
Smooth as foam can be—
The Mariposa lily, that is
leaning upon the young
stream's hem,
Speaking grandly to that
larger flower
That grows down toward the
sea, hour after hour
Hunting for the Pacific
storms and caves.*
50

"But often, for lone days he goes, exploring cliffs
  afar,
And chants his King James' Bible to tarantula and
  star.
I hear him read Egyptian tales, as he rides by in
  the dawn.   *Some words about singing
I am sometimes an Egyptian cat. My crudities   this song,*
  are gone.   *Are scattered this border
He spells, in Greek, that Homer, as he hurries on   along.*
  alone.
I hear him scan at Virgil, as I hide behind a stone.
He has kept me fond of Hawthorne, and Thoreau,
  cold and wise.
The silvery waves of Walden Pond, gleam in a bob-
  cat's eyes.
He has taught us grateful beasts to sing, like
  Orpheus of old.   60
The Boston forest ranger brings back the Age of
  Gold.''

A BACK-BAY WHALE

And then I contradicted him, in a manner firm and
  flat.
"I have never heard, in the cultured Hub, of
  rowdy men like that."
"So much the worse for Boston," said the Rocky
  Mountain cat.

And the cat purred on, in his great dream, as one
who seeks the noblest ends: — 65
"Higher than the Back Bay whales, that spout and
leap, and bite their friends,
Higher than those Moby-Dicks, the Boston Lover's
trail ascends.
Higher than the Methodist, or Unitarian spire,
Beyond the range of any fence of boulder or
barbed wire,
Telling to each other what the Boston Boys have
done,
The lodge-pole pines go towering to the timber-line
and sun.
And their whisper stirs love's fury in each panther-
ish girl-child,
Till she dresses like a columbine, or a bleeding
heart gone wild.
Like a harebell, golden aster, bluebell, Indian ar-
row,
Blue jay, squirrel, meadow lark, loco, mountain
sparrow. 75
Mayflower, sagebrush, dying swan, they court in
disarray.
The masquerade, in Love's hot name, is like a
forest-play.
And she is held in worship who adores the noblest
boys.
So miner-lovers bring her new amazing pets and
toys.
Mewing, prowling hunters bring her grizzlies in
chains. 80
Ranchers bring red apples through the silver rains.
In the mountain of my beauty-sleep, when storm-
flowers
Are in bloom,
The Boston of my beauty-sleep, when storm-flowers
Are in bloom. 85
There are just such naked waterfalls, as are roar-
ing there below.
For the springs of Boston Common are from price-
less summer snow.
Serene the wind-cleared Boston peaks, and there
white rabbits run
Like funny giant snowflakes, hopping in the sun.
The ptarmigan will leap and fly, and clutter
through the drift 90

Sing like the Mariposa to
the stream that seeks the
Speak like that flower,
With still,
Olympian jest,
And cuplike word
Filling the hour.

And the baby ptarmigans 'peep, peep,' when the
  weasel eyelids lift.
And where the pools are still and deep, dwarf
  willows see themselves,
And the Boston Mariposas bend, like mirror-kiss-
  ing elves.
White is the gypsum cliff, and white the snow-
  bird's warm, deep-feathered home,
White are the cottonwood and birch, white is
  the fountain-foam.   95

"In the waterfalls from the sunburnt cliffs, the
  bold nymphs leap and shriek
The wrath of the water makes them fight, its kisses
  make them weak.
With shoulders hot with sunburn, with bodies rose
  and white,
And streaming curls like sunrise rays, or curls like
  flags of night,
Flowing to their dancing feet, circling them in
  storm,   100
And their adorers glory in each lean, Ionic form.
Oh, the hearts of women, then set free. They
  live the life of old
That chickadees and bobcats sing, the famous Age
  of Gold. . . .
They sleep and star-gaze on the grass, their red-
  ore campfires shine,
Like heaps of unset rubies spilled on velvet super-
  fine.   105
And love of man and maid is when the granite weds
  the snow-white stream.
The ranch house bursts with babies. In the
  wood-lot deep eyes gleam,
Buffalo children, barking wolves, fuming cinna-
  mon bears.
Human mustangs kick the paint from the break-
  fast-table chairs.''

And then I contradicted him, in a manner firm
  and flat.   110
"I have never heard, in the modest Hub, of a stock
  ill-bred as that."
"So much the worse for Boston," said the lecher-
  ous mountain-cat.

And the cat continued with the dream, as the snow
    blew round in drifts.
"The caves beneath the craggy sides of Boston
    hold tremendous gifts
For many youths that enter there, and lift up
    every stone that lifts.   115
They wander in, and wander on, finding all new
    things they can,
Some forms of jade or chrysoprase, more rare than
    radium for man.
And the burro trains, to fetch the loot, are
    jolly fool parades.
The burros flap their ears and bray, and take the
    steepest grades.
Or loaded with long mining-drills, and railroad
    rails, and boards for flumes,   120
Up Beacon Hill with fossil bats, swine bones
    from geologic tombs,
Or loaded with cliff-mummies of lost dwellers
    of the land.
Explorers' yells and bridle bells sound above
    the sand.

"In the desert of my beauty-sleep, when rain-
    flowers
Will not bloom,   125
In the Boston of my beauty-sleep, when storms
Will not bloom,
By Bunker Hill's tall obelisk, till the August sun
    awakes,
I brood and stalk blue shadows, and my mad heart
    breaks.
Thoughts of a hunt unutterable ring the obelisk
    around.   130
And a thousand glorious sphinxes spring, singing,
    from the ground.
Very white young Salem witches ride them down
    the west.
The gravel makes a flat, lone track, the eye has
    endless rest.
Fair girls and beasts charge, dreaming, through
    the salt-sand white as snow,
Hunting the three-toed pony, while mysterious
    slaughters flow.   135
And the bat from the salt desert sucks the clouds
    on high

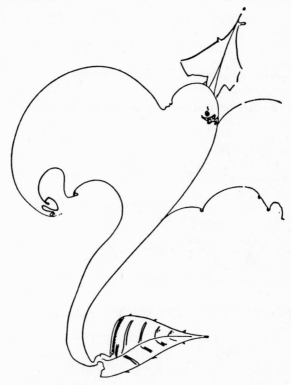

VACHEL LINDSAY 1922

THE BAT

Until they fall in ashes, and all the sky is dry.
Oh, the empty Spanish Missions, where the bells
   ring without hand,
As we drive the shadowy dinosaurs and mammoths
   through the sand.''

And then I contradicted him, in a manner firm and
   flat.   140
''I have never seen, in the sun-kissed Hub, cir-
   cuses like that.''
''So much the worse for you, my cub,'' said the
   slant-eyed mountain-cat.

And the cat continued with his yarn, while I stood
   there marveling: —

"I here proclaim that I am not a vague, an abstract
    thing.
I like to eat the turkey-leg, the lamb, the chicken-
    wing.   145
Yet the cat that knows not fasting, the cat that
    knows not dream,
That has not drunk dim mammoth-blood from the
    long-dead desert stream,
That has not rolled in the alkali-encrusted pits of bones
By the saber-toothed white tiger's cave, where he
    kicked the ancient stones,
Has not known sacred Boston. Our gods are
    burning ore.   150
Our Colorado gods are the stars of heaven's floor.
But the god of Massachusetts is a Tiger they adore.

"From that saber-tooth's ghost-purring goes the
    whispered word of power
In the sunset, in the moonlight, in the purple
    sunrise hour: —
That an Indian chief is born, in a teepee, to the
    west,   155
That a school of rattlesnakes is rattling, on the
    mountain's breast,
That an opal has been grubbed from the ground
    by a mole,
That a bumble-bee has found a new way to save
    his soul.
In Egyptian granite Boston, the rumor has gone
    round
That new ways to tame the whirlwind have been
    marvelously found.   160
That a Balanced Rock has fallen, that a battle has
    been won
In the soul of some young touch-me-not, some tiger-
    ish Emerson."

And then I contradicted him, in a manner firm and
    flat.
"Boston people do not read their Emerson like
    that."
"So much the worse for Boston," said the self-
    reliant cat.   165

Then I saw the cat there towering, like a cat cut
    from a hill: —

A prophet-beast of Nature's law, staring with stony
  will,
Pacing on the icy top, then stretched in drowsy
  thought,
Then, listening, on tiptoe, to the voice the snow-
  wind brought,
Tearing at the fire-killed pine trees, kittenish again, 170
Then speaking like a lion, long made president of
  men: —
"There are such holy plains and streams, there are
  such sky-arched spaces,
There are life-long trails for private lives, and end-
  less whispering places.
Range is so wide there is not room for lust and
  poison breath
And flesh may walk in Eden, forgetting shame and
  death." 175

And then I contradicted him, in a manner firm and
  flat.
"I have never heard, in Boston, of anything like
  that."
"Boston is peculiar.
Boston is mysterious.
You do not know your Boston," said the wise, fas-
  tidious cat, 180
And turned again to lick the skull of his prey, the
  mountain-rat!
And at that, he broke off his wild dream of a per-
  fect human race.
And I walked down to the aspen grove where is
  neither time nor place,
Nor measurement, nor space, except that grass has
  room
And aspen leaves whisper on forever in their grace. 185
All day they watch along the banks. All night the
  perfume goes
From the Mariposa's chalice to the marble moun-
  tain-rose,
In the Boston of their beauty-sleep, when storm-
  flowers
Are in bloom,
In the mystery of their beauty-sleep, when storm-
  flowers 190
Are in bloom.

  1922

THE ROCKETS THAT REACHED SATURN

On the Fourth of July sky rockets went up
Over the church and the trees and the town,
Stripes and stars, riding red cars.
Each rocket wore a red-white-and-blue gown,
And I did not see one rocket come down.   5

Next day on the hill I found dead sticks,
Scorched like blown-out candle-wicks.

But where are the rockets? Up in the sky.
As for the sticks, let them lie.
Dead sticks are not the Fourth of July.   10

In Saturn they grow like wonderful weeds,
In some ways like weeds of ours,
Twisted and beautiful, straight and awry,
But nodding all day to the heavenly powers.
The stalks are smoke,   15
And the blossoms green light,
And crystalline fireworks flowers.

1921-1922

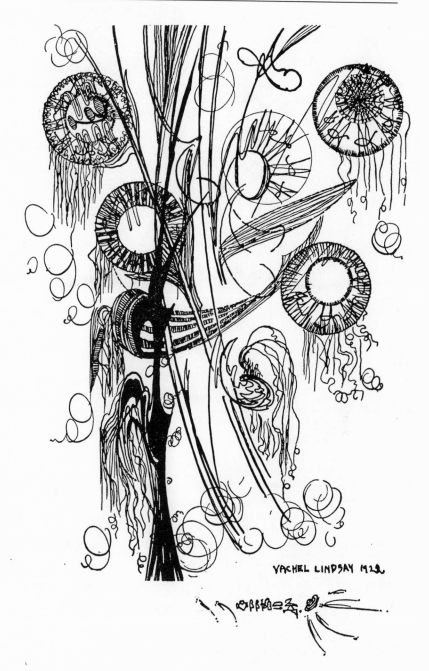

YACHEL LINDSAY 1922

MEDITATION

A spirit in soft slippers
Walked the Gulf Stream floor.
She opened many a cabin door
Of ships a long time underseas.
She read long-lost Egyptian books   5
And looked upon skull-faces,
And read their restless looks
Shining through the shadows
Of phosphorescent streaming waves, —
Impatient for the Judgement horn   10
To lift them from their purple graves.

     1923

ELIZABETH BARRETT BROWNING

Elizabeth Barrett Browning
Sat gossiping with Robert.
(She was really a raving beauty in her day.
With Mary Pickford curls in clouds and whirls.)
She was trying to think of something nice to say,   5
So she pointed to a page by her fellow star and
     sage,
And said: "I wish that *I* could write that way!"

     1923

SOME BALLOONS GROW ON TREES

For Betsy Richards

Some balloons grow on trees,
On rubber trees, indeed.
You plant old rubber-boots for seed.

Some balloons grow on trees.
If you want them red,   5
You pour red ink into the boots,
There in the balloon bed,

And blue ink if you want them blue.
But if you desire them green,
Just let it pass.   10
They will turn green to match the grass.

Some balloons grow on trees.
And if you do not spray them soon
With water-pots of hellebore
You will not have   15
One ripe balloon.
Mosquitoes will bite them in the night
Explode them like a thunder-storm
And give the town a fright.

Some balloons grow on trees.   20
If they grow too fast
And are not gathered every day
The infants stand aghast
To see them tear up by the roots
The trees on which they grew   25
And scatter dirt on the front walk
And disappear from view
Into the blue.

    Early 1922

BABYLON'S GARDENS ARE BURNING

There, on the shores of the river Euphrates,
Babylon's gardens are burning this morning.
Prophets warned,
Prophets prophesied,
But no one in Babylon heeded the warning.

    1922

BABYLON'S GARDENS ARE BURNING   VACHEL LINDSAY 1922

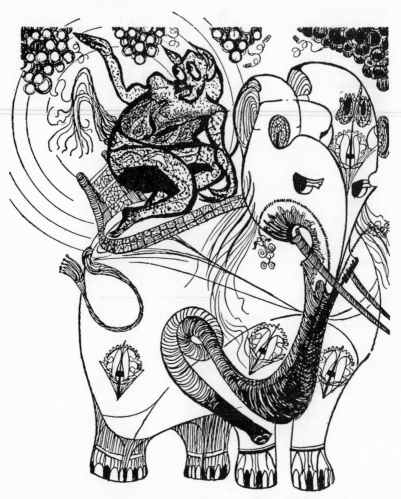

VACHEL LINDSAY 1922-

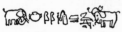

THE APE RODE THE JUMBO

IN THE BEAUTY PARLORS

A jumbo so vain, and fond of his shape
Had himself beautified by a gray ape,
Tattooed and gilded with elegant signs,
The latest and merriest monkey designs.
Then the ape rode the jumbo   5
And made the land gape,
As he sat at his ease in the elephant chair.
He had tattooed himself with designs from a shawl,
And he gathered a grape with a self-possessed air,
And threw down a twig at another fine ape.   10

    1922

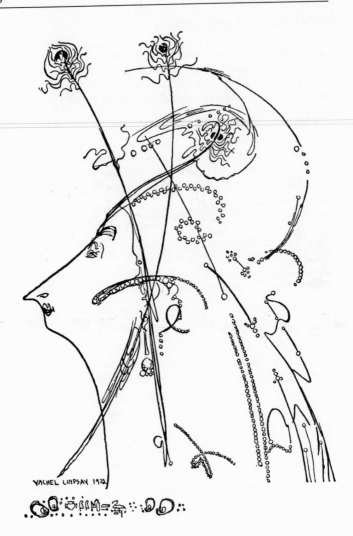

PEARLS

Now she was fond of jewelry,
The Lady-of-Fiddle-Dee-Dee,
So she built her house
Near an oyster bed,
Where the pearls were almost free.

1922

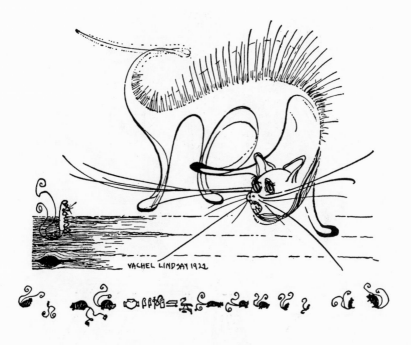

CONCERNING THE MOUSE WITH TWO TAILS

The cat was astonished
To see the mouse stand there,
Waving two tails,
With a confident air.

1922

WORDS ABOUT AN ANCIENT QUEEN

Inscribed with Apologies to Lytton Strachey

Queen Hat-shep-sut, pious and fat
Wore a hair net under her hat.
Queen Hat-shep-sut, restrained and refined
Wore a hair net over her mind.

1922

From THE VILLAGE MAGAZINE

Third Edition

Spring, 1925

IN MEMORY OF A GOOD PRINTER

N. M. Naylor of Springfield, Illinois
Died December 3, 1924

Brother, we take our earthly farewell now;
    Brother, buried in a Springfield grave,
And always buried in your craftsman's vow,
    By choice, and not necessity, a slave.

Never could I have been a man like that.   5
    I always liked to strut, and blow my horn,
And make my lion out of every cat,
    And call each horse my personal unicorn.

Yours was the broken heart, the faithful hand,
    Colossal patience, and the printer's pride.   10
Your inks were always black, your papers grand,
    Your margins always straight and proud and wide.

You knew a thousand ways to go to press,
    And every one was novel, clean and fine.
You could untangle fat fools in a mess,   15
    Could make their silly copy stand in line.

You made the bleared zink etchings come out right,
    Made honest half-tones out of tin-type smears.
While rich men cursed you, you could be polite,
    In short, a printer, through the years, and years.   20

I always dreamed my books like strange pine-brands
    American buffaloes, fairies, Buffalo Bill.
I always hoped that your fraternal hands
    Following the copy up and down the hill

Would pile my fires, and keep my dragons high,   25
    Produce my hieroglyphics the right way.
Who now will make Old Springfield's pamphlets fly?
    The notice of your funeral comes today.

Men like to think, with a good old-fashioned sigh
    Of homely customs in the better land.   30
And so, old-fashionedly, we prophecy
    Of your stern, patient, and correcting hand.

You give Mark Twain's long cuss-words ample space, —
   No editing angels hold you, or refine,
And print proud Altgeld's word without disgrace,   35
   And make as brilliant Wilson's sternest line.

You now make clear Roosevelt's marvellous shout,
   No matter how excitedly he brawls.
You now and then tactfully straighten out
   All the political saints upon the walls.   40

They scrawl cartoons, debate, and write in flame
   Then rush to press. You, gently, print them right.
Even in Heaven you do not sign your name.
   Dear N. M. Naylor, this is my good-night:

There you will have one friend—the Crucified.   45
   Your quiet toil the Christ will understand.
Yours is the loving heart, the wounded side,
   Yours is the broken heart, the faithful hand.

   January 1925

From COLLECTED POEMS

Second Edition

Spring, 1925

A MAP OF THE UNIVERSE ISSUED IN 1909.
THIS MAP IS ONE BEGINNING OF THE
GOLDEN BOOK OF SPRINGFIELD.

ROOSEVELT

(Written for the Illinois State Teachers' Association,
printed as a broadside, and read, and distributed the same
day: April 4, 1924.)

When the stuffed prophets quarrel, when the sawdust
   comes out, I think of Roosevelt's genuine sins.
Once more my rash love for that cinnamon bear,
Begins!

His sins were better than their sweetest goodness.
His blows were cleaner than their plainest kindness.   5
He saw more than they all, in his hours of black blindness.
The hour of his pitiful spiritual fall
He was more of an angel than all of this host,
When with Lucifer's pride his soul was burnt out,
When, still in the game, he gave up the ghost.   10

His yarns were nearer the sky than their truth.
His wildest tales, in his fish-story hour,
Nearer true than their truth.
When with art and with laughter he held supreme power,
He was white as the moon, and as honest as youth.   15

And now their sworn word is but barnyard mud.
And their highest pride is to hide in a hole.
They talk of "dollars" and "dollars" and "dollars"
And "dollars" and "dollars," and hate his clean soul.

(Oh money, money—that *never* can think,   20
Money, money, that *never* can rule,
Always an anarchist, always an idiot,
Always King Log—never King Stork,
Always rotting, reeking:—always a fool.)

Roosevelt was proud like a singer.   25
Roosevelt's pride was that of a scribe,
Or the pride of a father, the pride of a ruler,
The pride of the thoroughbred chief of a tribe,
The pride of Confucius, the pride of a student!
He hated a coward, he hated a fool,   30
He knew that money is always a fool.

When they tear each others' newspaper-hearts
I think of Theodore's genuine code.

He hated the paste-board, the smeary, the fake.
He hated the snake, the frog and the toad.   35

Oh a moose with sharp antlers!
Oh a panther of panthers—Oh a fox of foxes
Often caught in tight boxes!
Yet we know he would always bark out the truth.
He loved the curious political game:—   40
But we know he loved better:—truth, God, and *youth*.

A peacock of peacocks! An eagle of eagles!
Defeating, within himself, the quick fox.
A buffalo roaring—a world-lion roaring!
Defeating within himself the bright fox,—   45
Then ranging out through the wilderness trail,
Killing the jackal—felling the ox.

Megalomaniac, envious, glorious,
Envying only the splendors of worth.

Emulating the cleanest on earth,   50
(Those who were, therefore, the strongest on earth.)
Emulating thoroughbreds—always.
Peacock! Lion! Cinnamon bear!
Skyscrapers—steeples and plains for abode!
He was mostly the world's fine cinnamon bear,   55
He was mostly our glittering cinnamon bear,
Sitting there in an old rocking chair,
In the White House yard, taking the air.

He told us Aesop's new fables, each day—
President seven big glorious years!   60
Seven years of wonder. Must they all fade away,
In the quarrels of the rat with the loud-voiced cootie
Told by the zinc-throated, varnished ''loud-speaker,''
Told by wireless, while the world sits breathless,
Or by megaphone,   65
By line-o'-type, or by letter ripe:—
The quarrels of the angle-worm with the toad?

Who elected these pole-cats rulers of men?

Let us start a gay nation over again!
Let us start a circus as honest as Barnum's,   70
With three clean rings, and plenty to see,
Athletes, not snakes, on the trapeze tree.

Let us start our nation over again,
In the names of legitimate rulers of men,
In the names of the great, and the famous dead: —   75
Yes, the name of the glittering cinnamon bear,
Never so wicked or sore in the head,
But he fed the children honey and bread.
He taught them the names of the great and the dead,
From the Irish Sagas, to Carson and Boone.   80

He loved the villages, Deadwood, Medora,
Tuskeegee and Tuscarora,
Mexicali and Farmington,
Calexico and Bennington,
Arlington and Lexington,   85
Oyster Bay, Mount Vernon.

He loved the cities Denver, Manhattan,
And the wide great spaces
From the Amazon to Saskatoon —
He loved the heroes, Columbus, Whitman, Lincoln,   90
He loved the heroes! He loved George Washington! —
Who was honest as youth and white as the moon.

"Great-heart!" Roosevelt! Father of men!
He fed the children honey and bread.
He taught them the Ten Commandments and prayer,   95
Rocking there in his old rocking chair,
Or riding the storms of dream that he rode.

Join hands, poets, friends, companions!
Let us start a new world on the Roosevelt Code!

Let us start our nation over again   100
In the name of the honest, proud cinnamon bear,
Rocking there in his old rocking chair
Or riding the terrible storms that he rode!

The most-quoted phrase from the first edition of [CP is]* —
"That this whole book is a weapon in a strenuous battle-field." So this section starts with two broadsides, carrying out that idea, one on Roosevelt, one on Sandburg. "Roosevelt" was written, printed and issued in one day, after reading of the behavior of two middle western governors, that morning. I read the poem that night in East St. Louis for the Illinois State Teachers' Association, three thousand strong. It was distributed by Doubleday Page Book Shop, St. Louis. I

*See "Adventures While Singing These Songs" in CP.

read it in the loudest voice I could muster, holding the broad-
side up before the convention like a banner. It was an occa-
sion of some humor, but of even more seriousness, and the
New Republic telegraphed for a copy of the broadside at
once, and reissued it in abbreviated form. In this form it was
quoted with apparent approval by the Philadelphia *North
American*, and sent for by the Roosevelt Memorial Associa-
tion to be fastened on their walls. And the same day it was
politically attacked by the earnest Providence (Rhode Island)
Journal.

4 April 1924

BABYLON, BABYLON, BABYLON THE GREAT
(Inscribed to Carl Sandburg)

This poem is based on the episode of "Lincoln's Lost
Speech," too dangerous to print at the time, at Cooper
Union, his first appearance in the East.

Isaiah, the country-boy, marched against the jazz—
Babylon the shrewd and slick, Babylon the great.
Jeremiah, Ezekiel, Daniel, walked alone,
Alone against Babylon, alone against fate.
St. Paul walked alone, St. Peter walked alone,   5
Against that town to marvel on, Babylon the great.

Lincoln at Cooper Union, improvised and chanted,
Threw away his speech, and told tales out of school,
Changed from politician to God's divine fool.
Beside himself, beyond himself, set his old heart free,   10
The flame spread, the flame spread, every suppressed
      word was said,
Isaiah's voice from the dead;
Lincoln's great lost speech, nowhere written down,
But it burned every gate of the famous old town.

Lincoln at Cooper Union, called down fire from Heaven,   15
Overthrew jazz—Babylon, Babylon the great.

I have seen the burning of Babylon's gardens,
Many and many a noble day.
I have watched the ashes of that beautiful lost city,
Blown through many a year away.   20

Statesmen have torn down Babylon. . . . The gophers
  have buried Babylon. . . .
Coyotes lope through Babylon. . . . Prairie dogs bore
  the clay and sand. . . .
Texas cattle have trampled Babylon deeper in dung
  and dust. . . .
But forever stands Babylon, fresh in the sunrise, . . .
Foam upon the ocean . . . or granite on the land,   25
As new as the Devil, and the Devil's lust.

How our tales of Babylon multiply upon the ranges!
How old memories of victory renew!
Except for the warfare of the youngsters against Babylon,
The campfire songs would be few.   30

Troubadour! — March with bleeding feet against
  Babylon! —
(So, keep going to the sun! So, keep going to the sun!)
—If you would be a man. — As these have done before!
As lonely as Lincoln, dazed in Babylon,
Plod, plod, with a heartache, through the Devil's own
  door!   35
Tear up your set speeches, improvise once more!

War must begin against that city's music,
So — sing a silly song. Say: — "The sky is blue."
Sing a song of rainbow gems, unknown to Babylon.
Then improvise a song of the mick who lifts the hod,   40
Of the mick who sets in concrete the steel truss and rod,
Who builds the auto highways across the prairie sod—
(So, keep going to the sun! So, keep going to the sun!)
Improvise a cowboy song, of cactus and of dew,
And of raging on a mustang across the alkali   45
To where the snow-bright mountains of new mediation lie,
To the Indian basket-flowers, the ferns, the
  meadow-rue; —
Sing of beans in the pod, and of wheat in the shock,
Of hay in the stack, and windmills in the air,
Of castellated silos, and turkeys fat and fair,   50
Of chickens and of guineas, of pheasants, quails and
  eagles,
Of the High-School senior boys, foot-ball players,
  Sheiks and swells,
Of Lincoln-highway roses and sweet lovers everywhere: —
And the candies and the vanities of senior High-School
  belles,
(So, keep going to the sun! So, keep going to the sun!)   55

Sing a Kansas love-song, modest, clean and true.
Sing a Kansas love-song, modest, clean and true.
Then lift your psalm of the Manna of our God!
It is the only way to go into Babylon,
Call down fire from Heaven, and the world renew.   60

This is the only way a bard is a man.
So lift your proud word against the towers if you can.
Go on, with your guitar, through the Devil's breezy gate.
March on, with simple Lincoln against Babylon,
   Babylon, —
His dog-eared carpet-bag crammed with state papers,   65
His sweaty old duster flapping like a rag. —
Go, with prairie Lincoln against Babylon, Babylon,
Go with that tall prophet, again to Cooper Union,
March with mighty Lincoln against Babylon the Great!
(So — keep going to the sun! So — keep going to the sun!) 70

    In this poem I have exhorted Sandburg to improvise, but in
a way the opposite of jazz—for I have always hated jazz, as
our most Babylonian disease. This poem originally appeared
in Christopher Morley's Bowling Green column, in *The New
York Evening Post*, to celebrate a visit of Carl Sandburg to
New York City. Several months later it was printed in Mem-
phis, Tennessee, by the author, in anticipation of Carl Sand-
burg's visit to address Memphis in a recital for the Goodwyn
Institute, November 17, 1923. I issued it in a three-foot
broadside, with my picture of Babylon at the top as a kind of
hieroglyphic. It was distributed through the kindness of Mrs.
Dicken's Book-Shop.

    April 1923

PREFACE TO "BOB TAYLOR'S BIRTHDAY"

A Poem on "The Tennessee Orpheus"

A Rhymed Oration. Being the Phi Beta Kappa Poem,
Harvard Commencement, 1922.

Robert Love Taylor, the twenty-seventh and thirtieth gov-
ernor of Tennessee, was born in 1850, and died in 1912. He
was the greatest State governor America has ever had, to
me, a great statesman, indeed. This oration is dedicated to
the boys and girls of Tennessee. It is intended to be read to a

big crowd, out of doors, presumably July 1, Bob Taylor's birthday. If it is read while you sit down, in the house, it means nothing. Please, citizens of Tennessee, and others, assemble a concourse of neighbors with the children at a basket-picnic, on the Mississippi, the Tennessee, the Clinch or the Cumberland rivers, and read it so they all can hear, preferably after it is memorized, and every cadence adjusted and understood, as though they were all syllables of one musical word. After this kind of memorizing, it may be read slowly, as an oration, but not before. At natural intervals in the song, when finally given, let there be good tunes by a good picnic fiddler; — an old-fashioned, barn-dance, log cabin jig fiddler. At the proper moments solemn tunes, like "Old Hundred," and famous dances like "Money-Musk!" Then, after a moment's pause, let the orator resume, paraphrasing and improving on the poem, as he gets the swing. Please let the production be understood by the crowd as oratorical, to be cheerfully filled with local allusions, in the spirit of Taylor's own political speeches, and improvisations on his own fiddle.

We are so choked by the old arts. We need to improvise, but in the opposite of jazz. Watch Taylor again in fancy, running for governor against his brother, in that famous good-humored campaign, with the Democrats under Bob, using the white rose of York as their emblem, and the Republicans, under Alfred, the red rose of Lancaster, the boys fiddling on the big pine platform draped with flags and bunting. Think of the days when red or white roses were worn by every soul of Tennessee. Those were the days of improvisation.

So this is likewise, of all my productions, the one least intended for cold print. I urge all my friends to amend it as they read it. It is only in this way one can get much out of Bob Taylor's most famous oration—the basis of this poem: — Taylor's own reminiscent "lecture," "The Fiddle and the Bow," delivered from every Chautauqua platform in the United States and printed in his collected works: "The Lectures and Best Literary Productions of Bob Taylor," The Bob Taylor Publishing Co., Nashville, Tenn.

"Practical" people hated Orpheus, Homer, Milton.

Taylor is the livest and greatest new legend in America. As to his charms for "practical" people, I have no doubt some of them foam as they read this. How bankers do hate a poet in office! As to Taylor's actual appearance, mannerisms and quality, I refer you to Taylor's book, the very adequate pictures therein, and several charming school histories of

Tennessee, where the tale is told as marvelously as one in
any Gilbert and Sullivan libretto. But to this is added an
inventive and epic earnestness that is a tremendous sane
prophecy for American domestic art and religion and power.
Ask the Chautauqua man who met him in his very last days,
when he became a national figure in that fashion, and any
veteran senator, who met him in Washington, when he
became a national figure in that fashion (presumably the
supreme fashion). The element hardest to record is the
village apocalypse quality, this inventive, epic earnestness.
Some of us are beginning to see him the livest and greatest
new prophet in America, an unconscious prophet, far closer
to the future than Whitman, because actually elected to
office again and again. Whitman was a thwarted Tammany
brave.

My friend Frank Waller Allen, of Los Angeles, a man of
great Chautauqua experience, has talked to me about Taylor
at great length, the last few years. And I remember one very
pleasant evening with Bishop Gailor of Memphis, and the
poet Will Percy, talking about Bob Taylor. This summer
while visiting a charming Tennessee county seat, I carried
the manuscript of this poem with me, and I heard much
gossip of Taylor from fellow-politicians who helped him
toward the governor's chair. The *ideal* aspects of a fiddling
governor took stronger hold of me. They are now, frankly,
the main theme of this song, the *ideal* aspects of the
conception of a Fiddling Governor of a state of this Union.
We certainly have had enough of utterly sordid "practical"
governors, of late. The more Frank Waller Allen tells me
about Taylor, the more I feel that the Taylor ideal is a gigan-
tic piece of democratic genius and initiative and, for that
mere initiative, that costs so much in vitality—the ever-
lasting glory of his state. Tennessee, and the Union, should,
in the end, be held tranced by the ideal. It is as though
Tennessee said to the world: "You have business managers.
But we have an Orpheus. Unless you also get the immortal
soul of a musician, as a governor to rule you, we have put you
everlastingly in the wrong. Your business-managers seem to
be going to jail, fast." As I read in a Tennessee school-
history, a mere primer, the outline of the pretty story, I see
the beautiful children of Tennessee huddled together, listen-
ing entranced, being made over into artists, poets,
musicians, architects. Then I see all the children of America
being made over into these, and into statesmen, prophets,
saints and sibyls, tranced and listening to "Money-Musk,"
and looking up at a gigantic figure of Bob Taylor in a great
blue rocking-chair in the sky.

Now get the map of Tennessee, and look at the eastern counties. I was begging in East Tennessee, in the log-cabin region about which Taylor was always so eloquent, only a short journey from his ancestral mansion. I was between Flagpond and Greenville. I offered "The Tree of Laughing Bells" pamphlet, in exchange for a night's lodging to a man on the porch of a log cabin, just the sort of cabin Taylor pictured in his orations. The man on the porch welcomed me that night in the name of Tennessee's Fiddling Governor. It was the first time I had heard of Taylor. But it was like coming to the edge of a new, tremendous, eternal tradition. This was about 1905. Taylor had been Governor 1887 to 1891 and 1897 to 1899. In that time he had made himself a part of the soul-fabric of the American people, like Johnny Appleseed and, and—Roosevelt and *such diverse dreamers*! Death and time were no more, and a day was as a thousand years, a thousand years as a day. I had come for eternity beneath the wing of Orpheus. It was there or near there I wrote the Canticle of the Tennessee Rose, which is in "A Handy Guide for Beggars," page 109. The story of "Lady Iron Heels" is an adventure in the same region.

Bob Taylor is worth reading after. *He could teach any man in the world who would learn how to rule.* Here is a quotation from his famous lecture, "The Fiddle and Bow":

"It would be difficult for those reared amid the elegancies and refinements of life in city and town to appreciate the enjoyments of the gatherings and merrymakings of the great masses of the people who live in the rural districts of our country. The historian records the deeds of the great; he consigns to fame the favored few but leaves unwritten the 'short and simple annals of the poor,' the lives and actions of the millions. The modern millionaire, as he sweeps through our valleys and around our hills in his palace car, ought not to look with derision on the cabins of America, for from their thresholds have come more brains, and courage, and true greatness than ever emanated from all the palaces in this world. The fiddle, the rifle, the ax and the Bible, the palladium of American liberty, symbolizing music, prowess, labor, and free religion, the four grand forces of our civilization, were the trusty friends and faithful allies of our pioneer ancestry in subduing the wilderness and erecting the great commonwealths of the Republic. Wherever a son of freedom pushed his perilous way into the savage wilds and erected his log cabin, these were the cherished penates of his humble domicile—the rifle in the rack above the door, the ax in the corner, the Bible on the table, and the fiddle, with its streamers of ribbon, hanging on the wall. Did he need the charm of music to cheer his heart, to scatter sunshine and drive away melancholy thoughts? He touched the responsive strings of his fiddle and it burst into laughter. Was he beset by skulking savages or prowling beasts of prey? He rushed to his deadly rifle for protection and relief. Had he the forest to fell and the fields to clear? His trusty ax was in his stalwart grasp. Did he need the consolation, the promises and precepts of religion to strengthen his faith, to brighten his hope and to anchor his soul to God and heaven? He held sweet communion with the dear old Bible.

"The glory and strength of the Republic today are its plain working people."

I like this better than Whitman's "Song of the Broad Ax" or "I Hear America Singing." It is far nearer democracy, though much farther from the grand style. But it seems to me it will take only one more generation to lift the memory of lives like Taylor's into the real American art. It is nearer to the true beginning.

Bob Taylor could teach any man in the world who would learn how to rule. He had no "Bread and Circuses" to bribe the crowd, after the manner of the Roman demagogues who purchased the votes of the Republic. But between fiddlings, on a thousand platforms, he told stories like this, to people who came a hundred miles afoot to hear him:

The Candy-Pulling

"The sugar was boiling in the kettles, and while it boiled the boys and girls played 'snap,' and 'eleven hand,' and 'thimble,' and 'blindfold,' and another old play which some of our older people will remember—

    'Oh, Sister Phoebe, how merry were we
    When we sat under the juniper tree,
    The juniper tree Hi O.'

"And when the sugar had boiled down into candy they emptied it into greased saucers, or, as the mountain folks called them, 'greased sassers,' and set it out to cool; and when it had cooled each boy and girl took a saucer and they pulled the taffy out and patted it and rolled it till it hung well together, and then they pulled it out a foot long; they pulled it out a yard long, and they doubled it back, and pulled it out, and looped it over, and pulled it out, and when it began to look like gold the sweethearts paired off and consolidated their taffy and pulled against each other. They pulled it out, and doubled it back, and looped it over, and pulled it out; and sometimes a peachblow cheek touched a bronzed one and sometimes a sweet little voice spluttered out, 'You, Jack,' and there was a suspicious smack like a cow pulling her foot out of stiff mud. They pulled the candy and laughed and frolicked; the girls got taffy on their hair, the boys got taffy on their chins, the girls got taffy on their waists, the boys got taffy on their coat sleeves. They pulled it till it was as bright as a moonbeam and then they plaited it and coiled it into fantastic shapes and set it out in the crisp air to cool. Then the courting began in earnest. They did not court then as the young folks court now. The young man led his sweetheart back into a dark corner and sat down by her, and held her hand for an hour and never said a word. But it resulted next year in more cabins on the hillsides and in the hollows, and in the years that followed the cabins were full of candy-haired children who grew up into a race of the best, the bravest, and the noblest people the sun in heaven ever shone upon.

"In the bright, bright hereafter, when all the joys of all the ages are gathered up and condensed into globules of transcendent ecstasy, I doubt whether there will be anything half so sweet as were the candy-smeared, ruby lips of the country maidens to the jeans-jacketed swains who tasted them at the candy-pulling in the happy long ago."

This was finally crystallized in his formal lecture, "The Fiddle and Bow," into the above form, but not until told a thousand ways a thousand times to a thousand stump-speech audiences.

To tell such stories well is one of what Mr. Gilbert Sedles calls "The Seven Lively Arts."

Bob Taylor could teach any man in the world who would learn how to rule.

This "word-painting," just below, was doubtless the final climax of many a stump-speech, and amid the dancing, the devilled eggs and fried chicken, was an outdoor tribute to the abstract qualities of the most abstract art.

Music

"The spirit of music, like an archangel, presides over mankind and the visible creation. Her afflatus, divinely sweet, divinely powerful, is breathed on every human heart, and inspires every soul to some nobler sentiment, some higher thought, some greater action.

"O music! Sweetest, sublimest ideal of omniscience—
first-born of God—fairest and loftiest seraph of the celestial
hierarchy, muse of the beautiful—daughter of the Universe!

"In the morning of eternity, when the stars were young,
her first grand oratorio burst upon raptured Deity and
thrilled the wondering angels. All heaven shouted. Ten
thousand times ten thousand jeweled harps, ten thousand
times ten thousand angel tongues caught up the song, and
ever since, through all the golden cycles, its breathing
melodies, old as eternity yet ever new as the flitting hours,
have floated on the air of heaven, lingering like the incense of
its flowers on plumed hill and shining vale, empurpled in the
shadow of the eternal throne.

"The seraph stood with outstretched wings on the horizon
of heaven clothed in light, ablaze with gems and, with voice
attuned, swept her burning harpstrings, and lo, the blue
infinite thrilled with her sweetest note. The trembling stars
heard it and flashed their joy from every flaming center. The
wheeling orbs that course the crystal paths of space were
vibrant with the strain and pealed it back into the glad ear of
God. The far-off milky way, bright gulf stream of astral
glories, spanning the ethereal deep, resounded with its
harmonies, and the star-dust isles, floating in that river of
opal, reëchoed the happy chorus from every sparkling
strand."

This is what the old Southern orators used to call "sky-
painting oratory." It is indeed that, we confess, and deny it
not.

Read indoors, this quotation *is* a bit flowery. But, of
course, every one hundred per cent American believes in
democracy. Let the reader take it to a county fair, mount the
nearest box, wave his hand and read it in competition with
every Cracker-Jack seller on the place. Or just read it to
himself in that setting. He will suddenly discover it taking on
great dignity and proportions.

I have tried to write my tribute to Bob Taylor in the spirit of
these three quotations. Try the above quotation in front of
the grand stand, between horse races, or imagine yourself
doing so. Then try my own piece of "sky-painting oratory"
given below. I have tried to add a bit more of the pioneer
Tennessee County Fair point of view. The third quotation
above moves in the other direction. It is a great democratic
way of saying that art has some mysterious abstract occult
qualities. It is the outdoor or "log-cabin" way of reiterating
the dogmas of Walter Pater. I have tried to consider its
meaning.

In his school of "The Fiddle and Bow,"
He could teach every man in the world,
Who would learn how to rule.
His was no gladiatorial show,
By tears and kindness he ruled his democracy, 5
With never a wall flower, never an enemy.
With one bold fiddle, with a heart never cool,
Loving them all, serving them all,
Playing old tunes that conquered them all,
He brought his whole state to one violin school, 10
He brought his whole marvelling crowd
To one beautiful school.

On his birthday, he teaches his state to flower!
Unabashed orator, dropping his pearls!
Today, he is shaking the butterflies' thrones! 15
Orpheus stirs up the squirrels to be barking;
Bee-hives are ringing their phones,
Wasps their razors are honing.
Good wheat ripens, and whistles and drones,
Cotton fields fiddle a tune to the sun, 20
Cornstalks rustle tassels and ears,
Spiders whirl round with misgivings and fears.
Bob Taylor is teaching his crowd to flower,
Shaking the butterflies' thrones!
There are pinch-faced people that snarl and deride, 25
For a singer triumphant defiles their pride.

Where are the hearts born to power,
My darlings,
Where are the hearts born to power?
You boys and girls 30
With the frolicsome manner,
From the first and second and third and fourth reader!
Will you lift your conquering Tennessee banner?
Oh, children, born of McGuffey's old reader,
With your new little brothers and sisters, 35
Will you heed the prophecies,
Mellow and rare,
Of the governing fiddle of Governor Taylor,
As he rocks in his blue rocking-chair,
As he rocks in his blue rocking-chair? 40

Oh, his giant chair of sky and dreams
Of the Great Smoky Mountains and East County Streams,
Tennessee clover and Tennessee rain,

Mixed with natural laughter and pain,
While Taylor's birthday comes round, comes round,   45
As he rocks in his blue rocking-chair, my darlings,
As he rocks in his blue rocking-chair!
As he lends a new splendor to log-cabin hearthstones,
Till the oceans reëcho his violin tones,
Oh, where are the hearts born to power,   50
My darlings,
Oh, where are the hearts born to power?

Who has the wings of the eagle?
Who has the wings of the lark?
Who has the wings of the owlet   55
As he dives through the twilight and dark?
Who will fly in dance time, in the springtime,
To the Money-Musk of Governor Bob,
As he shouts the new war cry of spring at its height,
And his fiddle gives forth a sweet sob?   60
As he sits on a cloud in the moonlight,
As he shakes up the world and its bones,
As he shakes up the nations that lie in their ashes,
And his bow sweeps the stars and the zones, my
     darlings,
And his bow sweeps the poles and the zones?   65

There are pinch-faced people that snarl and deride,
For a singer triumphant defiles their pride.

But now let us go to each county seat,
Where the old county fairs make the harvest complete,
And friend meets friend with pride.   70
In the merry-go-round where we will ride
To the music of the far stars' hum,
And the music of the hearth-crickets' drum,
And the tunes of Governor Bob, that will never end,
In the merry-go-round that we will make,   75
Many queer things we will undertake,
While the children will break ambrosial cake,
Bears will bring us honey-bread,
And the turkeys bring us honey-bread.

In the merry-go-round that we will make,   80
The cricket will chirp, the bee will hum,
The cricket will chirp, the bee will hum,
While the spokes of the merry-go-round go round.
A world-wide merry-go-round we will make,
With a tall elm tree for the central stake,   85

(While the spokes of the merry-go-round go round!)
The lark will cry the world awake,
The lark will cry the world awake.
Kind hearts will cry the world awake.

And now let us tell just the same child story—   90
In other terms, and with other glory.

While today's young children group around us, clap their
    pudgy hands,
And tell each other tales of beasts of distant lands,
And tell each other stories of sheiks and desert sands,
While they rock in big Grand Rapids chairs, varnished
    hard and slick,   95
Let flames of his birthday fiddle, coming nearer, make
    them quiver,
Let flames of the Governor's fiddle
Light each spirit's candlewick.
Let there be repeated visions
Of this man in every cabin,   100
The statesman, the soul's visitor, the mystical vote
    getter.
Now, just before Taylor finds "you and me,
Behold a young fairy called Tennessee,"
Come to set souls free.
She stands on the nation's hearthstones,   105
In the homes of millions, debating—
And there for the presence of Taylor waiting,
And chattering there with our tiniest children
As they watch for our man at the window sills,
Stories of hunters and trappers relating,   110
Martha Washington parties, and Jackson quadrilles.

She is crowned with three burning Tennessee stars,
Her soul is Jackson and Taylor and Boone,
The white far-flaming soul of the West,
For Tennessee once was the world's Wild West,   115
And is still, in secret, the world's Wild West.
With the eyes of the dawn and the gesture of pride,
And a fairy's heart in her childish side,
A heart for magic—a heart for music,
A heart that will not be denied.   120
Now Taylor's birthday comes round, comes round.
He is rocking now, and swaying, and playing,
In this, the millennial hour.
And his fiddle, speaking with tongues, keeps saying,
"Behold, the young beauty, called: 'Tennessee.'"   125

Obeying the fiddler's merry command,
Tennessee,
In the shining form of a child,
Holds out her white hand.
Then a village Apocalypse indeed!   130
Taylor's news films of the future,
His merry Orphic games for his every dreaming creature,
Set to the Dixie tunes of "Kingdom Come,"
Tunes for stubborn souls,
No longer blind or dumb.   135

Threads of incense,
Then log cabins come,
Then Red Indian council halls,
Toys of the past,
Tossed up through the sky's blue walls,   140
And then,
From the white palm there,
Those toys, and those threads of smoke, become the
    world's World's Fair,
That floats, to merry robin notes,
And goes up, in shining power and authority and worth,   145
Till there a university of man's whole soul has birth,
From old McGuffey's reader style,
From toy-shop style, and play-room style, and baby
    Christmas mirth,
Spreading in terrible splendor, conquering the sad
    earth,
Spreading out like a Maytime field,   150
Coming down like an angel's misty shield,
A fair of the secret spirit, of the proud heart's comforter!

From the fairy comes a cry:
From that strange child comes a cry:
"Our pride is eternal, a tree no worm can kill—   155
It is older than the old oak trees, deathless like the sky."

And we go with the dream World's Fair,
We walk on its strange wide streets—
And the nation is the child and the child is the nation,
With pride in noble toys—   160
With the same firm, quick heartbeats—
Old toys grown great, now built anew—
Hilltop sunrise battlements set against the blue—
Set in cloudy streets of giant blue-ridge pines,
Where every kind of dewy flower vine shines.   165

And yet some childish towers have great pink ribbon
   bows,
And big bisque dolls,
And Indian dolls
Hold up some mighty roofs in pillared rows.
And jewelled city flags wave high,   170
And toy-shop mayors bow the knee
To those flags, unstained and wildflower sweet,
And the pouring crowds, set free.

Yet the fiddle cries in majesty of our nation's good
   and ill,
Great brains work greatly, with a will,   175
And the trees of pride no worm can kill
Grow stronger still.
While some wireless from Aldebaran
Rolls down from on high—
How democracy has swept the farthest stars—   180
Broken up Aldebaran's prison bars,
And the shout shakes and thrills
The nation's new-born, dream-born toy,
The Tinselled Oak Tree, priest of Truth,
And the new-born, dream-born toy,   185
Tinselled Mulberry, priest of Youth,
And the new-born, dream-born toy,
The Amaranth-Apple Tree,
White as the foam of the jasper-sea,
Priest of the Holy Spirit's grace.   190
And the new-born Golden-Rain-Tree,
Tinselled priest, at our honeyed feast,
Priest of the future Human race,
On our soul-paths set with fantasy,
Where the children of our hearthstones   195
Find the proud toys of democracy,
Find Majesty and Alchemy,
While Orpheus plays his fiddle there.

And look, there are Maypoles in a row,
And baskets pouring out strange flowers   200
For all the crowds that pass,
And tiny fairy Maypoles
And roller-skating rinks,
For all the squealing infant class,
In the nation that shall be,   205
Beginning with this lover—
Of innocent small children,

Beginning with this fiddler
And his fairy Tennessee—
On the borders of our prairies,   210
Our Middle-Western sea.
And our highest art will come in this Hereafter.
And in all the parks so gay
Sad young Shelleys, learning laughter,
Amid High-school yells, and college yells, and
   adventure yells,   215
Weird Confederate yells, weird Union yells,
In scandalous music, whispered, hissing, drumming,
While above the skylark flying machines
Of all man's future humming!
Playthings of the fancies of young Shelleys that
   shall be,   220
And their little brothers and sisters,
And the pouring crowds set free,
By the conqueror of death—
By the great Orpheus fiddler, and his fairy Tennessee.

Oh, the pinch-faced people still think we are drunk,   225
With this pearl-dropping orator's fair,
With this sky-painting orator's fair.
They call it *"the old Buncombe county bunk,"*
Deriding our village Apocalypse there,
Our old Happy Valley fair,   230
Turned to a world's World's Fair,
Though there are the glories of all creation,
Thoughts, from every ultimate nation,
Though the birds and the beasts are there—
Changed from the whimsies of first creation,   235
To things majestic from Revelation:—
Still, the pinch-faced people think we are drunk,
Curse us, and think we are drunk.

And now let us tell just the same child story—
In other terms, and with other glory.   240

Obeying the fiddler's command,
Tennessee in the shining form of a child
Holds out her white hand.
From her magic palm, strange doll books come,
Toys tossed up through the wide sky's walls,   245
They turn to boys' "dime libraries,"
They turn to girls' doll whimsies,
Snark-hunting paper flimsies,

They turn to children's Christmas books,
Alice-in-Wonderland looking-glass books,   250
And Pilgrim's Progress allegory books,
Singing bolder words as their leaves spread more and
    more
And up into the sky the flocks of beauty pour—
The flags of imagination on the page of the soul's sky,
Each gorgeous new day's print goes by.   255

And as the full years sweep along
Each old man reads his patriarch tome,
In the light of his dear hearth home,
And each child follows his new toy book
Though it flies across the world,   260
For always it returns
To his home-town hearthstone towers and bowers,
And childhood's wildflower banners unfurled.
So, each child keeps his soul alone,
As he keeps his ballot still his own,   265
True to the stars that gave him birth—
And the dreams he found in the wide earth—
To the Orpheus, to the fiddler and his fairy Tennessee,
And the pouring crowds, set free.

The night rolls round, stars light the land.   270
Obeying the fiddler's command,
Tennessee in the shining form of a child
Holds out her white hand.

And now let us tell just the same child story,
In other terms, and with other glory.   275

Now, hear the cry of all the nations,
Hear the cry of the generations,
Egypt to Utopia,
The hieroglyphic parallel written on the sky—
Following all the way—   280
The cry of the sun by day,
The cry of the stars by night,
The cry of the deep, deep earth,
The cry of the deep, deep earth.

She holds out her white hand—   285
From the incense, from the fairy palm,
From the wild cry in the air
White temples and pavilions there

From Adam's day to Kingdom Come,
Tossed up through the great sky's walls,   290
Petals before a humming wind,
And we watch them spread their delicate eaves
Amid quivering leaves—
Altars—then cathedrals,
Go up in long progression,   295
Growing greater,
Killing the gloom,
Till we see the white procession
All future forms of holy faith
Stand still and take possession   300
Of our nation that shall be,
Tremendous white Cathedral ships,
On our Middle-Western Sea,
Whose waves are fields of cotton, corn and wheat,
Orchard paths and boulevards   305
And pouring crowds, set free,
By the Orpheus, the fiddler, the conqueror of Death,
And his fairy, Tennessee.

And now let us tell just the same child story,
In other terms, and with other glory.   310

Oh, where are the child souls,
With the singers' pride,
Who will wake, refusing defeat and death,
Returning perpetually from the grave,
Generation on generation?   315
Where are the furious wills of the nation?
Oh, where are the hearts born to power?
"Oh, who is there among us, the true and the tried,
Who will stand by his colors, who is on the Lord's
    side?"
Who will rise each century, shout once again,   320
Who will wake in hot faith
With our cavalcade ride?
Send up their American souls from the grave,
And go forth in glory, aspiring,
Breathing springtime breath and noonday fire,   325
Armed with doll beauty perilous,
Armed with child glory marvellous,
Armed with Southern poems delirious,
Armed with grass daggers
They found in the ground,   330
Armed with old shields they dug up in the sky,

By the Archangel Mountains high—
Armed with long swords like the young crescent
　　moon—
Oh, who is there among us, the true and the tried,
Who will ride against Death and his endless cruelty,　335
However his legions conspire?
Who will ride against all grown-up foes of Democracy?
"Tomorrow, tomorrow," their marvelous tune—
"Tomorrow," their marvelous cry of desire—
Going forth with pouring armies　　　　　　　　340
Of the deathless young and gay,
Driving Death forever from the way.
Yes, who will sing in the follies of Heaven
To the Taylor-born Tennessee tune?
Who will follow the child Tennessee　　　　　　345
Armed with soul-swords like the young crescent
　　moon?
Who will follow her through the twilight,
Or in the morning, by the bright light,
Armed by her music, shouting her fame,
As she rides down the future with her boys all white
　　flame,　　　　　　　　　　　　　　　　350
As she rides down the future with her girls all white
　　fire?
Just in time to stop the charges
Of Death and all his hosts
That turn at last to beaten ghosts.

As she shouts down a thousand long years, my
　　darlings,　　　　　　　　　　　　　　355
Magic tomorrow the best of her tune,
Magic tomorrow her cry of desire. . . .
Her troops dressed in white for the spirits' delight,
She will stand in her stirrups a Torch of White Light,
The fairy child, Tennessee,　　　　　　　　　360
The soul of us, hope of us, helper and tyrant,
On her Pegasus horse of thunder and snow,
Round the merry-go-round she will go.

We dream we will make a merry-go-round,
While Taylor's birthday comes round, comes round,　365
A beautiful toy while the daisies laugh—
A picnic place for Taylor's sake
And his lovers, and little brothers and sisters. . . .

We dream we will build a merry-go-round.
Whose root is a flame in the ancient ground,   370
Whose flagpole is a tree to the sky,
A merry-go-round ten centuries high.
In the merry-go-round that we will make—
Of these Dixie thoughts of Kingdom Come,
In the merry-go-round that we will make—   375
The cricket will chirp, the bee will hum,
The cricket will chirp, the bee will hum,
The lark will cry the world awake,
Governor Taylor will govern the song,
Ten centuries will sweep along—   380
And the prairies and mountains will whirl around,
The prairies will whirl around, around.

In the merry-go-round that we will make—
The lark will cry the world awake,
Kind hearts will cry the world awake.   385
Toys will be men, dolls will be men,
And our sages and saints good dolls again.
Each painted reindeer will be a chum.
Not a single dingo or dog will be dumb.
And the horses will not be horses of wood,   390
Nor iron nor ivory, nor jewel nor jade,
Not hobby-horses whose paint will fade,
But Pegasus ponies on parade,
But Pegasus ponies on parade,
Whose hoofs are of ice, and whose wings are of fire.   395
White horses of Hope and the Spirit's desire,
White horses of Hope and the Spirit's desire—
On our horses of fire and thunder and snow
Round the merry-go-round we will go,
Round the merry-go-round we will go.   400

    December 1921 - May 1922

A SONG FOR ELIZABETH

    (Set to music by Albert V. Davies. Sung by Carolina
    Lazzari)

On the top of my red banner
Is a Psyche-Butterfly,
And I am very proud,
And would lift my banner high,
And march, perhaps, to somewhere,   5
Or on to splendid nowhere,

Or on to anywhere,
And tell this hour good-by,
And I am in a fidget
To hurry up and get there.   10

But I must be quite still
Or I will spoil my day.
I do not want my heart to die,
I do not want my soul to die,
I do not want that butterfly   15
To scare and fly away.

        1923

THE FLYING HOUSE, AND THE MAY QUEEN ETERNAL

Queen Venus, come now, be my heroine,
To form my pictures, and to scan my song,
And dominate that tall, enchanted house,
Invisible house, where I have lived so long.

Fast-flying house, that crosses sea and land.   5
House, always mine and empty but for me.
Fly near me, so your shadow may be near
And fall across my doors, and comfort me.

That house, all lights and shadows and no walls,
Has, for its doors and windows, barriers proud,   10
Closed wings for doors, or open wings for doors,
And, for its windows, wind-harps, singing loud.

Even your wing-whirr is a comfort there,
Your wireless whisper heard, though far away,
Makes you the heroine in that tall house.   15
The romance stays, if such fine honors stay.

Here I live on shadows, if I must,
Kissing one shadow's soft eyes to the end.
I will write out and draw new wind-harp rhymes,
Sons of your shadow's flesh and blood, dear friend.   20

(First contributed to Christopher Morley's Column in the
    New York Evening Post, "The Bowling Green," then
    reproduced in his book, "The Bowling Green.")

    1924

BILLBOARDS AND GALLEONS
   (Inscribed to Stephen Graham)

I

Each day is Biloxi's birthday party,
Splendid with many a sun-kissed wonder,
Splendid with many a swimming girl.
Oh, there is melted the heart of stone,
Fantasy, rhyme, and rhapsody ring.
From street car and Ford and yellow taxi,
Argosies crowded to shrieking capacity—
With moon-struck boy and sun-struck girl.
Tourists, residents, what you please—
From the whirling south, from the whirling north,
Bees near the hive,
Or far from home,
Dreaming of love like honeycomb.

"Barney Google" is what they sing,
"Mister Shean and Mister Gallagher,"
"Black Joe," and "Old Kentucky Home,"
"Swing Low Sweet Chariot," "Maryland," "Dixie,"
"Sometimes I feel like a Mourning Dove,"
"The Pullman Porters on Parade,"
Or hear, now, my "Song of Love."   20

But storms come down from the soul of the Universe,
Put the long coast in imminent jeopardy,
Despoiling felicity, quenching the ecstasy,
Hide my fantastical town from me—
Where every street is a valentine,   25
The kind we gave to love in youth
Where the lace is deep, three layers deep,
In, and in, and in you look:—
Gossamer book!
Fairy book!   30

Once, when such a storm was on,
When every spiritual hope seemed gone,
I was burning the world like a bridge, behind me,
I was walking in water so no one could find me—
In the edge of the waves, where the waves meet the
      beach—   35
Forest and sea waves, both within reach,
Far from my prairie home,

*This whole
poem is to be
read aloud,
with great
speed, and in
one breath,
as it were, as
though it were
one word,
rather than
one sentence.
This, over and
over, till the
metrical
scheme is
fluid in the
mind, a unit.
Then, of
course, read
very slowly.*
                                                      15

Far from the old hive, far from home,
Dreaming of love like honeycomb.

Twisted winds, coming down, from Heaven knows
    where,   40
Blistered feet were mine, seaweed was my hair.
Dream sea birds flew down on fanatical wings,
Flew down through tremendous red-rainbow rimmed
    rings.
They were speaking of glory, speaking of death,
Were shrieking creepy, fanatical things.   45
Many unwritten songs of mine, long forgotten,
And dim resolves, and loves forgotten
Swept in with the driftwood and foamy flakes.
Yet I said: "I will march till glory wakes,"
Yet I said: "My brain with marvelling sings   50
That courage and sleep, courage and sleep are the
    principal things."

March on, sleep-walkers, till courage comes
With invisible drums,
March, while the sad heart breaks,
Whirl on, like a leaf, then fight again—   55
Sleep and courage! Sleep and courage! The fate of men!
It was there, on the proud Spanish Trail I was walking,
And I thought of Don Ivan, my Spanish ancestor,
Friend of Columbus, and Isabel's guest,
From the stormy right   60
Came the green sea talking;
I was walking the Old Spanish Trail toward Biloxi,
So famous for legends of Spanish chivalry!
City of feathers, balloons and confetti,
City of hearties, of birthday parties!   65
Oh, streets of valentines in long lines,
Great garden of mocking-bird melody,
Oh, filagree city of fogs and mystery!
Far from the old hive, far from my home,
I was dreaming of love like honeycomb.   70
And startling pathways, starry-white,
Were revealed by the lightning and street light,
Revealed,
Revealed by the lightning and street light.

II

Buzzing autos, like black bees,   75
Like black bees,

Hurried through the magnolia trees,
Then billboards, to make nations stare,
Came in the vision flashy and vain,
Washed by the midnight sea-born rain,   80
Washed by the midnight sea-born rain.
They went like cliffs up to the sky,
America's glories flaming high,
Festooned cartoons, an amazing mixture,   85
Shabby, shoddy, perverse and twistical,
Shamefully boastful,
Shyly mystical.
Politics, with all its tricks, both old parties in a fix!
Donkey and elephant short of breath.
La Follette scorning them half to death.   90

The snappy *Saturday Evening Post*
Displaying, and advertising most
The noisiest things from coast to coast.
Exaggerated Sunday papers,
Comic sheets like scrambled eggs,   95
And Andy Gump's first-reader capers,
All on those billboards to the sky.
Who put them there, in the way, and why?
Pictured skyscrapers of the night,
Marble-topped, tremendous, white!   100
There were Arrow-collar heroes proud,
Holding their heads above the crowd,
Looking for love like honeycomb.
There was many an ice-cream vendor,
There were business kings in a daisy chain,   105
Then movie queens in a daisy chain,
Sugar-faced, unlaced and slender, dreaming of love
    like honeycomb.

Then all the rascals of the land,
All the damned for the last ten years,
Rising from their doom with tears,   110
Skeletons, skeletons, leather and bone,
Each dead soul chained to a saxophone—
Watching the roaring storm above,
Looking for honey-dreams and love.
All on those billboards to the sky,   115
Who put them there, in the way, and why?

Then a railroad map of the U. S. A.
Then a soul-road map of the U. S. A.
Showing all the flowers of the land,

But nowhere, love like honeycomb.   120
Only signboards, only billboards,
Washed by the midnight sea-born rain,
Washed by the midnight sea-born rain.

III

There were open boxes of fine cigars,
As big and bold as Pullman cars.   125
And on the brass-bound lids of these
Old Spain was pictured as you please.
And,
Here's the night's miracle began,
The greatest splendor known to man.   130

Flourishing masks and cigarettes,
Clicking their ribboned castanets,
Were Gypsies in high back combs and shawls,
Strutting through the Alhambra's halls.

Why were these billboards to the sky —   135
Who put them there, in the way, and why?

First I thought all the splendor had gone —
I was in darkness — I was in darkness — plunging on.
On the left were summer resort and lawn.
The flash of the trolley car,   140
The flash of the midnight train.
On the right — little waves, then great waves,
Then masts and shafts, then the wrecks of rafts —
Pirate ships of the Spanish Main,
Then the wrecks of the Galleons of Spain.   145
Red coins, then jewels,
Drowned parrots, drowned peacocks,
Then a tolling sound, a tolling sound,
Then the wrecks of the Galleons of Spain,
Rolling by, rolling on, in the rain!   150
Rolling by, rolling on, in the foam!

Love calls, death cries;
Drowned pirates, drowned Spanish beauties —
Drowned Incas, then drowned Montezumas;
First friars of Quetzal, then nuns of Quetzal,   155
Lost faces, sweet as the honeycomb.
First friars of Christendom, then nuns of Christendom,
Lost faces, sweet as the honeycomb.
Then a tolling sound, a tolling sound —

Pirate ships of the Spanish Main,   160
Then the wrecks of the Galleons of Spain
Rolling by, rolling on, in the rain,
Rolling by, rolling on, in the foam.

And I said: "I will march till my soul re-awakes."
And I said: "My mind with marvelling sings,   165
That 'courage and sleep, courage and sleep, are the
    principal things.'"

For there came dead eagles, then dead panthers,
Then, millions of men to the edge of the sky:—
Dead Spanish Legions, from the deep-sea regions—
While increasing rain whipped the sea and the air.   170
Then there came a noise like a vulture crying.
Then there came a cheering, cheering sound—
Bullrings slowly whirling around,
Bullrings, bullrings, 'round and 'round,
Bullrings, bullrings, 'round and 'round.   175
Then waves like ponies, waves like bulls,
Then waves like Seminoles, waves like Negroes,
Dragging up their chains from the deep,
Singing of love like honeycomb.
Then waves like tobacco fields, waves like cornfields, 180
Waves like wheat fields, turning to battlefields.
Then
Round-table crusaders, then world-paraders,
Tall kings in shining silver line,
As though for a miracle and a sign,   185
Singing songs like Spanish wine.

Then I saw the bad Pizzaro,
Then hours of dewy jungle-glow—
Dim Peru and Mexico.
Then the wild seeker, Coronado, singing of love like
    honeycomb,   190
With all his furious train, foaming by in the rain,
Singing in eternal sleep, lifted, singing from the deep.
Then the tall town of Eldorado,
Passing by, like a fog and a shadow.

And then I saw a girl more pale   195
Than any fairy ever shone—
A white light in the southern night,
As cold as the north Auroral light
Reigning over the sea alone!
My heart was like a burning world,   200

I saw it flame above the dawn,
Her robe, her footstool and her throne!
And she was like a moon and pearl,
And like an Alabaster stone!
So far away in the utmost sky!   205
Her beauty like the honeycomb,
The secret love,
Glory and Fate—
Her wings from the earth to Heaven's gate,
A pillar in the dawn apart.   210

Then she was gone—the dawn was gone—
Black storm! Black storm!
And I plunged on.

Then lightning bolts across the sky,
Then a great bubble like a dome,   215
In whirling, whirling, whirling splendor.

Then Sancho Panza! Then Don Quixote,
He who could not know surrender,
Glory's ultimate contender,
Singing in eternal sleep,   220
Lifted, singing from the deep,
Singing of love like honeycomb!
Then—
Windmills, windmills, 'round and 'round,
Windmills, windmills, 'round and 'round,   225
Windmills, windmills, 'round and 'round!
Then a great storm, a fearful cry, a bell of doom—
A tolling sound, a tolling sound, a tolling sound.
Then the wrecks of the Galleons of Spain—
Rolling by, rolling on, in the rain,   230
Rolling by, rolling on, in the foam.

By these ships, on the right, were the red waves cleft,
Then, again on the left, stood the billboards there,
Queerly fine to the zenith line,
Overhead to the zenith line—   235
Washed by the midnight sea-born rain,
Washed by the midnight sea-born rain,
Gleaming down, as the wrecks went by.
Looking at fair, lost Spain!
Between these visions I plunged on,   240
And straight ahead came to the wonder of dawn,
In that foggy dawn, storm-washed Biloxi!
The piers were wrecks, street cars were wrecks,

Sidewalks were wrecks.
Yet straight ahead arose from the dead,   245
The valentine, filagree towers of mystery,
The snow-white skyscrapers of new history.

Oh, fantasy, sugar and mockery!
Oh, mocking birds in their whimsy!
Oh, pretty, lazy Biloxi,   250
City haughty and fair, knowing not why: —
And looking high at the mast-filled sky,
Looking up at the ghost-filled sky,
Looking at fair, lost Spain.

Early 1924

HOW DULCENIA DEL TOBOSO IS LIKE THE
LEFT WING OF A BIRD

My child is like a bird's wing, a bird's wing, a bird's
    wing.
Slender like a bird's wing, curving like a bird's wing.
Her bones like those that leap and fling,
And make the quick bird's wing,
An elegant   5
And slender
Fairy-fashionplate design,
Plumed like a bird's wing, steel strong, but very tender,
Every curve of life to render.

And her motion, like a bird's wing, cutting higher,   10
She spreads above my sky,
A noble, an immortal thing,
A phoenix-wing of fire.
She spreads above my sky
An aurora and a sign,   15
An elegant and slender fairy-fashionplate design.

And then we are timid,
And infinitely small,
Two children playing house
In a pine tree tall.   20
Or she is then a wren's wing
Hiding a small-boy wren,
Or I am hidden like a hope, tied with a cob-web rope,
Beneath a humming bird's wing, a bird's wing, a bird's
    wing,

And then she is an eagle's wing, a hawk's wing, a Greek
    god's wing,   25
Teaching me, her son, to fly where tremendous stars
    sing.

But I have never gone through clouds that hide her
    everywhere,
Have only seen one wing emerge from fog or sea or
    cloudy air,
Her eyes,
Like the fixed eyes   30
On the butterfly's or pheasant's wing.

I have never seen her young soul's face,
Her hidden eyes, and the other wing,
I have never heard the word of grace
My hawk will cry, my swallow sing.   35

I have only seen the left wing,
One fair, emerging bird's wing.

My child is like a bird's wing, a bird's wing, a bird's
    wing,
A dreamy wing, a lone wing.

    Spring, 1923

THE PEARL OF BILOXI

Proudest pearl of the wide world,
Haughtier than an Inca's plume,
You and I, near this Biloxi,
Long were laid in a shell tomb.
There we slept like white blind kittens   5
Curled in a warm kitchen box,
While the friendly fist of the sea
On our roof made humorous knocks
Without breaking the shell box.

Grandest pearl of the whole world,   10
And so vain you are twice dear,
Kin to dragon flies and dragons,
Kin to larks and kin to larkspurs,
Kin to gold and white snapdragons
And hot bees that drink such flagons   15

You grew whiter year by year,
You grew slender, like a dawn ray
To the plume, and flower, and torch I find you here.

Plume, upon the sunrise crest,   20
Pride of the beach, and set apart,
Hearing me; if not concurring—
Do we not have one horizon?

Is there not a secret stirring,
Yes, a deep-sea-kitten purring,
Then the slow thump of the ocean,   25
Deep in your heart, and my heart?

Oh, your heart is sky and ocean!
Each fond heart a world-wide heart . . .
To a new religion set apart . . .
Set apart,   30
Set apart.

        January 1924

DOCTOR MOHAWK
    (Inscribed to Ridley Wills)

    (A most informal chant, being a rhymed commentary on
the preface, "Adventures While Singing These Songs" [see
Collected Poems], especially the reference to the red Indian
ancestor. To this to be added a tradition that one branch of
my mother's family came of the Don Ivans, of Spain.)

                        I

    Being a Seven-Year-Old Boy's Elaborate Memory
              of the Day of His Birth

In through the window a sea-mustang brought me,
(Smashing the window sash, breaking the law).
I was tied to his back—I do not know who caught me.

Up from Biloxi, up the great Mississippi,
Through the swamps, through the thaw, through the
    rains that grew raw,
On the tenth of November (the hail storm was nippy).
Up the slow, muddy Sangamon River—
(While we heard the towns cough and we heard the
    farms shiver),

*The poem to
be read
with the greate
possible speed
imitating the
galloping of a
sea-mustang,
each time
faster till it is
so memorized,
all the repeten
musically
blended, almo
as though the
poem were on
long word, the
of course,
read very slou*

The high wave rolled on. We heard a crow squawk,
With a voice like a buzz saw, destroying the day;   10
"Caw, caw, you are rolling to meet the tall Mohawk,
He will burn you to ashes and turn you to clay,
You will burn like a scarecrow with fire in the straw,
You are rolling and whirling on to the Mohawk,
Caw, caw,   15
Caw, caw."

We sighted and broke the high hedge of Oak Ridge,
We rolled through its tombs. We saw Incubi walk.
We leaped the snow mounds like a pack of bloodhounds.
Dead lawyers were shrieking: *"You are breaking the
    law."*   20
We spoiled and howled down the shrill cemetery sounds,
Swept townward: a green wave, a foam wave, a moon
    wave,
Up the dawn streets of Springfield, high tide in a cave,
Up to Edwards and Fifth street, and broke every
    windowpane.
They thought we were "cyclone," earthquake, and rain.   25
We smashed the front door. We ramped by the bed's
    head.
On the wall-paper pattern sea-roses bloomed red.

There, for a ceiling bent crab-thorn, hazel-brush,
Red-haw, black-haw,
(And the storm blew a horn),   30
There fluttered a carrion crow that cried: *"Caw!"*
A scarecrow so queer, and a crow that cried: *"Caw,
    Caw! Caw!"*

II

*Being my notion, as a Ferocious Small-Boy, of my Ancestral
    Protector.*

The porpoise was grandma. The Mohawk was doctor:
"Heap-big-chief-the-Mohawk," with eye like a
    tommyhawk.
Naked, in war-paint, tough stock and old stock,   35
Furious swash-buckler, street-brawler, world-breaker,
Plumed like an Indian, an American dragon,
Tall as Sun-Mountain, long as the Sangamon,
With a buffalo beard, all beast, yet all human,
Sire of the Mexican king, Montezuma,   40

Of Quetzal the Fair God, and Prince Guatomozin,
And that fated Peruvian, Atahualpa,
Of King Powhatan and his brown Pocahontas,
And of everything Indian serious or humorous,
Sire of the "Mohocks" who swept through old London,   45
(Too dirty for Swift and too wicked for Addison);
He was carver of all the old Indian cigar-signs,
Chief of all the wild Kickapoo doctors,
And their log-cabin remedies known to our fathers,
Sire of St. Tammany, and sweet Hiawatha,   50
Tippecanoe, and Tyler Too,
He was named Joseph Smith, he was named Brigham
     Young,
He was named Susquehannah, he was named Mississippi,
Every river and State in the Indian Tongue,
Every park, every town that is still to be sung: —   55
Yosemite, Cheyenne, Niagara, Chicago!
The Pride of the U. S. A.: —*that* is the Mohawk,
The Blood of the U. S. A.: —*that* is the Mohawk,
He is tall as Sun-Mountain, long as the Sangamon,
Proud as Chicago, a dream like Chicago,   60
And I saw the wild Star-Spangled Banner unfurl
Above the tall Mohawk that no man can tame
Old son of the sun-fire, by many a name.

When nine, I would sing this yarn of the sea,
With ample embroidery I now must restrain   65
(Giving the facts and omitting the flowers)
It proved new fantastics were coming to me.
The Mohawk! the Mohawk! the Mohawk! the Mohawk!
Doctor and midwife! ancestral protector!
Breathed Mohawk fire *through* me, gave long claws
     to me,   70
Told my father and mother they must soon set me free,
Told the dears I had lived with a pearl in the billow
In the Mexican Gulf, in the depths of that sea,
For infinite years. Put the pearl by my pillow.
(It was new as that hour, and as old as the sea) —   75
The Soul of the U. S. A. —*that* was the pearl.
It became a white eagle I could not understand.
And I saw the carrion crow fly away.
And I saw the boughs open and the sun of that day,
And I saw the white eagle in the clouds fly and whirl   80
Then soar to the skies to a Star-Spangled Land.

And I cried, and held hard to my mother's warm hand.
And the Mohawk said: — "Red man, your first trial
    begins."
And the Mohawk roared: — "Shame to you, coward and
    mourner!"
And the Great Chief was gone.   85

But my life was all planned.

I wept with my mother. I kissed and caressed her.
Then she taught me to sing. Then she taught me to
    play: —
The sibyl, the strange one, the white witch of May.
Creating diversion with slow-talk and long-talk,   90
She sang with girl-pride of her Spanish ancestor,
The mighty Don Ivan, Quixotic explorer: —
Friend of Columbus, Queen Isabel's friend,
Conquistador!
Great-great-great-grandfather.   95

I would cry and pressed close to her, all through the
    story
For the Mohawk was gone. And gone was my glory: —
Though that white-witch adored me, and fingered each
    curl,
Though I saw the wild Star-Spangled Banner unfurl,
Though a Spanish ancestor makes excellent talk.   100
I was a baby, with nothing to say
But: — "The Mohawk, the Mohawk, the Mohawk, the
    Mohawk."
And I knew for my pearl I must hunt this long way
Through deserts and dooms, and on till today.

I must see Time, the wild-cat, gorging his maw,   105
I must hear the death-cry of the deer he brought low,
And the cry of the blood on his pantherish paw,
And that carrion crow on his shoulder cry "Caw, Caw!
    Caw!"

III

One Brief Hour of Grown-up Glory on the Gulf of Mexico.

Far from the age of my Spanish ancestor,
Don Ivan the dreamer,   110
Friend of Columbus, and Isabel's friend,

Wherever I wander, beggar or guest,
The soul of the U. S. A.:—that is my life-quest.

Still I see the wild Star-Spangled Banner unfurl.

And at last near Biloxi, in glory and sport   115
I met Doctor Mohawk, while swimming this morning
Straight into the Gulf of Mexico Sun.
The Mohawk! the Mohawk! the Mohawk! the Mohawk!
From the half-risen sun, in the pathway of blood
Sea-roses swept round me, red-kissed of the flood.   120
And the flying fish whispered: "the First Trial is done."

Magnificent mischief now was a-borning.
First: I dived and brought up the cool dream called
   "The Pearl."
As far from the Mohawk as peace is from murder,
As far from the Mohawk as May from November,   125
As far from the Mohawk as love is from scorning,
As far from the Mohawk as snow is from fire.
Yet, the Mohawk arm lifted me out of that flood
(The blood of the U. S. A.—that is the Mohawk)
And he healed my sick heart where the thunder-winds
   hurl,   130
There in the fog, at the top of the sun
Cool were his foam-fins, majestic his graces,
Doctor, and glorious Ancestral Protector,
Exhorter, reprover, corrector.
Then we swam to the sky through crystalline spaces,   135
The clouds closed behind us, all the long way,
And a rainbow-storm priesthood that hour blessed the
   bay,
Medicine men, in tremendous array,
While he spoke to me kindly and yet with fine scorning
For hunting for favors with rabbits or men.   140
Breathed Mohawk fire through me, gave long claws to
   me
And told me to think of my birthday again:—
How the sun is a Mohawk, and our best ancestor:
I must run to him, climb to him, swim to him, fly to him,
And laugh like a sea-horse, or life will grow dim.   145
How only the Mohawks will call me their brother,
(We will flourish forever, breaking the law)
They are laughing through all of the lands and the oceans,
(And only great worlds make an Indian laugh)
They are singing and swimming their pranks and their
   notions   150

With poems, and splendid majestical motions,
And they will stand by me, and save and deliver,
With the pearl near my heart, they will love me forever,
An eagle, a girl, then a moon on the sand,
The bird of the U. S. A.—that is the darling—   155
Whirling and dancing, swimming with awe
In the light of the sun, in the infinite shining
Of the uncaptured future:—that is the darling.
The infinite future, that is the eagle,—
An eagle, a moon, a girl on the sand,   160
The Soul of the U. S. A.—that is the pearl,
Without flaw.

Note:—For the "Mohocks" read Gay's Trivia iii, 325;
Spectator Nos. 324, 332, 347; Defoe's Review, March 15,
1712; also Swift's Journal to Stella.

Summer, 1923

THE TRIAL OF THE DEAD CLEOPATRA IN HER BEAUTIFUL AND WONDERFUL TOMB

The trial opens B.C. 29. This is the date of the death of
Caesarion, shortly after the suicide of Cleopatra. Caesarion,
natural heir to the empires of Egypt and Rome, son of Cleo-
patra and Julius Caesar, was assassinated by his cousin
Octavian. This made Octavian Augustus Caesar sole heir of
Julius Caesar, made him ruler of the known world.

I. She Becomes a Soul, Flowering Toward Egyptian Resurrection, B.C. 29

Said Set, the Great Accuser: "You poisoned your young
  brothers."
But the mummy of Cleopatra whispered: "These were the
  slanders of Rome."
"You poisoned your faithful servants, you sold the Nile
  to Caesar."
But the mummy of Cleopatra whispered: "These were the
  slanders of Rome."
"You gambled with Marc Antony for the last wheat in
  Egypt,   5
But the mummy of Cleopatra whispered: "These were the
  slanders of Rome."

*   *   *   *   *

And Set, the soul defiler, the hyena, the tomb-violator,
Yet Prosecuting Attorney of gods and stars,
Eternal in the eternal judgment room,   10
Said: "Antony is again my witness
Again to declare this woman vile."
For the ninth time Thoth drew him on the wall,
Again, that ink was a green and sulphurous flame,
And Antony was pictured in his armor: —   15
Bacchus, turned soldier, painted on the stone.
For the ninth time Thoth gave that ibis cry,
And called forth that traitor from his tent.
He stood, a pillar of flame and smoking gold,
And spoke, but as the puppet speaks in shows.   20
Ancestral enemy of Octavian —
He took Octavian's part before these gods, —
Every praise of the Italian city
For Julius Caesar's nephew on the throne: —
Flattering that crowned Augustus in his seat   25
With all the slanders against Cleopatra
Invented by Rome's poets and her priests!
And slandering Caesar's child Caesarion,
Killed by Augustus' sword in Alexandria.

              *   *   *   *   *

A speaking mummy, neither living nor dying —   30
A human log, held upright by Anubis,
Once the goddess high priests make of girls,
The queen was more than mortal in her sorrow.
More than her thirst and hunger, was deeper still
A memory like old poison in deep wounds —   35

She whispered again, in the face of Set, the deathless: —
"Cleopatra, the young girl, died when Caesar died.
Only my shadow revelled with Antony,
Coming forth by day from this dark hall
To win the empire for Caesarion.   40
Coming forth by day to make my boy
The heir of Egypt, Rome, and the purple seas —
As all you high gods knew from the beginning.
Only my shadow revelled with Antony.
He was the plume of Caesar, nothing more.   45
Half-republican, then half-Egyptian,
Half-clay — half-god — the Roman clay prevailed,
He turned against his prince, Caesarion. . . .
Then lost at Actium the purple seas."

Held in a spell by Set, the god of evil,   50
In a drunkard's dream, Antony chanted then
Forgetting his life-hatred of Augustus.
He who had called himself before the Senate,
"Champion of Caesar's widow and her son."
There on the terrace of a million years,   55
In a big doll's-voice, Antony chanted then
A song the Swan of Avon yet should sing,
That all the poets of the world should know,
And all the singers of the world believe,
Till the good queen be lost in her wild name.   60

              *   *   *   *   *

Her eyes were like two rays of the great moon,
When Mediterranean storms destroy the ships.
She looked at him. And the eyes of Antony
Became the idiot eye-holes of a helmet,
The visor down. And his world-flashing sword   65
Was smoke and dust—his face a wavering flame.

In that dim court there stood the great iron scales;
"Scales of Justice," known to souls today,
In one side, the Feather of Perfect Truth,
In the other—the heart of the waiting dead.   70

              *   *   *   *   *

Appointed to devour all hearts rejected—
The crocodile called Ammit glowered and waited.

Then Thoth gave Cleopatra "Words of Power."
And Cleopatra called through the dusty court,
With the musical voice of all the women of time—   75
And the flaming heart there on the iron scales cried:
"Cleopatra died when Caesar died.
I am the heart of Caesar, nothing more."
And the Apes of the Dawn beside the scales gave tongue:
"She is the heart of Caesar, nothing more."   80

And then Cleopatra spoke alone:
"I have knocked at this inner door of my own tomb,
Waiting patiently for this my judgment,
As all you high gods know, since Caesar died.
We crossed the purple seas for Alexandria   85
Two clouds, blood-red, two storms against the moon.

He brought me here, that day, and you judged him.
Queens have been crowned, have reigned, and have
   grown old,
Have been sealed in holy tombs with 'Words of Power':
Have come to judgment and to resurrection   90
Since Caesar knocked with me upon this door,
While his body lay in blood in roaring Rome.
You set him free, you sent him to the skies!
Give me my throne today, beside his throne.
When Antony turned against Caesarion   95
I put the Asp against my naked breast;
My *Mummy* joined my *Shadow* at this door,
My *Heart*, and *Soul* and *Name*,
Came to one place.

"Why should the gods keep Cleopatra waiting,   100
A first, and then again a second time,
Suffering the mummy's peril and thirst and hunger,
Suffering the mummy's fear and hell-fire flame?
I, a dead log, cry to be made a god,
Above all memory and all forgetting.   105
I, Cleopatra, defy Set, the Accuser,
And I stake all on Caesar and our son.
I have called those witnesses now nine times nine,
Let Set prevent their coming nevermore!

"Why should this violator of the dead,   110
He who would tear the precious mummy-cloth,
He, to whom only mummy-thieves will pray,
He, who would rend the helpless flesh and tendon,
Stealer of vases of most precious ointment,
Counter of beads of lapis-lazuli,   115
Hyena-souled, small-minded, jackdaw-king,
Stealer of mummy-crowns and mummy-sandals,
Tearing them from the flesh of long-dead men:—
Be the wrecker of tombs of gods—stealer of suns?
Why should this mole steal heavens and suns from me? 120

"Why should this one defiler of the earth,
Prevent the coming here of Julius Caesar,
Egypt's dazzling Bird of Paradise,
The great cock-pheasant and peacock of the world,
And the beautiful young prince, Caesarion,   125
Heir of Egypt, Rome, and the purple seas?"

The silent gods half-opened their dull eyes,
Isis, in mercy, lifted one slender hand.
So, at last, the deathless prayer seemed heard.
Thoth, with his chisel, cut in the wall before them,   130
Then painted, Rome's giant hieroglyphic—
Dead Caesar, with his deep red flowing wound—
Then Caesar's boy,—Horus Caesarion,—
An exquisite god-prince, naked and fair.
Yet patience! Oh, mummy and prisoner, Cleopatra,   135
For that slow, cruel, humorous artist, Thoth,
Tantalizer of the souls of men,
Painted and carved, for many a racking day,
Sword-waving hieroglyphics, that, marching, sang
Only at the end: "Come shining forth,   140
Come forth, oh, deathless sons of Amon-Ra."

       *   *   *   *   *

Caesar and Caesarion at last,   *B.C. 20.*
Stepped from the wall to the side of Cleopatra   *Nine years*
And the great queen fell there, like a speaking log,   *later.*
Touching their feet. Her mummy case was wrecked—   145
A scattered, shattered chrysalis, and tomb.
But Cleopatra called through the dusty court,
With the musical voice of all the women of time—
And the flaming heart, there, on the iron scales, cried:
"Cleopatra died when Caesar died.   150
I am the heart of Caesar, nothing more."

But what then of the flame called Antony?
It merged into the majesty of Caesar, -
Walked with his stride, the shadow of his shadow,
Hid in his robe, lost itself in his wound.
Had neither vanity nor purpose of its own,   155
Was seen no more. And Caesar stood there, waiting.
Only his crown was brighter now: his whip
Shone like a torch above the dusty floor,
The light from his eyes like two rays from the moon,   160
When Mediterranean storms destroy the ships.

Then Set, the beautiful, the hard and proud,
Ignoring Caesar and Caesarion,
Called again to the old Egyptian gods,
Pointing at the high-throned Alexander,   165
Still the new-comer in that pantheon,
Pointing long fingers at the fallen queen—

The mummy cloth, still binding her dead knees,
Dried mummy wreaths fallen from her hair: —
"These are invaders, like the Assyrian kings!   170
What have the Ptolemies to do with Egypt?
What right had the Macedonian phalanx here?
Why are Roman legions on the Nile?
Are they enthroned by ancient Amon-Ra?"

Then to those gods, the golden Caesar spoke: —   175
"Oh, grief of Caesar in the heaven of heavens!
Without her, thrones are dim and lights are vain!

"She set me on my horse, to win the Parthian crown,
We were resolved to conquer utmost Asia,
Build again the empire of Thutmose Third,   180
And send the ardent arrows of Amon-Ra,
To ultimate Britain and ultimate India,
Win new empires for Caesarion,
Heir of Egypt, Rome and the purple seas.
But Cassius, Casca and Brutus struck too soon.   185
Caesar they could endure, but not his heir.
They could endure a king, but not a god.
They could endure a queen, but not a goddess.
And they hated my queen-goddess, Cleopatra.

"No blood was in her veins, but the sun's blood.   190
Sweet Hathor lived in her eyes and her dimpled knees;
And here, with open wounds, I praise her yet.
I was weary and old, with shadowy ambition.
She kissed me into pride and power again.
She was the Isis nations make of queens.   195

"She made me into a son of Amon-Ra,
Into Egypt's dazzling bird of paradise,
The great cock-pheasant and peacock of the world.
With one kiss of her girl-lips, long ago.
We dreamed of The Terrace of a Million Years.   200

"There on the island, where I met her first,
This priestess taught me the wisdom of old Thoth,
Who hears the wit, and even the sweet singing,
Uttered among the humorists of the moon.
And when she bore my son Caesarion,   205
We sailed with him on all the purple seas,
We climbed with him to every earthly throne,

"Thinking of things beyond all human speech.
We chanted 'The Chapters of Coming Forth by Day,'
Till Thoth, himself, flew in from the wide sea   210
(The ibis with the rakish wing and stride)
With the great chapters marching after him,
The hieroglyphic soldiers of his heaven,
That will go marching, flying and glittering,
In all the tombs and capitals of men   215
In all inscriptions of papyrus rolls,
In many languages, in picture-plays,
Waving stone wings through men's minds forever,
When all Rome's legions are but dust and bones,
When every arch of triumph has fallen down,   220
When men will fly with iron wings, and speak
Across the sky in words that bind the world,
And light can shine through earth, through steel, and
      granite.
Those hieroglyphics still will march and sing,
Defending gods and all the tombs of gods,   225
From Set and his innumerable train,
And all who violate your judgment hall."

The heart of Cleopatra in the balance,
Neither rose nor fell, and not one breath
Overthrew the Feather of Truth, in the scale.   230

        *   *   *   *   *

                                                      B.C. 11.
The god of spices, and incense, and embalming,   *Nine years*
God of the body's dim eternity.   *later.*
Anubis, the faithful jackal, kept the scales,
And warded off the wicked hands of Set.
The Feather of Truth, and the heart, kept balance,
      still.   235

But Set, the hard, the proud, the confident,
Set, with the crocodile, Ammit, at his side, —
Set, the beautiful, the hard and proud,
The devious, the diabolical postponer,
Tried still to outwear her heart, till it fall from the
      scales   240
Into the monstrous jaws to the second death.
He said: "Your fable is yourself in truth,
Your rumor is your soul, your name is you
To the secret caves of long reëchoing time."

Set, the Accuser, lifted his hand of stone   245
And sounds came up from the darkness under the sea
And the bones in darkness under all the sands: —
"She poured us out like water and like wine,
She wasted us in battle, let her die!
She wasted us in battle, let her die!"   250

But what have the gods to do with such complainers?
They love the beautiful, the hard and proud—
Only these can wake them from the night.

The law's delay among the gods is great.
They sleep on shadowy thrones. Their words grow
     gray.   255
Their ribs are basalt and their faces basalt
Cut by the hardest chisels of proud priests,
There on The Terrace of a Million Years.

High above in the light of each changing year,
Priests of the jewelled temples of Abydos,   260
Thinking not of forgotten Cleopatra,
Of Caesar, Caesarion, or Antony,
Sang their sweet songs of the soul's resurrection,
Songs to Osiris, "First of the Westerners,"
Thinking only of their unburied dead,   265
Of mummies to be sealed in their holy tombs.

          *   *   *   *   *

With quiet gesture and tremendous air   *B.C. 2.*
Set still held the gods' too-sleepy eyes.   *Nine years*
He pointed there to the pitiful prostrate one,   *later.*
Half-mummy, and half-living girl. Her lips   270
Had called in vain for water and for food
For years and years, for moments like centuries.
More than her thirst and hunger was deeper still
A memory like old poison in deep wounds,
Antony's treachery to Caesarion.   275

          *   *   *   *   *

Anubis, the faithful jackal, fed her smoke,
There with strong paws, beat down the snakes of
     death.
Unnoted and unknown to gods or ghosts,
To Set or to his suffering prisoner.

          *   *   *   *   *

Strange winds from the uttermost heavens swept the *Anno Domini 1.*
    tomb,   280
For Christ was born in the night in a town to the north,
And the world's first Christmas flamed on the sea and
    the air.

Said Set, the torturer, the king of hell-fire: —
"If you are the daughter of a god,
If you would change your name and take your throne,   285
Command these grave-stones to be made your bread
In my great name, proudly defying them.
I am the light-god, I am the king of the skies."
Her one virtue, a transcendent scorn,
Her one virtue: supernatural pride,   290
Thirst and hunger had made the great queen mad.
But still she cried and sang through the dusty court
With the musical voice of all the mothers of time,
And the flaming heart, too, on the iron scales cried: —
"Cleopatra died when Caesar died.   295
I am the heart of Caesar, nothing more."
Then, then, she was given in mercy The Wisdom of
    Thoth.
Then, though her mummy-face was in the dust,
She whispered against the tempter one last spell—
And the pride that would not break conquered the
    stars: —   300
"Must Set still violate the judgment hall?
Let the cold scales be the sole judge of my heart.
And as for the kingship of the universe
Hail to the true light-god, Amon-Ra,
And his Roman son, Caius Julius Caesar—   305
Egypt's dazzling bird of paradise,
The great cock-pheasant and peacock of the world!
Oh, wings of Caesar high above all mountains,
Wings of Caesar above the purple seas."

                *   *   *   *   *

Strange winds from the uttermost heavens swept
    the tomb.   310

                *   *   *   *   *

Now the steady hand of Thoth was trembling—   *Anno Domini 10.*
The artist, king of magic and miracle, —   *Nine years*
Physician, healer, merciful, at last.   *later.*

He touched her shrivelled hands with reverent love.
He touched her gilded eyelids and strained arms.   315
He loosed the mummy bands from thigh and shoulder,
Singing from the ancient Book of the Dead,
"Lift up thy head, oh thou who liest prostrate."

And she was again held upright by Anubis,
A speaking mummy, transfigured, and not dying.   320
And she stood pitifully by Caesar, there,
Half-mummy, but half-god: and beautiful—
A soul indeed—a human soul at last—
The Macedonian glory in her face,
Flowering toward Egyptian resurrection.   325

Anno Domini 19.
II. She Becomes a Goddess   *Nine years later.*

Strange winds from the uttermost heavens swept the
    tomb,
A mystery and a mercy, still unknown.

    *   *   *   *   *

The ghost of Caesar swayed like a weed in a storm.
And his flaming wound was great in his shadowy side.
Still the steady hand of Thoth was trembling   330
Amid his proud, unfaltering picture writing.
He shook his Ibis-wing, nodded his head:—
For the log had well-nigh changed into the goddess.
And the wisest woman of all the mothers of time,
Still the secret favorite of shrewd Thoth,   335
Heard now with him the rumors of all nations.
(For these two could apprehend and prophesy
Further than all those basalt gods there brooding,   .
Further than Set, the accuser of gods and stars.)
Strange winds from the uttermost heavens and uttermost
    tombs!   340
Dim dreams on the march above the universe!
Miracles on the edge of the Dead Sea!
The little river Jordan roared like doom!
There were shoutings and hosannahs among small
    peoples!
Wild fishermen on the Sea of Galilee!   345

Even Anubis lifted his jackal head.
There was the incense of a more merciful empire,

The beginnings of terrible justice, in the air,
Greater than the mercy of Osiris!
His power was waning in the Universe,   350
A power was gathering from the deeps and the heights.
As a great storm, this power was whirling down,
Blowing through mountain ribs, as through silk veils,
Potent to make real gods, even of these: —
Who sleep on shadowy thrones, whose words grow
    gray,   355
Whose ribs are basalt and their faces basalt,
Cut by the hardest chisels of proud priests.
Their hearts were softened while their thrones were
    shaken,
There on The Terrace of a Million Years.

And the cry of Anubis came like a temple gong.   360
And the cry of the woman rang through the dusty hall,
With the musical voice of all the mothers of time: —
"Oh gods of mercy and of majesty,
Oh gods of softening hearts and trembling thrones: —
When first I came to this my dark tomb door,   365
When I came clamoring for my goddess throne,
And Caesar knocked with me, a suppliant here,
You set him free, you sent him to the skies,
To mourn for me, to wait for me in vain,
Through years and years, and moments like centuries.   370
Give us our thrones today beside your thrones!

Still Set was opening his mouth in scorn,
"Your rumor is your soul, your name is you,"
She stretched frail arms toward all the gods and thrones
Arms at last unwrapped from mummy bands,   375
And sang above Set's accusing voice
With the voice of a child arising from long sleep,
"Why should the gods of Egypt believe the eternal
    Accuser,
Or the lying poets of Rome?
These were the slanders of Rome."   380

      *   *   *   *   *

Still Set cried on with his eternal spell,   *Anno Domini 28.*
With the old charge that would not be put down: —   *Nine years*
"Your granite hieroglyphic, still is you!   *later.*
The written rumor of your name is you,
To the farthest caves of long reëchoing time."   385

      *   *   *   *   *

The forty-two assessors and the nine great gods of Egypt
Were growing very old. And their daughter, the pale
   queen,
The last of royal Egypt, was thwarting the Great Accuser.
They watched with increasing flame in their vague, hot
   eyes
(Flame like the goldsmith's furnace melting brass)   390
Her still uplifted arms, her advancing step,
Her gentle increasing strength, as the years rolled on,
The years and years, the moments like centuries.
They saw from their rocking thrones, unafraid, unsmiling,
That the Feather of Truth fell not from the balance,   395
The flaming heart fell not. But it whispered still: —
"I am the heart of Caesar, nothing more."

Privileged doubter of all gods and stars!
Privileged prosecutor of gods and stars!
Privileged scourge of men, and gods, and stars: —   400
Set cried boldly: "Still you are Cleopatra!
Still mongrel in Egypt, like yonder Alexander!
Upstart! Parvenu! Usurper!
You are shamed in the eyes of all the women of time.
Gambler, Thief, Poisoner and Betrayer!   405
The world will believe my word in the mouths of the
   poets,
And these gods will believe all the golden slanders
   of Rome!"
Barking his terrible bark, he waited and harried,
With his ravening hungry monster at his side—
Set, who had broken the heart of holy Isis   410
Once, in the far beginning of the world: —
Set, who had murdered, then tried the good Osiris,
Before this very court of the basalt gods
Still stood unsmitten in the Osirian court
Though The Merciful King, now at the top of his
   stairway,   415
Ruled, and justified all the pure of heart.

       *   *   *   *   *

Strange winds from the uttermost heavens swept the
   tomb
Blowing through mountain ribs as through silk veils;
Then all the old years fell from The Merciful King,
New youth came with new mercy to Osiris: —   420
He, First of the Westerners, lifted his shepherd's
   crook,

Isis, The Mother, lifted one slender hand,
Thoth, the Great-hearted, lifted his Ibis wing
To the very roof of the black basalt hall.
And the walls were as the walls of the great full moon.   425
And that Macedonian Cleopatra
Glorious as Hera, blazing like Psyche the bride,
Was dressed now in strange spiritual snow-white.
And so, transfigured, and with power transcendent
In her arms, the little child, Caesarion: —   430
She fixed her eyes on mighty Alexander,
With the gods, a stone-carved son of Amon-Ra,
On the Trembling Terrace of a Million Years.
She prayed, with Caesar there by her snowy shoulder: —
"Oh son of Amon-Ra, called the Macedonian, —   435
Oh one man Caesar envied, Oh Alexander!
Oh conqueror, your great mother bore you
To Egypt's golden sun-god long ago.
And so it was you came to take your kingdom
In our beautiful oasis, Sekhet-Amit,   440
And there it was that Amon-Ra came down
To claim you, and my father, Ptolemy,
As Egypt's kings his Macedonian sons!
You set my fathers on Egyptian throne,
Giving, in love, their queens to Amon-Ra."   445
Then Caesar, Caesarion and the queen
Prayed toward the basalt throne of Alexander: —
"Give us our thrones today, beside your throne."
He stretched his priest-carved arms in miracle,
Stepped from the swaying terrace in strange might,   450
Stepped from the terrace with that wild assurance
He once rode trembling lands and fearful seas,
A blazing sun, hidden within that tomb,
A god and king and peacock of the world,
Unshaken, though the heavens and earth were shaken,   455
Caesar, his brother, there, eternally.

He gave into each right hand the terrible lotos,
That sends forth stars and suns in yellow pollen.
He gave them on their foreheads, holy seals
From the lotos cup of the Egyptian heavens.   460
The God-cup there ended the thirst of the dead.
And the flaming wound in Caesar's side was healed.
And the terrible lotos blooms dropped stars like jewels.
Gone was the hieroglyphic of Cleopatra
From the tomb-walls and from the coffin-lids.   465
Gone was the fabled wife of Antony.

Gone was all former meaning of her name.
The blood of Macedon had left her veins.

All the goddesses there on their thrones,
Shook sweet Hathor's sistrum like soft bells.   470
And they called her: "Hathor's-body-and-heart-and-soul."
And they called her: "Hathor's-laughter-and-true-name."

Her ears became the tiniest humorous calf's-ears,
Like sweet and humorous Hathor's masquerade,
When she dances among the half-grown girls and
    boys.   475
Then her white robe fell like snow blown from a cliff.
She stood there the brown Hathor, Queen of the Nile!
An airy, girl-Egyptian, full of whims,
Tender, innocent, marvellously young—
A black-eyed girl with body of tawny gold.   480
But still she cried, and her heart from the iron scales
    cried:—
"Cleopatra died when Caesar died."

Leaving the scales, where for long years it had waited,
Her heart flew back to her breast forevermore,
Justified! Justified! Before the good Osiris.   485
The Name, "Osiris," now blazing on her breast,
As on the breasts of Caesar, and her boy.

Leaving the scales, where for long years it had waited,
The Feather of Truth flew to the forehead of Isis,
Plume of the mother, the merciful mother, Isis,   490
Plume of the Queen, whose victory is the Truth.

Thoth cut the great verdict on the wall,
And the new names of the Queen, that the great gods
    cried,
Picture-names they invented each new hour:—
"Eyes-of-Love," "My Lady-Is-As-Gold,"   495
"Beautiful-Kitten," "Little-Wild-Lion-Girl."
The law's delay among the gods was ended.

Caesar, with the perfect eye of the elder Horus,
Wearing the ancient crowns of the south and the north,
The Queen, clothed in the ravishing form of Hathor,   500
And their beautiful son, the heir, Caesarion,
Heir of Egypt, Rome, and the purple seas;—
These three, the last of the Egyptian Triads—

Flamboyant, triumphant, magnificent,
Chanted "The Chapters of Coming Forth by Day,"   505
As in old days, chanted the golden chapters.

The "Words of Power" swept through the dusty hall,
Fulfilling there all the magic of Thoth,
The love of Osiris for the wise and just,
The love of Amon-Ra for his little children, —   510
Vindicating that strange wind from heaven
That still as one more mystery, shook the tomb.

There, there, was more than Egyptian resurrection.

III. She is Lifted with the Old Gods into the Western Sky

The walls widened, and were the horizon's rim.
The roof arched up, and was the infinite sky.   515
Where were those gods, who had lived in priest-carved
    stone?
Their souls were high above the universe.
Their outspread plumes now filled the uttermost heavens
In the marvellous west, where all our dead have gone.

Caesar, Caesarion, and the Queen,   520
(She who was no longer Cleopatra),
The last to be raised to heaven through heathen pride,
Wearing sandals of lapis-lazuli,
In a moment were one flash of ascending light.
They climbed blue steps, and sat with the good Osiris,   525
At the top of his stairway, "First of the Westerners,"
Bowered in the flowers of the deep western heavens,
There where the terrible star-lotos blooms.

They took their thrones with the forty-two assessors,
With the four sons of Horus, and with Sekmet,   530
With Thoth and Maat, and the Memphian Chivalry,
Anubis and King Menes and his train.
They took their thrones with Isis and with Nepthys,
Hatshepsut, Tiy and the strange Ikhnaton,
With Alexander, with the Ptolemies,   535
With Amon-Ra, and his Macedonian sons.

She stood with young Caesarion in her arms,
She stood with shadowy Caesar in that sky.
She kissed him into pride and power again.

Beneath their feet were every sun and star,   540
The Thrones and The Terrace of a Million Years,
And time, and fear, and the whirling universe.

And the Book of the Dead was rolled up for that day.
The judgment scene was ended. Far below
The priests of the jewelled temples of Abydos,   545
Thinking not of the forgotten Queen,
(She who was no longer Cleopatra),
Of Caesar, Caesarion, or Antony,
Sang their sweet songs of the soul's resurrection,
Songs to Osiris, "First of the Westerners,"   550
Thinking only of their beloved dead,
Of mummies newly sealed in their holy tombs.

            *   *   *   *   *

Set, the beautiful, the hard and proud,
Stealer of vases of most precious ointment—
Stealer of red, pitiful, human hearts—   555
Determined still to win the universe,
Set, the Accuser, victor in his fashion,
Since, to accuse, to him was victory,
Insulter of judges and stars to the highest sky,
He, who accused Job long ago,   560
In the judgment hall of Jehovah of the Jews,
Then laid his hand upon him through long years:—
Set, the Accuser, resuming his name of Satan,
Wearing sandals of hell-fire, laughing, not smiling,
Barking his terrible bark, marched far to the north,   565
There to accuse and tempt in the Dead Sea Desert,
And on a pinnacle of King Herod's temple,
And on a flower-decked mountain of meditation:—
The son of a girl, fairer than Cleopatra,
A son of Amon-Ra, prouder than Caesar,   570
And lovelier than the young Caesarion.

   On reading the latest proof of this poem, I have found a
book that elaborately confirms the political hypothesis:—
"The Life and Times of Cleopatra, Queen of Egypt—A Study
in the Origin of the Roman Empire," by Arthur Weigall,
published by Thomas Butterworth, Limited, 15 Bedford
Street, London W.C. 2; and G.P. Putnam's Sons, 2 West 45th
Street, New York City. But the same idea may be found in
Ferrero's "Greatness and Decline of Rome," in all the com-

ment on Cleopatra. I have outlined this poem of mine as a possible photoplay in "The Art of the Moving Picture," [Chapter XIX in both the 1915 and 1922 editions].

1922-1923

From THE VILLAGE MAGAZINE

Fourth Edition

December 1925

FOR A "SOCIETY" GIRL
do you want to be a lion?

A kitten born half lion,
Tossed back her mane
And sagely reflected:
"Where have I most to gain?
Roaring like a mountain lion,   5
Or mewing like a kitty?
Lions are more noble, kittens more pretty,
Half-grown kittens more witty.
A lion, long grown up,
Is a lion still;   10
A tabby-cat grown up
Is a fat cat still.
I'll roar myself to lionhood—
That I will!"

Summer, 1925

A SONG WHEN THE MAY QUEEN WAS
ANGRY AND WICKED

They used to sing in Sunday-School that "Time shall be
   no more,"
But Time is my avenger, and I hope he lasts awhile—
For at least a thousand years of ETERNITY, that there
I may make increasing progress toward your too-exclusive
   smile.

You will find it in the Bible that "Time shall be no
   more,"   5
But Time is my avenger, and I hope he lasts awhile—
For when he makes you kind, and so has made me kind,
The first noon will flame high upon the dial
Of the church-clock at the entrance of ETERNITY'S
   cool aisle.

The Mass-bell then will ring, the Body of Christ be
   broken;   10
We two, set free from silliness and guile,
Will kneel and take Christ's Body as we should,
At last, each by the other understood,
Time's children, who have journeyed the last mile.

Summer, 1923

GOING-TO-THE-STARS

May 1926

Sunrise on Sun-Mountain

THESE ARE THE YOUNG

I

"What new mob disturbs the days?
Who are these, with intrusive ways,
Who speak with an alien tongue?
Who are these Olympian-white
Butterflies of flame,   5
High upon Sun Mountain,
Invading now, every fountain,
Obeying their own captains
And to no man tame;
Whispering so low   10
We cannot hear at all,
Yet calling: 'Brother,' 'Sister'
Through the sun-mountain wall?
Who are these Olympian-white
Butterflies of flame,   15
Full of a holy grace?
Tell me their spiritual name."

The Answer

"This is a separate race,
Speaking an alien tongue—
These are the young!"   20

II

"Tell me of the Olympian-white
Aspen trees of flame,
And of the Olympian-white
Mariposa lilies,
Climbing great Sun Mountain,   25
Invading now, every fountain,
Tell me their spiritual name."

The Answer

"This is a chosen people,
This is a separate race
Speaking an alien tongue—   30
These are the young!"

III

"Tell me of the Olympian-white
Basket-flowers of flame,
The marching-plumes of flame,
Climbing great Sun Mountain,   35
Invading now, every fountain,
While our hearts grow greater
And our climbing songs are sung;
While the days grow later,
While the sun still lingers,   40
Or great storm bells are rung,
And now the lightning splits the hills,
And now, the falling fountain fills.
Tell me of these high-plumed tribes
Of Indian basket-flowers   45
That march up the Sun Mountain glacier,
Through the holy hours.
What is their spiritual name?"

The Answer

"This is a separate race,
Speaking an alien tongue —   50
These are the young!"

IV

"Who are these boys and girls on horseback
Who go by next day,
The horses loaded for camping,
No guides to lead the way?   55
Girls Olympian white
Or painted to the eyes,
Innocently wicked,
Innocently wise;
Innocently impudent,   60
Innocently gay —
Boys who are Young America,
Scholars, lean and white,
Or athletes red and gay,
Proud young man America,   65
Well on its way,
Girls most bewitching,
Boys most untamed,

Hotly praised and preached at; hotly, *very* hotly blamed.
Who are these? What is their aim?   70
What is now their game?
What is their spiritual name?"

The Answer

"This is a chosen people,
This is a separate race,
Speaking an alien tongue —   75
These are the darlings of my heart,
These are the young."

1922

An Oration, Entitled
"OLD, OLD, OLD, OLD ANDREW JACKSON"

"Our Federal Union, it must be preserved!" Jackson's
famous toast.

I

The Coming of Hope in the Heart of Old
President Jackson

I will speak of your deeds,
Andrew Jackson,
When I take the free road again.
Oh, the long, dusty highway!
Oh, the rain,
Oh, the sunburnt men!   5

I will think of you,
Strong old Indian god,
Old turkey cock
On a forest rock,
Old buffalo, knee-deep in the weeds,   10
Old faithful heart who could boast and strut;
I will think of you when I harvest again,
I will think of you in the forest again,
I will think of you when the woods are cut —   15
Old, old Andrew Jackson.

I think of you, Andrew Jackson,
Two o'clock in the morning,
In the White House, alone,
You stand there, Old Hickory,   20
Lean as a bone.
It is now
The fifth of March,
1833,
And you wonder   25
With an aching heart,
Have you set your people free?
You see the frontier skirmish-line
Of the western cabins, built
For man's escape   30
From Babylon,
From Europe's gold and gilt;
And yet you know this Washington
Is too fine
Too superfine,   35
Is full of sugar,
Cake and wine.

I dreamed when I was only a boy
Of this second inaugural night,
When you, a second time,   40
Had your way;
And your banners burned bright!
I saw you marching around your fire,
Tired, restless, fuming, dreaming,
Booted and spurred,   45
Till day.

Some are born to be bullied and chidden,
To be bridled
And ridden,
Born to be harried or whipped or hidden;   50
Others
Born
Booted and spurred to ride,
To make the aristocrats stand aside.
I dreamed, as a boy, of Andrew Jackson,   55
Relentless, furious, high in his pride,
Democracy irresistible,
Booted and spurred
To ride.

He broke the horns 60
Of all cattle who horned him,
He broke the bones
Of all who scorned him:—
Biddle or Webster or Clay or Calhoun.
The finest hope from the Cave of Adullam, 65
Since David ascended the throne:—
Old Andrew Jackson,
The old, old raven,
Lean as a bone!

Now his smart lackey, the wizard Van Buren is gone. 70
Van Buren's crawlers, bootlickers and toadies have gone,
But the best and the worst of "The People" stay on.
Young frontiersmen drink around Jackson,
Yet he sits alone,
Like a stone. 75

He is so cold,
He is so old.
The night is so empty, so weary, so dreary,
He is short of breath, he breathes hardly at all,
He wishes for death and the end of it all— 80
Old, old,
Old, old
Andrew
Jackson.
Why should he not be unsteady? 85
He is a legend already.
Though he leans here, the conqueror of the proud,
Harvesting here without fear,
He sighs for his coffin, his pall and shroud,
And calls for his Rachel aloud. 90

And he thinks of Van Buren and all such men,
Then stands up and laughs,
And laughs again.
For he thinks what all lions think of all jackals;
Then he thinks of the time when the world was young 95
And Rachel was young,
When he threaded black woods without guard, without
   guide,
And shot without trial all who slandered and lied;
He thinks of gigantic scoundrels he hung
In West Tennessee, when the Nation was young, 100
In Florida, when the Nation was young.

Then he thinks he will soon
Hang those
Nullifiers,
And make them a "terror to traitors" —   105
And especially . . .
John C. Calhoun!
Then, he thinks on,
To Heaven,
Where heavenly Rachel is gone.   110
And the boy frontiersmen sense the mystery
Of the far-off eyes and the destiny
Of this man who could never change his mind,
Who put strange fight into humankind.
Still cold as a stone,   115
Abrupt, alone,
Old, old,
Old, old
Andrew
Jackson.   120

He climbs to the roof.
He looks at the stars aglow;
One constellation
Seems like a buffalo.
He says: "The world is so queer and so wide!"   125
He wonders if that new notion is sound —
These rascals say that the world is round.
And he watches the fires on the edge of the sky,
Far-off delirious dancers go by: —
Democracy prancing on far-off hills,   130
Where the hard cider pours down
In rivers and rills.

Soon his back grows straight,
His manner more stern,
His breath turns fire,   135
His iron eyes burn,
More and more mysterious grows
The dawn,
Till he calls to his Rachel the rose.
He dreams,   140
As he walks,
Of the bride
Of his youth —
Her immaculate beauty,
Immaculate truth.   145

That game-cock look all over him now,
Don Quixote now, with a dangerous eye,
He inflexibly stands
With a Bible and picture there in his hands;
(And only in these will his heart confide!)   150
His wife's tattered Bible tight in his hands,
And her miniature there in his lonely hands: —
Old Rachel Jackson,
Our flag, our flag, in her capable hands,
Her faithful and deathless hands!   155

He tramp-tramp-tramps down the creaky stair,
With a rattle of spurs,
A rattle of spurs,
Jingling out
The old, old story,   160
Democracy's shame
And Democracy's glory,
A natural king
With a raven wing;
Cold no more, weary no more —   165
Old, old,
Old, old
Andrew Jackson!

Now the strong west wind with a loud song is singing,
Down the White House chimney the wild song is
    winging: —   170
"West Tennessee brought white horses for him,
Strong colts in relays, white horses in line,
Each steed had more splendor, fury more fine,
War horses, king horses, stallions divine.
Then the whole Nation brought white horses for him."   175

Only the rich want his name to grow dim,
To have the American people forget
How they brought great white horses for him.
Do you think that I want some fool,
Statistical,   180
To picture that second inaugural
Who has read all the diaries of that day
And all that the Adamses have to say?
And the speeches of Calhoun, of Webster and Clay?
I must ask a boy who has faded away.   185
I must ask my own heart when it was young
To speak of Jackson with a proud tongue,

As my father and my grandfathers taught me
To speak of Jackson with a proud tongue.
When I take the road and beg again,   190
In the first log cabin I will talk of Jackson.

There, the second inaugural night,
With a cane he drove the last revelers out,
For there were swine in the glamour and rout.
There were gourds on the floor,   195
Empty hard cider kegs,
Broken-up tables,
And broken chair legs.
But, far on the edge of the Maryland hills,
Bonfires burned high, the revelers danced,   200
Steeds and riders snorted and pranced;
Thebes had gone down,
Sparta gone down,
Babylon fallen,
Rome fallen,   205
London Tower fallen,
The Bastille fallen!
Gone were the blasphemous breeds—
Mankind was made new.
The only crown was Democracy's crown,   210
The only town left was Democracy's town,
And Jackson was king of it, too.
And the hard cider poured down the hills and the trails,
And men drank up glory from gourds and from pails.

In the empty White House the chieftain was still.   215
His face was a talon,
His hands were talons,
George Washington's old armchair was a throne,
The high-heeled women were weeping alone.
Rachel Jackson's old ghost   220
Was queen on the throne.
He thinks of New Orleans,
Then of the day
He sent Calhoun's messengers furious away,—
The green logs hissing a sinister tune   225
While he thinks
Of Calhoun.

He hears louder shouting,
The bonfires afar
Shine on the hills like his mighty north star;   230

He hears his followers boasting, bantering,
With the end of his sword he stirs up the embers,
And he thinks of secessionists,
Counts all their numbers,
But he looks in the embers and sees his white horses,   235
Cantering, cantering, cantering, cantering.

II

The Coming of Day in the City of Washington, March 5, 1833

I will speak of your deeds,
Andrew Jackson,
When I take the free road again,
Oh, the long, dusty highway,   240
Oh, the rain,
Oh, the sunburnt men!
I will watch all your storm clouds,
On the wing,
I will hear your red robin sing.   245
Only the rich want your name to grow dim,
But the robin will sing again your wild hymn.

The neat little town
Has no peace,
No rest,   250
Backwoodsmen have poured in from the whole West!
Oh, the hard cider crowd drinks him down by the gallon!
His long hands are talons!
His face is a talon!
Oh, this is the secret that shakes him forever: —   255
The Star-Spangled Banner that stands near his side
Is his furious heart's immaculate bride,
That flag is Rachel Jackson to him,
And the light of that lady will never grow dim.

Strange indeed are the ways of the Giver,   260
Pouring out the people forever.
From forest and field,
They will ever renew,
But the Jacksons are few.

When I take the free road again,   265
I will hide from the rich forever,
Like an under-the-desert river,
The better to learn the ways of the Giver.

Let us think of Democracy's proudest son,
The *wilderness*, brought to Washington,   270
The *frontier*, brought to its place of power,
To its proudest hour! —
Bull-buffalo, tramping again the weeds!
Victory
There in his eye,   275
He thinks of his speech
On last Fourth of July,
And many a farther off Fourth of July.

He hears a far Yankee Doodle tune,
He thinks he will soon be hanging Calhoun: —   280
That new-made aristocrat, John C. Calhoun—
The green logs hissing
A sinister tune,
While he thinks of Calhoun.

Long he leans there,   285
Over George Washington's chair,
And he visions his Rachel throned dimly there,
Till his eyes have a curious,
Furious glare.

More and more mysterious grows   290
The dawn till he calls to his Rachel the rose;
Again, and again, and again, till the day,
He opens his shirt,
He beats his breast,
He takes out the picture of Rachel his pride,   295
Of old Rachel Jackson,
Our flag in her hands,
His furious heart's immaculate bride!
Oh, miniature carried against his lean side,
Hung round his neck by a great black cord,   300
Carried in battle, and duel, and storm,
Always kept by his battle wounds warm.
Oh, the light of that lady will never grow dim!
She was always the Star-Spangled Banner to him!
The binding touch of that great black cord   305
Filled his heart with the love of the Lord,
And the wrath of the Lord.

"The kings and the commons against the world—"
Where have we heard that story before?
How soon will we hear it one time more?   310

In the name of that cause I will knock at your door—
Of that natural king
Soon come begging again,
Oh, free American women and men.

I see Andrew Jackson kneel by the fire, —   315
Then—
He heaps hissing logs till the fullness of day,
With that terrible fixedness in his look,
He kisses the picture of Rachel again,
He reads again from that tattered book.   320
Full day has come,
The bridegroom is young,
He strides about! And he strides about!
And he rattles around with his spurs and his sword,
And he tramples down every slanderous tongue;   325
Democracy's old, old heart has grown young.

The green logs give forth more mysterious fires,
The hickory logs hum a more sinister tune,
While he thinks of Secessionist
JOHN C. CALHOUN;   330
And he thinks he will soon
Be hanging Calhoun—
The new-made aristocrat, John C. Calhoun,
Who would wreck the Union—
John C. Calhoun.   335

III

The Coming of Tomorrow to the American Democracy

And today,
My darlings,
Victory
Burns in his eye;
Our Democracy's dreams ride westward with him,   340
Around the bright world, in valor and pride,
For he has learned that the world *is* round,
And the cries for his reign in all nations abound.

So from Sun Mountain,
When cliff shadows deepen,   345
I look to the west
At sunset, at moonrise,
Beyond where the sun

Has ended its journey, and stars have begun,
And I sing my song in valor and pride,   350
How Jackson still on white horses will ride.
Looking into my campfire,
There on Sun Mountain,
A fiery fountain: —
A hissing,   355
A showering,
A more and more unaccountable flowering!
I watch there all night
Till the last logs burn down,
And I see in the bright   360
Immaculate coals the Pacific foam;
I see in the bright
Immaculate coals Jackson's horses of white!

Oh, horses in relays, horses in line,
Each steed has more splendor, fury more fine,   365
War horses, king horses, stallions divine!
He rides the Pacific on clouds red and white,
Our Democracy's children ride westward with him.

Now the new west wind a loud song is singing
Again and again and again till the day: 370
    "Some men are born saddled and bridled to be ridden,
    Others born booted and spurred to ride.
    I sing the song
    Of Andrew Jackson,
    Born   375
    Booted and spurred to ride!
    West Tennessee brought white horses for him,
    Strong colts in relays,
    White horses in line;
    Each steed grew in splendor, with fury more fine—   380
    War horses, king horses,
    Stallions divine!
    Then the Nation
    Brought white horses for him
    Old, old,   385
    Old, old
    Andrew
    Jackson!
    Then Death brought white horses for him."

And I lift my eyes from my all-night campfire,   390
And I see him ride the high clouds of desire,

For he was born booted and spurred to ride —
Booted and spurred to ride!
My darlings,
Born   395
Booted and spurred
To ride!

This oration was given for the Jefferson's Birthday Dinner,
April 15, 1925, at Spokane, Washington, for the local organi-
zation of the Democratic party. It was a source of satisfac-
tion to me to have it accepted definitely as a political oration
for a definite party, and not as a parlor poem. It is to be read
aloud, in the way one would read a political speech from the
newspaper at election time, when such issues are really be-
fore the people.

February-March 1925

VIRGINIA

When I was asked to look at a gold model of the *May-
flower* in a Bank in London.

Oh, Mayflower, made of filigree gold,
"Hear now my song of love, melody immortal,"
Virginia, Virginia!

Land of the gauntlet and the glove,
Virginia, Virginia!   5
Horseback land of sash and plume,
Where they rode to wisdom, wonder and doom,
Virginia, Virginia!

They took their axes and their Bibles,
They took their guns, they took their fiddles,   10
Dancing the old Virginia Reel,
They went West to the new blue grass,
When it was still Virginia.
When people say "Kentucky," they mean Virginia.

And they were very proud and high,   15
Remembering a southern shore,
The Potomac, and Virginia.
Then west, to escape from western ways,
Days too hasty and too thin,

The tribe went on to the furthest west,   20
Where the oldest thoughts again begin,
Still dreaming of Virginia.

They took their schoolbooks and their wagons,
They took their scythes, their rakes and flagons,
They took their fiddles, Bibles and guns,   25
They took their sons, and their sons' sons.
On to new Missouri;
And they were very proud and high,
And danced the old Virginia Reel,
Remembering Virginia.   30

They took their glories and their shames,
They took their trifles and their rags,
They took their sects and tribes and names,
They took their cloaks and moneybags;
They went west to the silver mines.   35
And they were hoity-toity high,
Remembering Virginia,
Remembering Virginia,
The strutting, prancing glory,
The sweet dancing glory,   40
The wonder, the heartbreak,
Virginia, Virginia!

They went northwest to the tall woods,
On to Kootenai,
On to Going-to-the-Sun;   45
To the mountains called Olympia,
To the river called Columbia,
To dew and mist and roses.
And they were very proud and high.
Chin-high, breast-high, thoughts-in-the-air,   50
Remembering a southern shore,
Remembering Virginia.

We can make fun of their every-days,
But, "hear now my song of love, melody immortal" —
Virginia, Virginia!   55
Land of the gauntlet and the glove.
Virginia, Virginia!

Pocahontas, Powhatan,
Rolfe and Raleigh and John Smith,
Jefferson, Washington —   60

First families of Virginia.
Mount Vernon, Monticello,
And that ancient University
Founded by wild Jefferson,
The place where young Poe learned to sing —   65
Virginia's University!
Remembering the wandering walls,
The proud pillars, the strange halls,
Of that old University —
The brain of old Virginia!   70

They went northwest to the tall woods,
They went northwest to the pine woods,
And they were touchy and quite high,
Remembering those ragged men
That followed hard the Stars and Bars,   75
The Potomac running mud and blood,
While Lee reigned in Virginia!
Remembering Lee and all his men,
Remembering daguerreotypes, tintypes, books and
    photographs
That once came from Virginia —   80
And thinking deeply all the while
Of the growing dimness of that land,
And the ruin of Virginia,
And the ruin of Virginia.

At the Seattle water front   85
The lovers stood there, eye to eye,
Their passage booked for India,
West, to escape from western ways,
Days too hasty and too thin,
To the farthest West and the furthest East,   90
Where the oldest thoughts again begin.
Starting Walt Whitman's journey there,
The passage to India.
Paying in heartbreak for their pride,
Like all the great who lived and died —   95
Remembering Virginia.

Oh, lovers, standing eye to eye,
Remembering a southern shore,
Remembering George Washington,
And the dim land of Virginia.   100
"Hear now my song of love, melody immortal" —
Land of the gauntlet and the glove,
Virginia, Virginia!

If your dust in far Thibet
Shall sweep across the desert walls   105
And mix with the wild desert snows
Beyond the heights of India,
Something will whisper:
"Washington, Jefferson, Virginia,
Poe and Virginia,"   110
The melody immortal—
"Virginia! Virginia!"

        April 1924

THE FLOWER-FED BUFFALOES

The flower-fed buffaloes of the spring
In the days of long ago,
Ranged where the locomotives sing
And the prairie flowers lie low: —
The tossing, blooming, perfumed grass   5
Is swept away by the wheat,
Wheels and wheels and wheels spin by
In the spring that still is sweet.
But the flower-fed buffaloes of the spring
Left us, long ago.   10
They gore no more, they bellow no more,
They trundle around the hills no more: —
With the Blackfeet, lying low,
With the Pawnees, lying low,
Lying low.   15

        April 1924

THREE HOURS

The moon was like a boat one night,
And like a bowl of flowers;
Three butterflies were riding there,
Named for three lovely hours.

The first hour was the hour the night   5
Was a great dome of peace;
The second hour was when the night
Gave my heart release

From all old grief and all lost love.
And the third hour was when   10

I found that I was reconciled
To Heaven and Earth and men.

1924-1925?

THE ANGEL SONS

We will have angels and men for sons,
For I have gone out to you
Wearing the wings of desire,
In the rain, in the storm, in the dew.

Strong men, stronger than any we see,   5
Strong angels, stronger than any we see,
Singing of love round the poppy bed,
For they have soft eyes, and they weary of waiting
For our souls to reach the ultimate mating,
Weary of waiting, worn with waiting,   10
Till half of their glory is dead.

My soul has gone out on their poppy song,
Wearing such wings of desire
That our angel sons will have strength to the uttermost,
Beauty and dreaming power to the uttermost,   15
Veins filled with snow and uttermost fire,
Snow from the top of the Great Sun Mountain
Fire from these flowers of desire!

They will rule our sons who are merely men,
Enforcing our will on the earth again,   20
Beginning, beginning at Great Sun Mountain,
They will make over the land,
They will make over the age,
Granite each angel house,
Crimson each written page.   25

They will rule our sons who are merely men,
Earth sons with this elder brother start!
Born from beneath your earthly heart!
Born from your lily side,
Strong, with the sternest eyes,   30
They will conquer the land and its pride.

Dear girl, when these wild years die,
When other lovers go by,

Playing Sun Mountain games,
With faith that their love will also save   35
Their pride of love from destruction's breath,
Their sun-born stock from uttermost death,
And their earth-born stock from uttermost death,
These lovers will say our names,
And climbing Sun Mountain high,   40
Will stop where our bodies lie,
And leave as the sign of faith
A poppy upon your grave,
Yes—
A mountain poppy upon my grave!   45

      Winter, 1925-1926?

SUNRISE

To drink the cup of Faust, and find youth waiting,
To drink Lord Byron's cup, and find youth gone,
Or drink Christ's fearful cup of crucifixion,
Or Buddha's cup, that great renunciation—

I think that I would rather be this mountain,
Lifting my head, drinking the cup of dawn.

      April 1923

RAIN

Each storm-soaked flower has a beautiful eye.
And this is the voice of the stone-cold sky:
"Only boys keep their cheeks dry.
Only boys are afraid to cry.
Men thank God for tears,
Alone with the memory of their dead,
Alone with lost years."

      April 1923

WHAT THE WILD CRANE BROUGHT

A wild crane came flying
With music around his head,
Not his cry,

But little cries
Of thoughts white and red,
The thoughts you have,
The thoughts I have,
That we have left unsaid.

   1923-1924?

NANCY HANKS, MOTHER OF ABRAHAM LINCOLN

   "Out of the eater came forth meat; and out of the strong
came forth sweetness." Judges 14:14

A sweet girl graduate, lean as a fawn,
The very whimsy of time,
Read her class poem Commencement Day—
A trembling filigree rhyme.

The pansy that blooms on the window sill,   5
Blooms in exactly the proper place;
And she nodded just like a pansy there,
And her poem was all about bowers and showers,
Sugary streamlet and mossy rill,
All about daisies on dale and hill—   10
And she was the mother of Buffalo Bill.

Another girl, a cloud-drift sort,
Dreamlit, moonlit, marble-white,
Light-footed saint on the pilgrim shore,
The best since New England fairies began,   15
Was the mother of Barnum, the circus man.

A girl from Missouri, snippy and vain,
As frothy a miss as any you know,
A wren, a toy, a pink silk bow,
The belle of the choir, she drove insane   20
Missouri deacons and all the sleek,
Her utter tomfoolery made men weak,
Till they could not stand and they could not speak.
Oh, queen of fifteen and sixteen,
Missouri sweetened beneath her reign—   25
And she was the mother of bad Mark Twain.

Not always are lions born of lions,
Roosevelt sprang from a palace of lace;

On the other hand is the dizzy truth:
Not always is beauty born of beauty.   30
Some treasures wait in a hidden place.
All over the world were thousands of belles,
In far-off eighteen hundred and nine,
Girls of fifteen, girls of twenty,
Their mamas dressed them up a-plenty—   35
Each garter was bright, each stocking fine,
But for all their innocent devices,
Their cheeks of fruit and their eyes of wine,
And each voluptuous design,
And all soft glories that we trace   40
In Europe's palaces of lace,
A girl who slept in dust and sorrow,
Nancy Hanks, in a lost log cabin,
Nancy Hanks had the loveliest face!

     May 1924

THE JAZZ OF THIS HOTEL

Why do I curse the jazz of this hotel?
I like the slower tom-toms of the sea;
I like the slower tom-toms of the thunder;
I like the more deliberate dancing knee
Of outdoor love, of outdoor talk and wonder.   5
I like the slower, deeper violin
Of the wind across the fields of Indian corn;
I like the far more ancient violoncello
Of whittling loafers telling stories mellow
Down at the village grocery in the sun;   10
I like the slower bells that ring for church
Across the Indiana landscape old.
Therefore I curse the jazz of this hotel
That seems so hot, but is so hard and cold.

     Winter, 1924-1925

A CURSE FOR THE SAXOPHONE

    (Originally appearing in the *Spokesman-Review*, Spokane, December 16, 1924.)

When Cain killed Abel to end a perfect day,
He founded a city, called the City of Cain,

And he ordered the saxophones to play.
But give me a city where they play the silver flute,
Where they play a silver flute, at the dawn of the day,   5
Where the xylophone and saxophone and radio are mute,
And they play the Irish Harp at the end of the day.

When Jezebel put on her tiaras and looked grand,
Her three-piece pajamas and her diamond bosom-band,
And stopped the honest prophets as they marched upon
    their way,   10
And slaughtered them, and hung them in her hearty
    wholesale way,
She licked her wicked chops, she pulled out all her stops,
And she ordered the saxophones to play.
But give me a Queen whose voice is like the flute,
Queen of a city where the saxophone is mute,   15
Who can dance in stately measure, in an honest solemn
    way,
When they play the Irish Harp at the end of the day.

For the Irish Harp moves slowly, though the Irish heart
    moves fast,
And both of them are faithful to their music at the last,
And their silence after music is the conqueror at last.   20

What did Judas do with his silver thirty pieces?
Bought himself a saxophone and played "The Beale
    Street Blues."
He taught the tune to Nero, who taught it to his nieces,
And Rome burned down to saxophones that played "The
    Beale Street Blues."
Now it comes by wireless, and they call it news!   25

When Henry the Eighth of England married his last wife,
He carried underneath his coat a well-edged butcher
    knife,
But he affected to be glad, affected to be gay,
And he ordered the saxophones to play.

But give me a wedding where the silver flutes at dawn   30
Bring visions of Diana, the waterfall and fawn!
Give me a wedding where the evening harp is singing,
And Irish tunes bring Irish kings, their strange voices
    ringing,
Like songs by William Butler Yeats or noble Padraic
    Colum,

Give me a wedding that is decent, sweet and solemn,   35
Not based on brazen dances or hysterical romances,
When they order the saxophones to play!

When John Wilkes Booth shot Lincoln the good,
He hid himself in a deep Potomac wood,
But the Devil came and got him and dragged him below,   40
And took him to the gate—and the rest you know.
Twenty thousand pigs on their hind legs playing
"The Beale Street Blues" and swaying and saying:—

"John Wilkes Booth, you are welcome to Hell,"
And they played it on the saxophone, and played it well. 45
And he picked up a saxophone, grunting and rasping,
The red-hot horn in his hot hands clasping,
And he played a typical radio jazz;
He started an earthquake, he knew what for,
And at last he started the late World War.   50
Our nerves all razzed, and our thoughts all jazzed,
Booth and his saxophone started the war!

None but an assassin would enjoy this horn.
Let us think of the Irish flute in the morn,
And the songs of Colum and the songs of Yeats,   55
And forget our jazzes and our razzes and our hates.
Let us dream of the slow great seraphim wings
Of the good and the great sweet Irish kings!

    This "Curse for the Saxophone" was dictated by me with
Stoddard King at the typewriter offering valuable amend-
ments and suggestions including "The Beale Street Blues."
Mr. King could claim at least half the poem if he chose, not
only as an inspiring but also as a constructive artist. In short,
he helped me write it.

        Late 1924

WHEN I WAS A TREE

When I was a tree, an aspen tree,
An Indian wigwam hid by me,
And a great big redwood sheltered me,
And a great big mountain sheltered him.
But a white man came and cut him down   5
To make cheap shacks in a dirty town,

And shot the Indian in my shade,
And I wondered why young trees were made.
I stood alone, sunburnt and slim,
And the mountain stood. Those men left him.   10

1924?

CELESTIAL TREES OF GLACIER PARK

A Song with Hieroglyphs

Celestial forests grow in Glacier Park
Invisible to all but faithful eyes.
Those who are wise
See each new tree spring with its aureole.
Every dawning brings one more surprise   5
Shining in heaven between them and the sun,
Or nodding where the cold rivers run,
Or hovering over granite, shale, and snow,
The ghostly trees like rainbows come and go.

I

These are the trees: The Stable for the Deer,   10
The Bee's Skyscraper, The Angel's Spear,
The Daisy's Tower, The Storm Wave of the Land,
The Old Clock Tower, The Manitou's Hand,
The Mountain's Giant Flower, The Dreamer from
    the Seas,
These are the trees.   15

II

These are the trees: The House of Honeycomb,
The Ball Room of the Winds, The Great Green Torch,
The Buffalo's Pride, The Pillar of the Sky,
The Bear's Home, The Tall Fern That Will Fly,
The Priest of the Morning, The Giant's Knees,   20
These are the trees.

III

These are the trees: The House of Honeycomb,
The West Wind's Evening Lodge, The Red Man's
    Temple Dome,
The Waterfall's Big Brother, The Frost Defyer,
The Planet's Nest, The Root's Achieved Desire,   25
The Sun's Bride, The Fire That Will Not Freeze,
These are the trees.

IV

These are the trees: The Chipmunk's Tenement,
The Icicle's Retreat, The Fire Bird's Flat for Rent,
The Flowering Sword, The Planet's Hair,   30
The North Wind's Dress, The Fir Bough Stair,
The Moss That Dared, The Dreamer from the Seas,
These are the trees—these are the dream trees.

Summer, 1925

These are the Dream-Trees

THOSE CLOUDY RIDERS

When they floated by, those cloudy riders,
Eager to go I know not where,
They thought I would join them, those cloudy riders,
And sleep in the flowers in the great tree's hair,
Sleep in the heart of the apple blossoms,   5
Deathless, blooming since ancient days.
Some day I may join them, those cloudy riders,
For my sweetheart sleeps in those flowers always.

    1924?

JACK-IN-THE-PULPIT

Jack-in-the-Pulpit preached today,
His congregation came on wings—
Thoughts of far-off wild pink roses,
And other diaphanous thoughts with stings,
Thoughts of investigative nettles,   5
Of blackberry bushes cut and slashed,
Thoughts of distant poison ivies,
Came all the way with their green teeth gnashed,
Thoughts of serpents, of whippoorwills,
Thoughts of dragon flies, wasps, and bees,   10
And thoughts of sour old apple trees.

A flattering crowd, from the whole wide woods,
All much alike, these thoughts, these wings,
Forgot that they had teeth and stings.

Our Jack read scripture from the skies;   15
Our Jack preached, "Put your stings away,
"Be like little clouds at play."

They liked Jack's eloquence. They said:
"How well that scripture verse was read!
"He thunders like his papa thundered,   20
"And like his papa nods his head!
"The farmer's bull should hear this man!
"That bull needs preachers just like these
"To bring him to his wicked knees!"

    1924?

LADY LONDON

There is a Lady London
Whose face I hardly know.
I turned away from London
Because I feared her so.
But the whisper of young London   5
Goes farther than the sword—
Far across the water,
She calls to me. I go.
For my mother loved young London;
And centuries far back,   10
Some one walked in London
Before he found the track
Into our agéd wilderness,
Some Austen or Frazee,
Walked in foggy London   15
And never thought of me.

     1924?

THE PANSY WEDDING
   For Laura Wheeler

Oh once I ate a pansy bud
When I was short of bread:
The rascal had been drinking dew;
The liquor filled my head.

I saw a pansy king and queen   5
And dowager sail by:
The haughty dowager was fat:
The little queen was spry.

The stately king was like a cloud
In lazy summer days: 10
He stood beside his pansy girl
And whispered solemn praise.

I forgot that I was hungry
His cooing was so grand:
She slapped him when he kissed her   15
And tried to hold her hand.

I almost died a-laughing
At the funny things she said.

So feed your lover pansy buds
When you are short of bread.   20

April 1909

THE FOUR SEASONS

I saw my muse go walking,
Her path was day and night!
The rake of Autumn in her hand:
Her hair was Winter-white.

But she was clothed in Springtime   5
She bore a fairy fan—
The wind of Love and Summer—
That comes to every man.

April 1909

THE SPOKANE APPLE FAIRY

Her hair like curly sunbeams,
Her voice a bell,
I saw a fairy come
From an apple as it fell;
She was scattering little flowers,   5
And she spread her little hand
With a blessing for the grass
And the orchard land.

1924?

WARMING UP THE MOON

"The moon is too cold," I said to the Mohawk,
"The creature is dusty and gray.
"And I must sit on this beach all night
"And wait for a dreadful day."

So the Mohawk came down from his tent in the north,   5
And built me a fire on the sand
Of live-oaks and straws and of Spanish moss,
And of gems from a ring on his hand;

And seven hairs from his black coarse braids,
And an eagle plume from his war bonnet high.   10
And the fire turned a wonderful red,
And he took down the moon from its shelf in the sky—
He shoved it deep in the red-hot bed—
"Now there is your moon," he said.

1924?

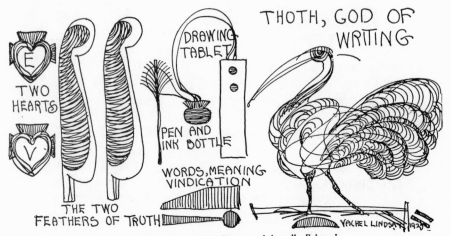

Part of my Hieroglyphic Signature, Informally Enlarged

THE MOTH AND THE UNICORN

"What does that unicorn eat for his meals?"
Asked the moth from the closet one day.
"My wings are bright fur, for I live upon fur,
"My legs are all wool, for I live upon wool,
"My plumes are fine feathers, I live upon feathers.   5
"My children at college, who still are mere worms,
"Live upon feathers, and soon will grow feathers—
"They eat up one good coat a day.
"But what does that unicorn eat for his meals,
"That vulgar young unicorn eat for his meals?   10
"I darkly suspect he eats hay!"

"Why, yes," said the fellow so vulgarly mellow,
"Why, yes, as a rule I eat hay.
"Once I ate bacon with Lindsay and Graham,
"But day after day I eat hay!"

1924?

TWO POEMS GEOGRAPHICAL

I. Hieroglyphics on the Gulf of Mexico

A Primer Lesson in Hieroglyphics

And now we set aside our whims
And try once more to be quite wise
With the new day shining in our eyes.

Egyptian hieroglyphic for the rising sun—
And I swam this morning toward that same big sun   5
In the Gulf of Mexico.

Egyptian hieroglyphic for the setting sun—
This hour is gay, serene, and slow.
This evening seems the loveliest one,
And I swim tonight toward the western sun   10
In the Gulf of Mexico.

EGYPTIAN HIEROGLYPHIC FOR THE HEART

Egyptian hieroglyphic for that vase, the heart:
And the heart is still an urn of flame,
Though temples come and go.
The floors of Thebes and Abydos   15
Are ash heaps, but their spirit fires
Leap the sea, flame and grow
In the winds that sweep across the shores
Of the Gulf of Mexico.

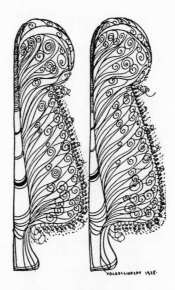

EGYPTIAN HIEROGLYPHIC
FOR THE TRUTH

Egyptian hieroglyphic for the Plumes of Truth   20
For the truth twice-told, for the Justice Hall
Where the feathers may yet outweigh us all.
Truth is no steal or dynamite thing,
No reader lesson from old McGuffey,
Or editorial noisy and huffy   25
Puffing a senator with a boom,
Truth is a downy double Plume,
Truth-in-the-balance still the same,
Resilient; and not fixed or tame,
Upstanding, quivering, moon-beam fine,   30
Shaken by all the storms that blow,
Yet defying all the storms that blow, —
As it was in the old Egyptian sign,
As it was in Osiris' Judgment Room,
Weighing the heart on the day of doom,   35
As it is on the Gulf of Mexico.

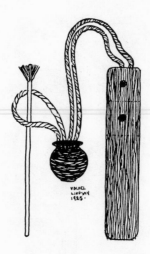

EGYPTIAN HIEROGLYPHIC FOR
A SCRIBE, INDICATED BY
INK-BOTTLE, PEN AND
WRITING TABLET

Egyptian hieroglyphic for the learned scribe
And his funny tablet, ink bottle and pen,
And the loops to go over the scribe's lean shoulder,
(For over the shoulder they wore them then).   40
And if we take to these styles again,
We might be picture-writing men,
And set all the poets in a glow,
With our letters marching around the world,
Hieroglyphic, mural painting,   45
Photoplay and scenario,
From the Park on the Gulf of Mexico.

EGYPTIAN HIEROGLYPHIC
OF THOTH, GOD OF
WRITING

Egyptian hieroglyphic for the Great God Thoth,
King scribe of the Sun and the Truth,
The god of epics and of art,   50
Patron of electric signs,
Patron of billboards, and cartoons,
Of all our new and queer designs,
And the movies, in their youth.
Arch, humorous, feathery, soft,   55
On the old Nome standard still aloft,
A friendly strutting Ibis-king,
Ibis-god who can wink and sing.

   Come let us march with him and fling
Bright inks about, paint up and shout —   60
Paint country places, gild our faces,
And tell to the farmers all we know, —
Hold our Festival of Thoth
On the Gulf of Mexico!

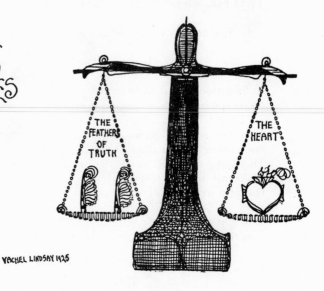

EGYPTIAN HIEROGLYPHIC FOR THE SCALES OF JUSTICE AFTER DEATH

VACHEL LINDSAY 1925

And here is the greatest sign they wrote,   65
For the mummy on the coffin lid,
And it meant: "No dead man here lies hid.
"He kneels in the hall of the Plumes of Truth,
"He speaks, is tried, is justified,
"He is standing by Osiris' side,   70
"The name of Osiris is on his breast,
"The merciful god's immortal guest."

There is a truth that still redeems,
And I swim tonight where the sunset streams
On the Gulf of Mexico,   75
And my heart is as light as the truth of truth,
I feel at one with the feathery tide,
And my heart is weighed in my flaming side,
While I know the sunbeams flow
From my forehead to my splashing feet.   80
And a thousand songs from the far west come
With a strange gift to bestow,
With a fury of storm like a lightning flash
New victory comes with that furious beat,
My soul and the west made one, complete,   85
On the Gulf of Mexico.

1925

TWO POEMS GEOGRAPHICAL

II. Saskatoon, Saskatchewan

The Shakespearean Christmas Tree

In Saskatoon, Saskatchewan,
Shakespeare's voice seemed in the air,
And something in the prairie line,
Something in the wheat field fair,
Something in the British hearts   5
That gave me welcome in my need
Made my soul a splendid flower,
Out of a dry and frozen weed.

And something in the stubbly fields
And their young snow to end the year,   10
Brought a sob and a great wind,
Each snowflake was a frozen tear.
The sky rained thoughts, and a great song
In the Elizabethan tongue
Swept from the Canadian fields!   15
New broken sod, too sad, too young,
Yet brother fields to Kansas fields,
Where once I worked in sweat and fire
To give the farmer his ripe wheat,
And slake my patriarch desire,   20
For wheat sheaves for my eyes and arms
A satisfaction vast and strange.
And now I reaped dim fields of *snow*
And heard the song from the wide range.

All prairies in the world are mine,   25
For I was born upon the plain.
And I can plant the wheat I choose,
In alien lands, in snow or rain.
I heard a song from Arden's wood,
A song from the edge of Arcady.   30
Rosalind was in the snow.
Singing her arch melody,
Although the only tree there found,
In alien, cold Saskatoon,
Was heaven's Christmas Tree of stars,   35
Swaying with a Shakespearean croon.
The skies were Juliet that night,
And I was Romeo below.

The skies Cordelia and Lear
And I the fool that loved them so.   40
I shook my silly bells and sang
And told young Saskatoon good-by.
And still I own those level fields
And hear that great wind's noble cry.

        November 1922

GEOLOGY

Said the wind to the mountains of Glacier Park—
    "My friends, am I wearing you out?"
Said the mountains then to the wind,
    "You will in a million of years, without doubt!"

        1924?

THE MOUNTAIN ANGELS

He who has loved the mountain angels
Is always lonely-hearted;
He will hear them rustle, rustle,
Their wings against the pane;
He will hear them singing, singing,   5
Far, far upon Sun Mountain,
While he is hid in cities,
Brooding in the rain.

        1924?

Heaven's Sun

THE BLOSSOMS THAT HAVE CHERUB'S WINGS

The blossoms that have cherub's wings,
And grow in Heaven's greenest grass
Fold them down when twilight sings,
And watch the stars and midnight pass,
Then spread them again to Heaven's sun,   5
On gossamer threads they toss and rise,
Then break their threads, and leap through the clouds,
And flap wide plumes in the sun's eyes.

1925

CELESTIAL FLOWERS OF GLACIER PARK

A Song with Hieroglyphs

Celestial flowers spring up in Glacier Park.
Invisible to all but faithful eyes.
Those who are wise
See each flower springing with its aureole.
Every dawning brings one more surprise,   5
Shining in heaven between them and the sun,
Or nodding where the cold fountains run,
Or hovering over granite, shale, and snow,
The ghostly flowers like rainbows come and go.

I

These are the flowers: Lettuce for the Deer,   10
The Bee's Book, The Clouds Appear,
The Angel's Puff Ball, The Chipmunk's Big Salt Cellar,
A Daisy Gone Wrong, The Sparrow's Fortune Teller,
The Fountain of Feathers, Idle Hours, —
These are the flowers.   15

II

These are the flowers: The Bear's Bridal Wreath,
The Glacier's Dance, The Summer Storm's White Teeth,
The Frost's Temple, The Icicle's Dream,
Going Toward the Rainbow, Sunlight on the Stream,
The Mountain Carpet, The Red Ant's Towers,   20
These are the flowers.

The Bee's Book
The Angel's Puff Ball   The Chipmunk's Big Salt Cellar
                    A Daisy Gone Wrong
Lettuce for the Deer   The Fountain of Feathers
              The Sparrow's Fortune Teller

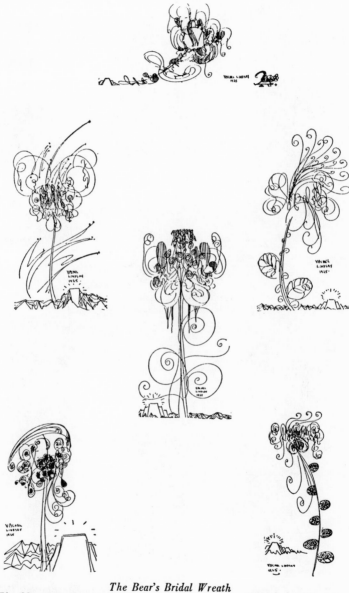

The Bear's Bridal Wreath

The Mountain Carpet

The Icicle's Dream

The Frost's Temple

Going Toward the Rainbow

The Glacier's Dance

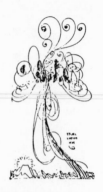

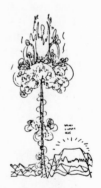

Wall Paper for the Sky
The South Wind's Lady
The West Wind

The Eaglet
The Amazing Dawn
Companion of the Fern

III

These are the flowers: Wall Paper for the Sky,
The Eaglet, The East Wind's Eye,
The South Wind's Lady, The Amazing Dawn,
The West Wind, The Vision of the Fawn,   25
The Companion of the Fern, The Dragon-Fly Lowers,
These are the flowers.

IV

These are the flowers: Going-to-the-Stars,
Going-on-Vacation, The Moth's Train of Cars,
Going-to-the-West, Going-to-the-Snow,   30
Going-to-the-Honey, The Indian's Bow,
Going-to-the-Moon, The Perfumed Bowers,
These are the flowers.

V

These are the flowers: The Flapper's Pride,
Ribbon for Your Hat, The Lover's Guide,   35
The Golden Garter, The Sheik's Plume,
Clocks for Your Stockings, Torch for the Gloom,
The Mirror of Fashion, The Crab-Apple Sours,
These are the flowers.

VI

These are the flowers: Romeo's Cap,   40
Kisses on the Mountain-Top, Diana's Lap,
A Thought from the Waterfall, Juliet's Bed,
The Midnight Wind, The Robin's Head,
The Breasts of Pocahontas, The Shadowy Powers,
These are the flowers.   45

VII

These are the flowers: The Sugar Candy Bun,
The Mohawk Fantasy, Singing-to-the-Sun,
Going-to-the-Stream, The Cricket from the Sea,
The Outdoor Corsage, The Baby Peach Tree,
Going-to-the-Winds, The June Time Showers,   50
These are the flowers, these are the dream flowers.

Summer, 1925

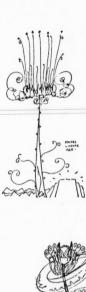

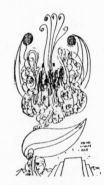

Going-to-the-Stars
Going-to-the-West
Going-to-the-Honey

Going-on-Vacation
Going-to-the-Snow
Going-to-the-Moon

The Flapper's Pride

Ribbon for Your Hat   The Golden Garter

Torch for the Gloom
The Sheik's Plume

Clocks for Your Stockings   The Mirror of Fashion

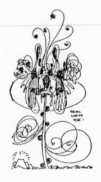

Romeo's Cap
A Thought from the Waterfall
The Midnight Wind

Kisses on the Mountain-Top
Juliet's Bed
The Breasts of Pocahontas

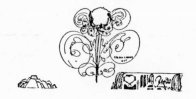

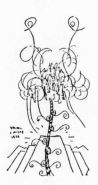

The Mohawk Fantasy

Going-to-the-Stream

The Outdoor Corsage

Singing-to-the-Sun

Going-to-the-Winds

THE CANDLE IN THE CABIN

A Weaving Together of Script and Singing

Fall, 1926

THE MOUNTAINS WITH STORMS FOR WAR-BONNETS

The mountains with storms for war-bonnets,
The mountains with earthquakes for ponies,
Ride on through the hundreds of millions of years,
Talking and laughing through rain, wind and tears;
Volcanoes their brothers, their chieftains, and cronies.   5
We, too, are their brothers and cronies.

They bathe in the oceans then lift up their heads.
They leap from the deep, from the old coral beds.
And conquer the shores again, moving by ages,
While seemingly still as old books with closed pages.   10

Beware the mountains, Oh Babylon men!
The mountains await you, outstay, ride you down.
They charge by like lightning in the sight of slow heaven,
And will conquer the earth ere the sun tumbles down.

1925

RISING WOLF

Rising Wolf, Rising Wolf, Rising Wolf, the brave beast,
Looms up past the ranges
And leaps through the roof
Of the star-sky at twilight
And puts to the proof   5
All the ten dogs in my wolf-hunting heart,
Snarling, defying them there all day long,
And giving the cry that the wolves call a song.
And my dogs bark in circles, but keep well aloof
From the proud Rising Wolf, Rising Wolf, Rising Wolf.   10

Rising Wolf, Rising Wolf, Rising Wolf, the brave beast,
It will take a hundred brave dogs at the least
To hunt down and beat Rising Wolf, the brave beast.

There are ten great dogs in my heart and no more
To hunt and to hound Rising Wolf, the brave beast.   15

But when will I have the strength of ten men,
And have one hundred brave dogs at the least?
In my heart are ten hounds
As small as small flowers,
When I turn them loose they are great as the hours: 20
They fill the valleys, they fill the rivers;
They leap to the stars, they leap to the sun;
They stand in a circle and bark at the snarling one.

And they think it is strange and very surprising
They cannot conquer the wolf in his rising.   25
They bark, but their bark is uncertain surmising;
And they beat back and whine, consulting, advising,
Back there on the prairie amazed at his rising,
And wonder what has delayed their great feast
On black Rising Wolf, Rising Wolf, the brave beast.   30

Where are nine strong men to go with me now
That the hundred strong dogs in our hearts may rush down
From the clouds and the sun and the stars on the crown
Of black Rising Wolf, Rising Wolf, the brave beast,
And beat the beast down,   35
Till we chain him, enslave him, and make him our own,
This river and snowstorm and stone,
This mountain unconquered, whose hair, bone, and blood,
Are those of the deeps in their primeval flood,
Are those of the winds to the west of the sky,   40
Are those of the highest Red Warriors on high?

        1925

THE HUNTING DOGS

The ten hunting dogs in my heart
Have captured forty-six years
In a wood that is dewy with tears.
The ten hunting dogs in my heart
Have captured, as hunting dogs should,   5
That is, without wounding at all,
All the wild birds that call
In my rustic cage in my house in the wood.
The ten hunting dogs in my heart
Have helped tame the chipmunks and small baby bears,   10
They drive mountain lions back, back, to their lairs.
They help me to feed on elk meat,
And my heart must beat to their rustling feet.
And these are their names:
America, Beauty, Song,   15
Religion, Love of Lone Games,
The Indian, the Lover, the Brother, the Proud One,
The Chief No Man Tames.

        1925

CONCERNING HIS INSIGNIA

To Stephen Graham

Brother, who went a-climbing across Asia,
Tramping with big boots through the mysterious places,
The wide world is your parish,
And new pathways
Beckon you farther through still further races.   5
We will be meeting soon on many boundaries:
We crossed the Canadian Border for a sign.
We will cross and claim a thousand oceans,
And each side will be yours and each side mine.

Restless of heart! Always overshining   10
Every path you found, the Cross gave light.
There in that light you found your hope and wisdom,
Tramping on, still fevered, through the night.
You will tell world's-end of the other world's-end;
You will tell borders where far borders are;   15
You will yet reconcile such separate races—
You will look down, a conqueror, from your star.

        1925

WORLD-MAPS

To Stephen Graham

I would draw rich maps of the whole world
And every classic nation of the past—
The spread of each religion, age by age,
The plot of each soul-empire and the cast:
The states that rose and fell after Christ's death,   5
The nations that turned flowers in Buddha's breath,
The states Prophet Mohammed made too brave,
The states Osiris wakened from the grave.

        1925

THE HOUSE OF BOONE

The smoke from the house
Of Daniel Boone,
More than a century ago,
Turned to a Kansas sunflower
In the sky,
Then to a vision
Of the Colorado mountains,
Then to the Northwestern mountains,
Row on row—
Then to the
California mountains,
With their cloudy snow.

   1925

THE RANGER'S CABIN

The Ranger's cabin keeps its light all night,
Just as the lighthouse on the terrible shore.
If you are lost, upon the high passes,
Fight toward the light, then wander never more.

   1925

THE SNOW BY RISING WOLF PEAK

By Rising Wolf Peak
There's a canyon of snow,
Heart-shaped,
Fair, and white.
It turns to blood-red   5
If you climb there
And stare,
Through
The long night.

   1925

THE CHILD-HEART IN THE MOUNTAINS

On Rising Wolf Peak
Is a canyon of snow
Heart-shaped and
Strange and wild.
The pilgrim
Who climbs
To the canyon of snow
Returns
With the heart of a child.

1925

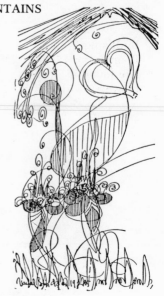

THE BRIDE'S BOUQUETS

By Rising Wolf
We saw the bride's bouquets
Tied to the New Moon.

1925

BONNETS

By Rising Wolf
Bonnets for Country girls
Are found in
Flowery swirls.

1925

THE LADY-SLIPPERS

By Rising Wolf
The lady-slippers
Grow on a green ladder
In a pretty row.

1925

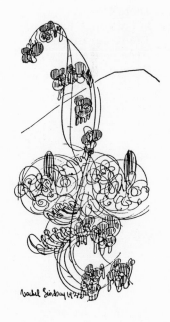

THE PENNANT

Where the forest-fires had blackened
Old Rising Wolf with shame
After
The first healing storm
The pennant
Of the green-grass soldiers
Came.

1925

"COEUR D' ALENE"

There blooms
In the Lodge-Pole forest lane
The flower called
"The pointed heart"
Or, sometimes
"Coeur d' Alene."

1925

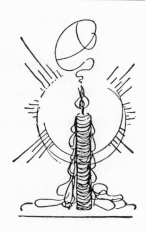

THE HALL OF JUDGMENT

The Forest-Ranger's Courtship

To this vague court of judgment we appeal
To this tremendous wind-swept range we call—
Be with us through the fall;
Though we are far away, and this majestic hall
Seems alien to the eastern falling leaves,   5
October apples and October sheaves.
We have the dream of conquering all the maps,
Of taking our twelve sons around the world:
We will not be stopped by rain or snow,
Or caught in little traps.   10
We would be unchained from dusty houses;
We would enjoy, then leave the largest towns.
We would enjoy and love the oldest neighbors,
Worn only here in the flowers' hall of justice,
Worn only in this great court of appeals,   15
Here would our tribe judge and be judged forever,
Here we would be sealed with sacred seals,
Till none can move us, or distress
Except the wilderness;
Till none can comfort, harry, or caress   20
Except the wilderness;
Till thus, by being free
And filled with the waterfall's mirth,
Our house, our twelve bright sons,
And our own souls   25
Explore and conquer the wilderness of earth,
All trails of the earth.

1925

THE PIGEON DRAGON-ROSE

The rose that bloomed
In the waterfall
Turned to a Pigeon Dragon-Rose
More sturdy of frame,
More icy of thorn
Than any garden-blossom
That blows.

1925

THE TWIN WATERFALLS

The Twin Waterfalls
That were jealous
Over a huckleberry bush
Swept down the mountains
With a quarrel and a push.

1925

THE CURLING WAVES

The curling waves
Of Iceberg Lake
Wind and wind
Before they break.

1925

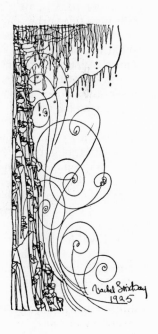

THE MOUNTAINS ARE THE MEMBERS OF OUR FAMILY

The mountains are the members of our family to defend
  us.
They fight us by the campfire but are for us in the
  street.
They gather round the fire log, insulting and accusing.
They curse the cat, they kick the dog,
Step on each other's feet,   5
Full of open feuds, with us, and one another;
But when it comes to war with men
Each mountain is our brother.
In Babylon we speak of them,
Each mountain is our brother.   10

    1925

THE BABBITT JAMBOREE

When I see an Indian dressed for war
Yet dancing for a Babbitt jamboree
In plumes no Babbitt ever dares to wear,
An anger rises in me
Like high tide in the sea.   5
These are my own, these Indians. I know
What makes the breeds more bitter than the bloods.
There's just one drop of Indian blood in me,
Yet in tremendous tides and floods
It seems to sweep upon me when I watch   10
Those who have owned this land turned to a show.

And when I put a feather in my hat,
It is with thoughts the Babbitts cannot know.
Woe to the pale face then who thinks it is for show!

That little feather stands for a whole war.   15
It means I beat the tom-toms in the rain;
It means a scalping knife is in my belt,
That I will lead the young braves not in vain.
It means when all these silly days are done,
Sons of this soil will come into their own,   20
Sons of the Mohawk,
Sons of Pocahontas,
Bred of these rocks and mountains, blood and bone.

    1925

THE MOUNTAIN WITH WINGS

Red Eagle, Red Eagle,
The red man's own mountain!
Red Eagle, Red Eagle,
The mountain with wings,
Where the butterflies fly in white rings,   5
Where the chipmunks display an especial fantastic
And seem to be spreading red wings.
Red Eagle, Red Eagle, where sunrise and sunset
Seem to be spreading red wings.
Red Eagle, Red Eagle, where waterfalls shake the walls   10
Seem to be splitting the canyons and valleys,
Seem to be spreading red wings.

Red Eagle
Where he
Who sleeps under   15
That wonder,
The aspen,
Dreams that its whiteness is wrapped round in fire,

Till it seems to be spreading red wings,
And climbed by a feathered green serpent that stings.   20

Oh mountain, endowed with the pride of the bird
That sings not, but rules every songster that sings,
And sets me to singing and lifting my head,
And spreading my sky with red wings, red wings!

Red Eagle, Red Eagle,   25
The red man's own mountain,
That seems to be spreading red wings.

    1925

THE RED EAGLE LOVE SONG

   The Forest-Ranger's Courtship

We would be stakers of homesteads and ranches,
Yet have our homes regal.
Then,
We would be breakers of underbrush branches
On that mountain, Red Eagle.   5
We would be rakers of alfalfa and hay,
By sweat earn our bread.
Yet: —
We would be lazy and sassy and gay,
By the moment be led.   10

We would be bakers of clams, in lost island sands,
Far from good people;
Be great forsakers of prim and restraining hands,
And the church steeple.
We would be eagles red,   15
Blazing through all the year,
Lovers of Red Gods and unknown to any fear.

By Red Eagle Mountain I make you my love song,
By Red Eagle Mountain, I lift up my voice, and rejoice.

    1925

THE PARABLE OF DEEPNESS

"In Glacier Park is a bottomless lake," said a guide on
    the east side to me.
"If you tie a big rock to a system of clothes lines,
Tied end to end, forever and ever,
You will find it more deep than the sea."
"Now where is this lake?" I asked the smart guide.   5
"West of the Ranges," said he.

"In Glacier Park is a bottomless lake," said the guide
    on the west side to me.
"If you let down a system of trout lines and wire,
Tying on more, all your heart may desire,
With a horseshoe for plumb on the end of the string,   10
You cannot determine the depth of the thing.
You will find it more deep than the sea."
"Now where is this lake?" I asked that gay guide.
"East of the Ranges," said he.

"In the ocean there sure is a bottomless place,"   15
Said a sailor in New York harbor to me.
"If you let down a cable with plummets to fit
You will find it more deep than the bottomless pit.
It's a terrible place to get drownded at sea—
We cannot dive down and rescuers be."   20
"Now where is this water?" I asked the salt sailor.
"Just south of the North Pole," said he.

"In the ocean there sure is a bottomless place,"
Said a San Francisco sailor to me.
"The sea spiders come when we ship in that sea   25
And they fasten their threads to the ribs of the ship,
Shark-proof-silk, resisting the lip
Of sharks of the highest or lowest degree.
And the spiders spin down, and swim down, and dive
    down,
And bite everything in the green-weed-town,   30
And clear things away, and swim down, and say:—
'Oh where is the floor of this fathomless sea?'
But the sea is as deep as the bottomless pit.
No spider has ever dived down into it,
Not a spider of highest or lowest degree."   35
"Now where is this water?" I asked the proud sailor.
"Just north of the South Pole," said he.

Now the China boy there in the chop suey dive
Serving us whisky in tea
Sat down and continued the epic of deepness,   40
Delighting the salt and his sweetie and me.
He said, ''There's a well in Confucius' back yard
Overhung by a plain little cinnamon tree.
The well has run dry, but is deep as the sky.
There's a star day and night you can see   45
If you put your fool head in the shadowy boughs,
Looking down through black leaves of the cinnamon tree.

''You can let down a kite string as long as a river
And tie on bright jades that will glitter and quiver,
In the light of the star in the depths of the well.   50
It goes down like the slenderest glittering dragon,
And passes all side-doors and cellars of Hell,
Making dry rainbows there in the flagon.
No thread has ever gone down to the star,
The jewelled lost hub of Confucius' blue car.''   55
''Now where is this well?'' inquired the gay sailor.
''I would like to go there with a spider and trailer.''
''In Confucius' back yard,'' said the boy with a stare.
''I'm American born and have never been there,
But I heard my great-grandfather say it was there.''   60

When I climb on Sun-Mountain and look up at noon
Then new revelations of glory come soon
And the sky is a lake more deep than the dream
Of cowboy or sailor, or China boy gay.
And I need no kite strings to measure the way.   65

When I sleep on that height
There is midnight more deep
Than the bottomless pit, or the seas, or the wells,
Or the wise men's great tales of sea spiders and hells.

When the great moon comes up   70
I lie in a sea
Where the moon is the ship of God comforting me,
But between are wonders more deep than ever may be
In the lonely and strange lost green floors of the sea,
Or the deep drowned flowers in the depths of the Polar
    Sea.   75

    1925

THE BEE

The Bee that left a smoke trail
In the sky,
After he kissed
The Fireweed Bloom good-by.

  1925

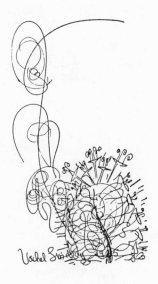

THE DRAGON FLIES

The Dragon Flies of the
Silver Lake
Were flying machines
Of an ancient make.

  1925

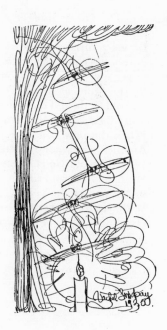

PATHFINDER OF THE AIR

With a Medal for Lowell H. Smith, Inscribed by the Explorers Club of New York "Circumnavigator and Pathfinder of the Air."

Pathfinder of the air, the nations honor you.
They envy the adventure and the goal.
They honor the hard pathway of Ulysses
The wave-surmounting cloud-compelling soul,
The courage of Columbus in new oceans   5
And Magellan's circumnavigating glory.

Like great migrating birds, their wings in rhyme
All men may fly around the world today,
Because you did it first, and for all time,
And made Magellan's victory your own story.   10

1925

BY THE MOHAWK'S BUCKSKIN DOOR

The Forest-Ranger's Courtship

Do we return to the Rockies?
Surely we camp once more
There on the peaks of tomorrow
By the Mohawk's buckskin door.
The old Gods and the new Gods   5
Must fight in student hearts.
When the new tribes seem most sleepy
Another war-whoop starts.
When the old Gods seem but basalt,
We hear a sistrum ring.   10
In the end of the years
Will Thoth, the scribe,
Or the Mohawk be our king?

1925

THE MOHAWK COMES

Bring my green-gold weeds and trees
To speak of his approach,
  The Mohawk.
Bring my roaring waterfalls
To speak of his approach,   5
  The Mohawk.
Bring the fearful glaciers
To speak of his approach,
  The Mohawk.
Bring the terrible mountain forms   10
To speak of his approach,
  The Mohawk.

For when weeds and trees are visions blazing
 through the midnight black,
When waterfalls are like great ghosts that walk
 across the storm and wrack,

When visions of vast glaciers bring the ghosts of
   rocks of old,   15
And the mountains seem to march and earthquakes
   with new clouds enfold,
Then the Mohawk brings the ages, brings the Indian
   ages back!

   1925

CONCERNING THE MOUNTAIN IN GLACIER PARK CALLED "ALMOST A DOG"

Almost a dog
But really a prologue,
To a wind song whose rhythms make ripples in creeks.
Almost a dog
But really a dialogue   5
Between my sick soul and the guardian it seeks.
Almost a dog
But really an epilogue
To an epic of hiding and seeking for weeks.
Almost a barking dog   10
Really a monologue,
A mountain that barks of itself at the sky,
And all the invisible things that go by.

Almost a dog
But really a thunder cloud,   15
Changing again to a mystery and mist.
Almost a dog
But really a fire-log,
Really a sunset where rose clouds are kissed
By storms that keep troth and keep tryst.   20

Almost a dog
But really a Mohawk's arm,
A tomahawk held in a warrior's fist.
Almost a dog
But really a jewel,   25
A vast and incredibly deep amethyst.
Almost a barking dog
Really a monologue,
A mountain that barks of itself at the moon,
Yet a sod so friendly, so shaggy, so wagging,   30
When one lays a tired hand in the deep bear grass;

The mountainside turns like a friend to you soon
To guard you and guide you home under the moon,
A dog like a friendly bear under the moon.

Almost a dog   35
Yet really a monologue,
Of the heart-roaring Mohawk singing in wonder
How mystery hangs like tree-moss from the heavens.
Almost a dog
But really the thunder—   40
The Red Indian Thunder, the Thunder, the Thunder!

1925

THE RED INDIAN BRIDE

The Forest-Ranger's Courtship

There is a bridal hour
In my ancestral story
That comes each year with overwhelming power.
I remember the wild pioneer
The younger son from England and from Spain,   5
Who took the Red Indian bride
On the mossy rock in the rain,
Somewhere in Virginia,
Or somewhere in Tennessee,
And set the Picts and Scots forever free,   10
And turned loose on America
The Saxons and the Angles,
Wearing Odin's raven wings
And Thor's war-bangles;
Wearing the sort of feathers   15
Fit for man—
The feathers of Black Hawk and Powhatan,
And made me an Indian chief.
Though I am worlds away
(There are mountain ranges between us)   20
Yet that deep-wood yesterday
Is nearer to my bridegroom blood
Than all other natural things.
If I have sons, let them be red,
Painted Red Indian kings.   25

1925

THE FLYING PAPOOSES

We have seen the Flying Papooses
Climbing Hawaii's crown;
We have seen them in visions in Mesa Verde,
In Yosemite's out-door town
Of towers that never will tumble down.   5

We have seen the Flying Papooses
In dreams, in the great redwood trees,
Flying and dancing in air,
Above the sequoia's knees,
We have seen the Flying Papooses   10
In the Yellowstone Park in our dream.
They jump into boiling waters,
They sing in the geyser steam.
We have seen the Flying Papooses
Diving in Crater Lake,   15
And marvelous medicine make,
There with the birds and the wildflowers
On the steep bank of Crater Lake.

We have dreamed of the Flying Papooses
Using snowshoes on Mount Rainier;   20
And climbing to dawn stars in snowshoes,
And riding the skies on moose-backs and deer.
We have dreamed of the Flying Papooses
How they captured Glacier Park,
Changing for an hour   25
From Flying Papooses
To young wolves that race and bark.

We have seen them fly up Mount McKinley
From the deep of the valley to where
The peak lifts tremendous snowstorms,   30
And throws them like flowers through the air.

In all of the Parks of the nation,
By these wings is your spirit set free,
The wings of the Flying Papooses,
In the mountains like primitive temples,   35
The forests and cliffs like the sea.
By the wings and the cries of the Flying Papooses
Is your soul long in prison,
Given its pride,
And its sails,   40
And set free.

    1925

THE FOURTH RETURN TO SUN-MOUNTAIN

The Forest Ranger's Courtship

From clear St. Marys Lake to the high blue
We saw the angels climb in sunset light, their wings
    all new.
And so in rain and storm and rainbows
We swore to climb, too,
To climb those celestial ladders every one,   5
Past the mountain peak called Going-to-the-Sun.

A double mind was ours.
We saw those angels as we see the flowers,
And yet we felt ourselves as Indians
Without aureoles   10
Serving Red Gods whose names were never written
On old scrolls;
Serving storms and stars
Alien to that angel band.
So while the angels filled the sky   15
The Indian storm Gods danced upon the mountain peaks,
The glaciers, the forests, the water and the land.
And yet with Indians and angels we were one,
All going, going, going,
To the Sun, the Sun, the Sun!   20

    1925

IDOL OF THE DEER

Behold: —
The steps to the
Idol of the deer,
The idol was a
Cloud in the highest sky,
The steps were clouds
Above Sun-Mountain.

    1925

THE GOLDEN ORCHIDS

The Forest-Ranger's Courtship

In the snow-born waterfalls, we found the golden orchids,
Nodding in the moss beneath the thunder.
Though many a snowstorm, there, had come and gone,
Though many a wind had deeply snowed them under,
They nodded there, and slept in spite of thunder,
In delicate, serene, and golden wonder.

1925

TO THE TALLEST ASPEN OF GLACIER PARK

The Forest-Ranger's Courtship

You are marvelous in your power to soar.
Too white to be a tree,
Too slim to be a tree,
And yet so strong, outshining all
The bright-boughed pines around;   5
Making the stream about your feet
Sing with a holy sound
From the consecrated ground.
You are a gate of Paradise,
The only one today that we have found.   10

1925

THE OLD MAIL COACH TO BELTON

The Forest-Ranger's Courtship

The old mail coach to Belton
Seemed to sweep the purple seas:
The old mail coach to Belton,
In the drizzle and the fog.
The old mail coach to Belton   5
Went through an old burnt forest,
Past blackened mast and log;
But our hearts were gay with the conquest
Of the world and all the seas.
Our hobnailed shoes were water-soaked,   10
We were mud up to the knees;

But with the ancient silken sails,
We swept purple seas,
For our hearts were tides within us,
Greater than all the seas. 15

1925

THE FAWNS AND THE STRANGER

The Forest-Ranger's Courtship

The fawns across the farmyard in the rain
Leap with a grace astonishing the eye.
They know the farmer, and they trust the farmer,
But watch the stranger with a weather eye;
And if the stranger quivers but a feather,
The fawns leap over the fence and say "good-by."

1925

THE DEER OF QUARTZ RIDGE

The Forest-Ranger's Courtship

The deer of Quartz Lake, Quartz Creek, and Quartz Ridge,
Leap to a rhythm that sets me afire.
They jump the rail fences, jump the barb wire.
They live in their leaping, they hold their heads high,
These quivering, shivering, delicate wonders,
The deer of Quartz Lake, that rush by.

1925

THE WRITHING, IMPERFECT EARTH

The Forest-Ranger's Courtship

Dear love, if you and I had perfect love,
No doubt we could not face the imperfect earth.
We have a little, struggling, deathless love,
Struggling up through the writhing, imperfect earth.

We who would make of every breath a song,   5
We who would make of every vista, peace,
Struggle up like rooted growing things,
Like pines at the mountain top in stony earth,
Struggling up through the writhing, imperfect earth.

Yet now, dear love, we proudly remake our vows,   10
Standing like gods beneath the noon or the moon.
Yet we bend with love flowers on our brows,
Renew them soon if they wither soon.

Yet, my darling, darling, though we wound,
Misunderstand, and struggle for our peace,   15
Still kisses, dearest kisses, give release;
And the sod blooms with a flower of deathless worth,
And secret heavenly mirth,
The flower of faith.
The angel flower of faith,   20
That strange scrap of snow,
That magical sweet wraith,
Struggling up through the writhing, imperfect earth.

    31 August 1925

BEGGING PARDON

    The Forest-Ranger's Courtship

There is only one way to forgive,
With a whole heart.
There is only one way to forgive,
Take a new start.
There is only one way to beg pardon,   5
And that is abjectly, completely.
And so I beg pardon,
And will you forgive me
Sweetly?

    1925

I SAW A ROSE IN EGYPT

The Forest-Ranger's Courtship

I saw a rose in Egypt
Where many a lotus blooms.
In Egypt, in my dream,
I saw a rose.
Alone there in the sand,   5
The glory of the world,
In Egypt, by the stream,
I saw a rose.

1925

WHEN YOU AND I WERE SINGERS IN THE MOUNTAINS

The Forest-Ranger's Courtship

When you and I were singers, were singers in these
   mountains,
A million and a million years ago,
We built a nest of silk
From the fireweed of these mountains,
And sang and sang, and saw the summers go.   5

When you and I were singers, were singers in these
   mountains,
We built our nest in echoing Indian Pass,
But we called it in bird-language: —
"The place of echoing grass."

The longest sweetest echo the world of birds may know,   10
We heard there, we heard there long ago.
We could sing long sweet sentences
And hear the whole come back—
A whispering of trembling lovers' words,
A whispering of ardent little birds.   15

When you and I were singers, were singers in these
   mountains,
We were just such mountain larks as sing at dawn,
Now making great cantatas with a chorus of dim echoes,
Calling sweet lovers to this sacred lawn,
Saying: "Set free your hearts and sing to the dawn!"   20

1925

THE HOUR OF FATE

The First Song of the Forest-Ranger's Honeymoon

The log cabin hearth fire dies away;
The embers turn to ashes, and we wait;
It is the hour of fate.

Here, by these two dim candles, we bend,
Each to each, at the riotous day's end.   5

Oh, the tremendous leaping of our souls
At dawn this morning because of the mountains' gold!
Till we improvised in song: meter and rhyme.
Oh, the tremendous leaping of ambition
When new strength came with the wind, and the high
    climb.   10
How we planned and plotted against gloom,
Against the sorrows of the world and time,
The gray hairs of the years,
The sod of the grave.
How we planned and plotted against tears.   15

Now we remember the red rocks at noon,
The great blue rivers and the yellow moss;
Now we remember the white aspen bowers;
Now we remember the purple lake, and how we swam
    across;
Now we remember the crimson Indian paint;   20
Now we remember the orange autumn leaves.
The embers turn to ashes and we wait.
It is the hour of fate.
Either the mighty bridal hour or the closing of love's gate.

    31 August 1925

BY AN OLD UNLIGHTED CANDLE

By an old
Unlighted candle in the cabin
In the moonlight
Strange flowers
Went up like arrows   5
Shot into the air.

Love-darts sprang up
By an old unlighted
Candle in a cabin
In the moonlight.

1925

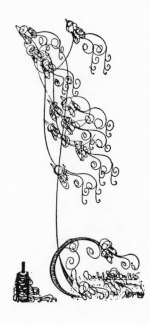

FINDING THE MYSTERIOUS CABIN

The Forest-Ranger's Honeymoon

We found an empty cabin
By a bend in the river,
In a forest of poplars, of aspens, lodge-pole pines,
In a circle of the steepest cliffs our eyes had ever known,
All of weird designs.   5
The narrowest, strangest valley
Our souls might hope to own,
Full of bewitching signs,
And deep as to the center of the earth
It seemed this morning   10
As we peeped down round the pass,
To take the reckoning,

And watch the dawn adorning
Glacial snow and grass.

Here in the empty cabin, we found our heart's delight,   15
And whispered plans to make the world all rhyme;
And whispered plans to find the golden heart of this
    strange time;
And planned deep deeds in this deep place
Throughout the forest night.

1925

THE JOURNEY TO THE CENTER OF THE EARTH

The Forest-Ranger's Honeymoon

Going-to-the Sun is Going-to-Tomorrow,
Going-to-Adventure, ''with bells on,'' as it were.
Once upon a time,
We had a strange adventure,
When we were dressed in feathers, leaves, and fur.   5

We found a very deep and quite extinct volcano,
With many circles of tall spruce around it,
And devil's club around it.
On and down we wandered when we found it;
Round and round we climbed inside around it.   10

The volcano was so wide
The eagles soared across it;
The echoes of its corridors were wonderful to hear;
And when we threw down pebbles, the thunder kept
    increasing,
And sent a deep earth trumpeting, to the inner ear.   15

Round and down we wandered,
Hand in hand kept going,
Eating huckleberries and blueberries all the way;
Killed and cooked big game, as down and down we
    wandered,
Till the blazing hour of noon was all we had of day.   20

All the flowers of Glacier Park bloomed down to the
    center.
A whispering wildcat soon made friends, and led us
    farther down.

He beckoned and he whined,
He skipped and rolled and signed,
With manners like a chipmunk's, —   25
Until he brought us to a wildcat-town.

Each cat had a tree,
Each cat had a cave,
Each cat took his turn at keeping deer, on the slope.
They fed us on deer's blood: —   30
They were like old friendly Indians,
And sent us farther earthward, with good-will signs,
    and hope.

In and down we wandered, following little streams,
Finding jeweled pebbles and Aztec designs
On the mattocks and the picks and drills of the jewel
    mines.   35

In and down we wandered,
Past many jeweled wonders,
And as the shadows tried us,
And as the nights grew longer,
The fireflies flew before us.   40
We lit brush fires to guide us,
We carried tall pine torches,
And the fireflies helped beside. . . .
And then new lights began to shine
On a phosphorescent tree,   45
That was our guide.

A tree like a giant aspen
That grew on a narrow roadway—
One side of each aspen leaf shone with silvery white;
Who had put the trees here   50
In a winding path transcendent
To guide us when the sun no more gave light?

The way was never lonely,
The way was never weary,
For we had one another and loved as now today.   55
The wonders all went past us,
We played and we adventured,
And took it all for granted, as this cabin here today.
We do not know who built it,
It seems left for half a century.   60
Its history in the forest is as unknown and as strange
As that wild lost volcano we found behind the range.

Down and down we wandered,
The aspens, giant candles,
Lit our way as these two candles   65
Light our shack tonight.
We had our loving there as here,
Our big pine beds of hearts' delight.
And love's eternal rite.

Down and down we wandered,   70
To the wild earth's center.
There we found strange bluebell flowers whose music
    could be heard,
And wore them for our pleasure,
Frolicked and were absurd.
And there we found a nest of birds with eggs big as
    the moon,   75
Round as the moon.
They broke their bright shells singing,
And soon with father and mother,
Up the whirling whirl were winging,
Up the whirling fantasy   80
Were whirling, soaring, singing soon.

One of them stayed to beckon,
One of them stayed to whisper,
Just as the wildcat whispered,
With manners like a chipmunk, though as big as any
    moon.   85
There, with bluebells all over us,
He tied us to one feather,
And then all three together
Went up, went up, to his volcano tune.

Cry of a lost volcano!   90
Cry of the dear earth's center!
Cry of a dream volcano, where the fire is now a bird,
A bird and yet a giant ghost, singing a giant word!
A word that means great bird-love,
A word that means bright nesting,   95
A word that means dim wings of fire,
And love and vast unspent desire.
And this he sang, as on he sprang;
He was tender with us, too,
And left us here beside this shack, while he leaped
    into the blue,   100
And we waved at him with bluebells
While he leaped into the blue.

We called him "Going-to-the-Sun"
And "Going-to-Tomorrow."
If these were our adventures, in our silly yesterday,   105
(With bells on, with bells on)
We are going to adventure now.
Going-to-Tomorrow;
And it is just past midnight, and the candle flames
    are gay.

The great fire-logs are roaring,   110
Whispering and singing
The love song of tomorrow and adventure and new day.
Going-to-the-Sun is Going-to-Tomorrow
And is going out to frolic and to play.

    1925

THE CANDLE IN THE CABIN

The Forest-Ranger's Honeymoon

When you and I were driving herds and ranching on
    the sun,
Skinning mules and building towns and cooking for
    the boss,
Living where the mountains and the plains and rivers
    cross,
We had our vast adventures and our blood-letting days.
For cattle thieves are mighty on the trails of the sun;   5
When they capture big-bull prizes, their day of glory
    rises.
But we caught them and we lynched them
On the great plains of the sun.
And those were cruel realistic days.
Yes, we kept our cattle safe, the cattle of the Sun-chief.   10
Bulls like the Bulls of Texas bellowed there,
And we rode their backs like gods and frolicked there.

The great sea in the sun is like the air;
And the great wind in the sun is like the sea;
And we rode the bulls of wonder   15
Through the ocean round the year,
Over the ocean floor;
And gloried without fear.

When we were cook and cowboy in the tremendous sun,
We built a shack of silver rocks and rain.   20
For the light is like the rain
In the storm-clouds of the sun,
And our magic harnessed clouds and rocks and rain.
And we built a rainbow shack of rocks and rain,
And lit a wax-flower candle in the night there in the
    rain;   25
For night comes there despite the blazing rain.
We lit a little candle made from wax from wax-flower
    berries,
From the highest forest of the mountain heights.
And there we kissed and sang,
As here we kiss and sing,   30
Teaching one another dear delights.

When you and I were children of the tremendous sun,
Serpent-stranglers, and horse-wranglers,
Bull-whackers and mule-skinners,
We hardly knew   35
Just what to do.
We had the strength and leisure,
(We had ten thousand years)
So we rode a great red eagle
Through the blaze and blue.   40
We looked down on our mountains,
We looked down on our cities,
We looked down on our oceans,
On our bull herds, proud and vain,
And on our playhouse built of rocks and rain.   45

Then we flew to Glacier Park,
And turned to aspen trees,
Here on great Sun Mountain, and dreamed here,
In the sunshine, rocks and rain,
Dreamed again of Going-to-the-Sun,   50
And saw April going and returning,
And forest fires and years,
And saw Red Eagle turn into a mountain,
Through the years.

Then we were born as lovers,   55
Singing as we are now,
Singing, desiring,
Burning a little candle in a log house in the rain.
And the shadows thrown by candlelight
Are light, not midnight darkness.   60
They fill the midnight darkness with the starlight of
    our pain: —
Our hearts' celestial revel,
Sun-born, without stain,
In that rain called the starlight,
In that rain called the sunshine,   65
In that candle-flame, called rain.

    1925

BY THE OLDEST TRAILS

The Forest-Ranger's Honeymoon

The moose they say is a whimsical beast.
The pack rat is a curious thing.
The wood wasp, too, is a curious thing.
But a stranger thing was on the wing,
A flying machine, the fire patrol,   5
Heard from behind a tremendous mountain,
Humming on like America's soul.

It was hid behind the mountain top,
Yet humming and humming again and again.
Then we slept all night in a cabin unused,   10
Yet a telephone spoke again and again,
The ringing pulse of America's blood,
Calling us back by its very sound
To America's streets again and again.

So deeper and deeper on we climbed   15
To where the fallen cabins are found
By the oldest trails, a lifetime old.
And the waterfalls roared to keep us proud,
And not be misled by the hum and the ring
Back to where the skyscrapers swing.   20

1925

THE DRAGON FLY GUIDE

The Forest-Ranger's Honeymoon

A dragon fly by bright Waterton Lake,
And a flying machine in the sky,
Ran competition for our admiration
The day that summer went finally by.
The flying machine disappeared in the west   5
Across hundreds and hundreds of trails,
The dragon fly dallied in buckler metallic
Fish and reptilian scales,
Whizzing this way and that,
By bright Waterton Lake,   10
And seemed to be showing the way we should take,
While the underbrush dragged at our knees.

Then the dragon fly led
To a dimmer lake,
The home of a somnolent, indolent breeze;   15
The dragon fly led
To one lone lake,
The true lovers' own,
The sweet secret lake,
Past hundreds and hundreds of trees,   20
Hundreds and hundreds of trees.

1925

WHY DO WE NOT RETURN?

The Forest-Ranger's Honeymoon

Dear, we were in Egypt
Not so long ago.
We sailed the Nile,
We saw the sacred Ibis come and go.
We sailed among Papyrus reeds,   5
We saw the temples burn
In the light of the desert dawn.
Why do we not return?

Here by our cabin candle,
With Red Indian Gods in the air,   10
We look at our hieroglyphic book
Till Thoth is standing there.
We look at the hieroglyphic book
Till Hathor shakes her bells,
Till Ra comes from the heavens   15
And Set comes from the hells.

Man is a mixed breed ever,
Remembering yesterday.
He looks to the East for wisdom,
Westward for his play.   20
He looks East in old memory,
Westward in new hope.
We rope the wild-west horses,
But scribe Thoth weaves the rope.
We stoop to kiss sweet Hathor   25
Who sleeps by our fire there;
But just as we have touched her lips,

There's a wild call in the air—
The Mohawk comes, the Mohawk comes,
And we hear his drums roll near   30
From great Red Eagle Mountain,
Next moment he is here!

1925

THE INDIAN GIRL—MY GRANDMOTHER

The Forest-Ranger's Honeymoon

I think of just one bride
Beside this pale bride here,
It is my Indian grandmother
Of a far yesteryear.

I think of her so often,   5
Her baskets, feathers, and knives.
I know she was good to her man,
The bravest of wives.

I am nearer her kin by far,
Than the British who strut and boast   10
That they are kin of William the Norman,
And his ravishing host.

And I back my one drop of blood
From this Indian girl
Against all the blood of the Normans,   15
Where the British flags unfurl.

1925

BEHIND SUN-MOUNTAIN

The Forest-Ranger's Honeymoon

We climbed to the glacier beyond the trail,
Beyond the flowers and the shale and the woods.
We built a campfire there in the rain
Of three old roots, broken to punk,
And our discarded goods.   5
The campfire burned against the fog,
Against the ice and the rain and snow,
And we asked what the wise in glaciers ought to know.

Then on we climbed, and down we climbed,
And built a better fire,   10
In the night, in the rain, in the fog and snow,
And watched the long night go,
Dry and warm by a glorious furious fire.
At midnight, for an hour, the sky
Was clear as a crystal pool,   15
Every star in its place,
Each mountain stood in its place
And spelled its name
In the happy midnight hieroglyphic school.
But soon the fog came down again,   20
Soon to renew the trial.
The great fire dried the rain in the fog,
And dried our shoes and our coats with a smile,
And there we slept awhile.

   1925

THE FOG COMES AND GOES

The Forest-Ranger's Honeymoon

In the valley of ten thousand flowers
The fog came down, we built a fire
That wiped out fog and dark and rain,
And gave a golden glory to desire.
And there, on a bed of deep pine-boughs   5
We gloried, and told tales of old.
Strange beasts were rustling in the bush—
We feared not, for one night were bold.
We dragged great logs from the mist's edge.
We built that fire to the great sky,   10
And midnight saw the great fog lift,
Clear stars and mountains fill the world,
While on that fir-bough bed,
Like mountain-lions in their cave we curled,
Two lovers, conquerors of the fog,   15
Sheltered by ten great fire-logs,
And conquerors of the world.

   1925

A GREAT SHADOWY DAY

The Forest-Ranger's Honeymoon

Looking out the window
Of the little log cabin
We found in the lone lorn wood,
We saw the green world passing by
Throughout the shadowy day.   5

Under Mount Custer,
We saw the shadows and we called them good;
Under the high trees,
Under the shadow of the bushes on the cliff,
Under the shadow of the flowers,   10
And the misty valley's flowery hours,
We saw the shadowy day go by
And found it a pageant and a play.
We found a joy in that great shadowy day.

    1925

THE BREATH OF THE WIND

The Forest-Ranger's Honeymoon

The winds that come across the pass tonight
While I watch the fire, hour after hour,
Come from the west, speak of the western sky
That changed from rose to gray,
And gray to rainbow butterfly   5
And to carnation flower.
All those strange colors change now to strange sounds;
In winds the twilight speaks the whole night through,
And so I heap new logs upon the fire,
And think, my sleeping sweetheart, still, of you.   10

Hid there beneath the fir-bough shelter, built
By our own hands at sunset,
Now a dark and darling mystery,
With deeper mysteries to keep.
I hear your breath, oh, sleeping sweetheart,   15
As you stir in sleep.
So the dark transcends both time and death—
Your whispered breathing is immortal breath.

    1925

THE QUAIL RECEIVES A GUEST

The Quail on her nest
Received a little dream-cloud
For a guest.

1925

THE BABY THAT CAME FROM THE FERN

Behold: —
Where the Honeymoon trails
Meander and linger
And tangle and turn
The Baby that came
From the curling fern.

1925

THE TIME WHEN THINGS HAD BETTER NAMES

The Forest-Ranger's Honeymoon

These flowers and beasts and birds and trees,
Mountains and bees,
Have not the splendid names
They once had long ago,
When you and I sat round the fire,

5

Our twelve strong sons there in a row,
Centuries ago.
They brought new names
For each new thing
They brought into the campfire ring,   10
Words our eldest son, the poet,
Then began to sing.
We wove those names into a world,
Centuries ago.

These rocks and lakes are much the same,   15
But the old names pass.
We had better names for rivers,
And for the white bear grass.
We had better names for every mountain
And for every tree.   20

We almost hear them in the night,
Alone by candlelight.
If we wait here by the light,
The names may come to you and me.
Elusive now, hiding now,   25
The dawn may set them free,
And bring those twelve strong sons
And the eldest son, the singing chieftain,
Back to you and me.

        1925

THE BAT

By the Candle
In the Cabin
I heard the voice
Of a great Pack-rat.
It spoke,   5
And the vision came—
Just
Like
That.
"The United States   10
Wears a great black hat.
Behold:—
The Descent
Of the Night
On the Mountains—   15

In the form
Of a great
Black Bat.''

    1925

The Candle of the Dream

*A Whirlwind Going
Up a Flower*

ONCE MORE

When the thousand love-gods
Knocked at the door,
We lit the candle of the dream
Once more.

    1925

THE WHIRLWIND

Said the Red Indian
Medicine-Man to his son: —
When you take your bride
Be a bull of power.
Be an eagle   5
Flying over red-eagle,
A whirlwind
Going up a flower.

    1925

The Arrow of Sunshine

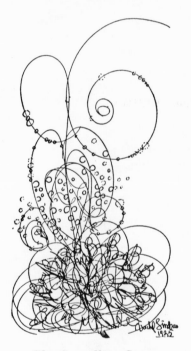

The Crystalline Crown

THE SUMMER ARROW OF SUNSHINE

The arrow that bent
In the summer wind
Was straight
And terrible
In the storm.

1925

THE CRYSTALLINE CROWN

The blossom
That came
When the storm died down,
Was decked with a dewy
Crystalline
Crown.

1925

THE RAT-SOULED FOE THE CITY FEARS

The Forest-Ranger's Second Honeymoon

When you and I were in the lands
Far to the west of this strange camp
(It seems to us but yesterday)
We lit a purple-flaming lamp—
No, a lantern—at the dusk   5
And walked through a still street
And heard no feet but far off feet.

We clambered at the guarded gate,
Of the inner city there.
We said, "A whispering foe comes near!   10
We heard him on the stair,
High on the tower of the outer gate.
We know that he will come,
We have owl's eyes, we have owl's ears,
The rat-souled foe the city fears   15
Will come."

But they woke not at the city gate.
We left the city to its fate.
We stole away at the dawn of day,
We reached the forest far away,   20
We saw the city burning down,
The far off, terrible, heedless town.

But no foe came to spoil delight
In our wooded cabin, day or night.
Our dream rolled on for many a year   25
Till we woke dreaming, singing here,
And saw the city and its fire
In this fir-bough bed, our heart's desire,
In these knapsacks,
All of life and play   30
And saw all cities burn away;
And saw all dreams come and go,
Except star-sky and sunlit sky
Over the forests and mountains high.

1925

A MEMORY OF BOYHOOD

The Forest-Ranger's Second Honeymoon

Once, alone in the wilderness I built myself a fire,
In an island in a little stream, alone,
And the water spoke,
With one hundred thousand voices,
Till the day broke.   5
How the mists rolled down from the mountain,
Bringing happiness;
How the trees were friends to heal my loneliness;
How the trembling island seemed the cloud of my pride;
The campfire was a chariot where my Elijah soul could
    ride.   10

How the mariposa lilies in the dim light gleamed,
The stately dress of the wilderness
Where I lay and dreamed.
Oh, once alone in the wilderness I built myself a fire!
Now, my love and I, this night, build again a fire,   15
And the strange God-breath of the wilderness
Turns to desire.

    1925

THE CITY OF GLASS

The Forest-Ranger's Second Honeymoon

Beside the lake we call "The City of Glass"
We watched our red, dear afternoon go past,
Red with Indian-paint and heart's blood hours —
Innocent were all the other flowers.
What rhyme of love or shout of love can sing   5
Of that deep grass and secret rock and spring?
Of your sun blaze of whiteness and your laughter
My still heart must remember ever after?

    1925

THE PICTURE OF THE HEART-BOAT

Behold: —
The boat called "wonder,"

Called: "Calm after thunder,"
It is painted with hearts.
The boat on the lake called: —
"The City of Glass."

    1925

THE FISH WITH THE BRACELETS

Through the candle of dreams
We saw them pass—
Each wearing a beautiful
Bracelet of brass,
The little fish
Of the lake called: —
"The City of Glass."

    1925

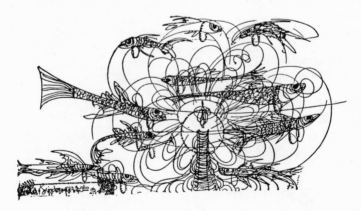

THE FIR-TREE

Heavy with secret shadows
That are sweet
As kissing rhymes,
The Candle in the Cabin
Is a fir-tree
Sometimes.

1925

THE APPLE TREE

Bearing two sweet apples
As sweet as kissing rhymes,
The Candle in the Cabin
Is an apple-tree
Sometimes.

1925

THE MUSICAL WIND

To the strange flower
On the mountain—
A Poet from afar,
A wind from the North Star
Made secret rhymes
As sweet as kisses are,
Rhymes that kissed each other
Many times, —
Laughing little rhymes.

1925

THE DRIFTWOOD BED

The Forest-Ranger's Second Honeymoon

The little driftwood bed
By Dragon Fly Lake,
Under the noon sun,
Cure for a little heart-ache.

The little driftwood bed,   5
The song of the dragon waves,
The free love, the free north wind,
And a thousand sorrows in their graves.

The little driftwood bed,
The pillow of pebbles and sand,   10
And our hearts again wedded
Like the water and the land.

      1925

LIKE THEIR FATHERS OF OLD

The Forest-Ranger's Second Honeymoon

Far from the world and its wrong,
They love as the pioneers loved,
Kissing by firelight and candlelight,
In the cabin there in the woods.

Face turns to shadowed face,   5
Body to body's grace,
All for Love's delight,
Kissing the whole night long,
Through the terrible storm
In the cabin, pine-ribbed and strong.   10

Lovers in far away places
Kiss by electric light,
By bright automobile light,
By movie theater half-light,
By wriggling street sign light.   15

But like their fathers of old,
These are kissing by candlelight,
Through the terrible storm

And hearing a night bird's song,
The night-raven's song.   20

1925

THE ASPEN LEAF LOVERS

The Forest-Ranger's Second Honeymoon

Two happy lovers on one pillow in the forest,
One pine bed in the forest,
Singing the night away!
The moon was almost full;
The little lake was still;   5
The aspen leaves were gay
Against the midnight blue,
Quivering all night through.

The lovers kissed—
Their lips were like the leaves—   10
And their hearts quivered, too.

1925

THREE LITTLE FLOWER-SHIPS

Three little
Flower-ships
Went sailing by,
With butterflies
For sails.

1925

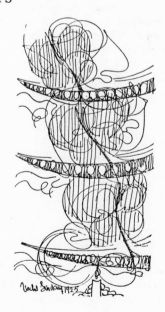

THE MUSICAL BUTTERFLY

The musical
Butterfly,
Whose wings are a harp,
And the dots
Are the notes
Of the tunes
That he plays.

1925

THE STORM-BLOWN BUTTERFLIES

Two
Storm-blown
Butterflies,
Kings of the Storm,
With their little Crowns
Quite groggy.

1925

THE PRAIRIE BUTTERFLY

The prairie butterfly
That dreamed of mountain-birds,
(Birds that were veiled
Like brides)
Was followed by
His dreams
Into the mountains.

1925

THE BUTTERFLY CITIZENS

Indian Pass is golden green,
Indian Pass is high;
Over it, the glaciers,
Under it, scraps of sky.

We climbed over Indian Pass   5
And thought of Springfield Town,
Far away in Illinois,
While the wind roared down,
Springfield seemed a star afar, a far off jewel flame,
Our home-town was a wonder-point,   10
Or merely one more name.

The real town, the one town,
Was the sod beneath our feet,
With city streets complete:
With the Indian Paint, the bear grass,   15

The ferns that toss, the fireweed floss,
The hundred sorts of mountain moss;
And up and down, across, across,
Flew the mountain citizens,
The shining snow-line butterflies   20
With peacock-winged eyes.

 1925

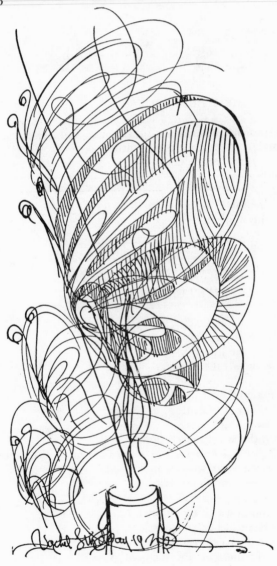

THE PROCESSION POLITICAL

Each insect
Flings off
His repression!
The butterfly
Torch-light
Procession!

1925

THE PRESIDENT

The butterflies
Chose for their president
A great big lily of glass.
We saw their
Election-rockets pass.
And the
Mountain-rocket flower
Turned to a rocket
And flew past
The lily of glass.

1925

SNOW-BORN BUTTERFLIES

The Forest-Ranger's Second Honeymoon

When you and I were white, white snow-born butterflies,
When you and I were butterflies,
When these were new-born mountains,
Back there a million geologic years,
The loves of fearful beasts went on   5

In all the valleys,
And love was shame and fury, blood and tears.

But we found new ways of loving
In the hearts of mountain flowers,
Close to glaciers, and the snow-line places.   10
We read a shy delight in the wooing red and white
Of all the tree-buds in their breeds and races.

And we bound ourselves together,
And flew through the blue air,
Fluttering in naked sweetness in the sun.   15
That was the day that this day on the fire-grass was begun.
Still we are tender, and flower-taught,
In the light of the sun.

Love is not death and fury, blood and tears;
Love holds no secret fears.   20
Love is the naked glory
Of the white, eternal, snowy, splendid summits of the years.

        1925

SEPTEMBER ENDED

When September ended
The palettes and brushes
Of autumn descended.

        1925

THE LEAVES FALL

The Indian Summer wind grieves
With the falling of
The first leaves.

1925

THE MOHAWK WAR-BONNET

Again—
Darkness, sweetness and scandal—
Trailing his Mohawk
War-bonnet—
The Butterfly came
And extinguished the Candle.

1925

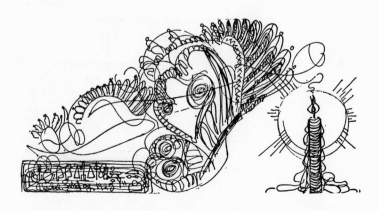

BUBBLES FROM BLACKFEET GLACIER FALLS

Bubbles
From Blackfeet Glacier Falls,
In the dream that
Hovers
Near the
Blown-out candle
In the Cabin
In the Moonlight.

1925

EPILOGUE

ONE MORE SONG

All I can bring is one more song,
Though I have brought you a thousand and one.
So it will be till my life is done.
I would set right the old world's wrong;
I would outbuild New York and Rome.
But all
I can bring home
Is one
More
Song.

1925

EVERY SOUL IS A CIRCUS

October 1929

EVERY SOUL IS A CIRCUS
(Bearing in mind the Chicago World's Fair, 1933)

I

My Brothers of the Poet-trade

My brothers of the poet-trade,
Leave your ivory towers, and stand
On the porch, and watch this ardent band
And praise, with me,
This Masquerade.   5
From a cloud by the dark Art Institute
That old Barnum comes,
Followed by serene Greek Gods,
And the lake-breeze hums.
There, on Michigan Avenue,   10
The fellow who led the game,
On his arm sweet Jenny Lind,
Her splendor yet the same.
Neat escort! Open carriage! Foaming horses!
For a singer unafraid.   15
So then behold her midnight dream-parade.

Passing the dim Art Institute
Her cavalcade glides on,
Nonsense and inconsequence
We had thought forever gone.   20
We see it with our spirit-eyes,
And sing, to the wise,
And join the song of Jenny Lind,
An arrow above the town: —
"Go find the wonders of the dawn   25
And bring the wonders down,
Bring, bring the wonders down,
Bring, bring the wonders down."

With marble gods we march to the song,
And they spread the street with wonders,   30
The bright Athenian violets,
And the cupid babes turned loose.
Then come the slow thunders of the throne of Mother
    Goose,
Drowning out the wise guys
Who are crying: "What's the use?"   35
Though Barnum's Show is gliding by,

Now the silence is so deep
We can hear the farthest feathery clouds
Whisper in their sleep.
Then whisper the sleepers of this racking, roaring
    place,   40
Joining immortal Jenny Lind
With the songs of our new race.
But Buffalo Bill interrupts us still
With the scalp of Yellow Hand.
Then comes Grizzly Adams with his grizzly band,   45
His bears blowing cow-horns, his bears blowing pipes,
Wearing boots like forty-niners,
Steaming like ocean-liners,
Then see stark-naked Indians, painted in stripes.
Then   50
The Deadwood coach.
Then
See approach
Sikh horsemen cruel and lean.
Then   55
Cassocks in green.

Then
Again we hear our Jenny Lind
In a white hoop-skirted gown,
Standing in Barnum's carriage   60
With a song for beast or clown,
Victoriously singing, over the sprawling town,
"Go find the wonders of the dawn
And bring the wonders down,
Bring, bring the wonders down,   65
Shower, shower the wonders down,
Ring, ring the wonders down,
Go, find the wonders of the dawn
And bring the wonders down,
Bring, bring the wonders down,   70
Bring, bring the wonders down."

II

A Million Singing Circuses

See, a million singing circuses
Come marching to the star!
Then a hundred million circuses,
None greater than the other,   75

All in a family unity,
Big sister and big brother—
Marching from the hearts that sleep,
Hearts in the nation buried deep.
Hail, turkey-gobbler, yak, and osprey,   80
Boa constrictor, and snake-charmer, and triumphal car!
Tiger, jackass, horse and zebra, gnu, tarantula, armadillo,
Strong man and clown,
Set free to find The Great North Star
To bring the wonders down,   85
Bring, bring the wonders down,
Bring, bring the wonders down.
And the whisper of Chicago
Grows sharper than its roar,
And haunts the handsome do-do birds,   90
The storks, the cranes, the cassowaries,
The ostriches and llamas,
And all the mixed menageries
That flap their wings,
Or dance,   95
From every door.
Our trance-wrought United States
Sends them forth to war,
Sweeps among the wagons
And haunts the marching train: 100
For Chicago is the Nation,
California and Maine.

For every soul is a circus,
And every mind is a tent,
And every heart is a sawdust ring   105
Where the circling race is spent.

Now march from their caves the mammoths
Of old geologic time,
And mastodons rerisen from the six first days of slime.

Behold the wild boars of Cathay,   110
Sacred cats of Menes' day!
Then elephants of Buddha's day,
Elephants of Hamilcar,
Elephants of Amritzar,
And elephants Adam Forepaugh bred   115
In the wilds of the U.S.A.
In his happy Yankee way—
Spreading out umbrella ears

To hear the whisper sent
That sweeps from the top tent.   120
Elephants from sophisticated, modern Lincoln Park,
And Genesis animals two and two, two and two, two
    and two,
Genesis animals two and two
From Noah's crowded ark,
All spreading out their searching ears   125
To hear the whisper sent,
For the heaven-born WORD is all they love
That sweeps from the top tent.

III

The Long Street Lifts

Now—the long street lifts toward The Great North Star
Of Liberty and Wonder.   130
They hear its canaries trilling
And its prophet-choirs thunder.
And they hear a call, so far below
(A hard, an alarm-clock call they know)
It is turned to a breath like a daisy's death,   135
And they laugh to hear it turned to a breath:—
"Chicago, go
Chicago, Chicago, Chicago, go,
Go Chicago, go Chicago, Go, Go, Go;"

Then follows fast the call above,   140
The cry from out of the far North Star of Liberty and Love.

So come, let us be bold with our songs, brothers,
Come let us be bold with our songs.

IV

The Pontoon Bridge Miracle

Prophets, preaching in new stars,
Have come in ships of sleep   145
And built a ghostly pontoon bridge that Michigan
    Avenue
Can keep.
Have built a causeway bright with sails
Where hares and tortoises may creep,

Where burbling bullfinches, laughing hyenas,
   whinnying Shetlands   150
Climb the steep.

Oh the harp-song of our sand-dunes
Up this arching avenue,
Oh the voices in the prophet-sails
Oh the lovers strolling slowly, two and two!   155

Though every Yankee patents some iron animals
   at last,
And does invent his own World's Fair,
And World's Fair tunes to cheer the air,
This is wild America, not orderly Timbuctoo.
So Barnum's old procession holds proud Michigan
   Avenue,   160
Again moves by up the pontoon bridge
To the Prophet Avenue.
The thought goes again through the night so dark,
Going up to the North-star ark,
Ostriches two and two,   165
Kangaroos, two and two, behemoths two and two,
Hippogriffs two and two, chimeras two and two.

Oh Radio, Oh Saxophone, Oh Slide Trombone, Oh Horns
   that moan: —
The lion, the lion, goes roaring from his cage,
Ten thousand years before your jazz he roared a deeper
   rage.   170
And Jumbo, great Jumbo, goes swaying left and right,
Ten thousand years before your jazz his trumpet shook
   the night.

But Jenny Lind outsings him still upon the heaven-born
   wind,
Stands up in Barnum's carriage on that bridge across the
   vast,
That pontoon span of comet-boats arching above the
   past,   175
That silvery bridge of dawn across the cold.
In the rigging of their ships the prophets old
Sing with her their songs across the cold.

So, come let us forget our ivory-towers, brothers,
Come let us be bold with our songs.   180

V

Beside Her Carriage

Run, run, beside her carriage now, up and among the
    stars,
Up Michigan Avenue, rainbow-high, above Chicago's
    carts and cars.

We will look adown, adown, in the circus-moods of
    slumber,
Then straight on, to the chaos-seas and the North Star
    coming near.
While these mastodons are singing and trumpeting
    away   185
At the joy-bells without number and the top stars that
    they hear.
While underneath us all, everyone belongs,
There's a cry from every house,
From the weirdest and the tiniest,
From whale and from snail,   190
From walrus, seal and porpoise,
From hare and from tortoise,
From leviathan and mouse,
For menageries, like rivers, pour roaring from each
    house.

For every soul is a circus,   195
And every mind is a tent,
And every heart is a sawdust ring
Where the circling race is spent.

And the lake-storms and breezes
Are but nets to save the brave,   200
And the planets are trapezes,
High, high above the grave.

So, come, let us be bold with our songs, brothers,
Come, let us be bold with our songs.

        *   *   *   *   *   *   *

And Jenny Lind sings at shrill noon   205
Sweetly above the town:
"Go, find the wonders of the star

And bring the wonders down.''
Victoriously singing,
Over the sprawling town: 210
''Go, find the wonders of the star
And bring the wonders down,
Bring, bring the wonders down,
Ring, ring the wonders down,
Shower, shower the wonders down,   215
Ring, ring the wonders down,
Go, find the wonders of the star
And bring the wonders down.''

Note: This poem is not to be set to musical notation. It is
not to be identified with any form of musical composition or
orchestra. It is to be read with a bardic and troubadour chant-
ing according to the spelling of the words, the manner of
Welsh preaching and praying to this day. Let the whispered
passages be whispered. Let the leader select certain refrains
to be chanted antiphonally with the audience. Let the poem
feel at home at an Eisteddfod.

Early 1928

A CHRIST CHILD BOOK

To my own tunes I will chant my words,
Let no men bring their tunes to twist them.
Some are words to the Christmas moons
That swept so low I could not resist them.
Those twelve half-moons, last Christmas eve   5
Arranged in a ring round a cloud of wonder!
And they turned to snow-bird nests on a bough
Tossed in the night-wind's organ-thunder.
Each nest had snow-birds flying around.
As the thunder ceased, they spoke like dreamers.   10
And they turned to angels in the nests, —
Now boats of the air with tinsel streamers.
Will I let some other man sit down
And spoil with his dots on his music-paper
Sea-ripples I alone have heard,   15
While the ships grew great, each mast a taper?
Each mast a taper tall as the sky
With fire on the top more bright than moon-fire.
From the twelve gilt ships, with singing lips
Souls called my name as they passed the church-spire.   20

They sang lost words I had whispered before
Awake all night till the Christmas day-break.
A baby boy in my trundle bed,
Who had never known a grown man's heart-ache.
When I ran bare-foot from my singing nest   25
To that Christmas tree in that long lost Springfield,
There were twelve gay candles, twelve balloons
And candies sweet as the clover May-Field.
Noah's arks, and apples fair,
And my shouting cousins running the show there;   30
And a filigree fairy lair for me: —
A Christ Child Book, on a bough bent low there.

And to my own tunes I crooned to the book.
Let no men bring their tunes to twist them.
Words from my own especial heart.   35
I hear them yet, and cannot resist them.

        Late 1927

RIGAMAROLE, RIGAMAROLE

Three Russian musicians, classical court composers,
    slept in an attic,
An East River Attic, in a state of mind splenetic.
A sky lighted turret of the Fish Market Tenements!
    Sorrow was their seneschal!
Sorrow was official, made them medieval, was steward
    and majordomo,
For each ceremonial.   5

The cutest was the flutist Brubenstein Ktchaikovsky.
    The slide tromboner
Was the moaner: — Abalakireffz Zkorsakoff.
    Psapellnikoff Psaffonoff was a scoundrel, a rounder
        and a bounder, and violinist,
Yet loyal to the turret and the hall.   10
    Listen to the story of their fall.

Neighbors in that castle hall tried to stop their squall.
A wop electrician in especial gave Sunday papers to keep
    them quiet,
Gave fifteen cents on rents, crusts and hot dogs by way
    of diet,
Rags   15
To wrap their bones withal.

By Brooklyn Bridge, all year through composing classical
  symphonies!
The cutest played—"Higgledy, piggledy, rilly-ra-loo,
  rigamarole, rigamarole!"
On a flute of crystal, bird-like tone. Yet made it blow
  Slavically, with a groan.
The Moaner played —"Lolly-pop, eat the pup,
  belly-mo-lay,   20
Kersniff, kersniff, eat him today, rigamarole,
  rigamarole!"
But Slavically, on his slide trombone, as he sat all alone
  by the telephone.
Psaffonoff seemed saying—"Alas, alas, poor Cock
  Robin lies under the glass."
Classically, classily, Slavically, slowly, playing his
  speaking violin,
Having for speed a great incapacity; touching the
  strings with fingers thin,   25
And a hint of rigamarole.

Sorrow was their seneschal, sorrow was their all.
Excuse me if I cry into my handkerchief.

Under the skylight they watched for the daylight,
  scrawny, half dead,
Blood royal and bar sinister!   30
And flames in the head.
  With Slavic Asiatic emotionalism, they quarreled
    all night over
Cannibalism,
And Ivan Pre Skootsky Skay Var.
In general, just raising helpless Hell,   35
Yelled about sex and behaviorism, Dostkoyeffsky,
  Turgeneff, Kropotkin,
Rachmaninoff, and Marie Whatya Macaller, Tolstoy
  and some other feller,
Eugenics, aesthetics, aromatics and the like!
Dialogued about physiology, pathology, astrology,
Elections, electrons, atoms, molecules, morons,   40
Psyco-analysis, mythology, the Soviet, the Universal
  Strike,
And spoke with a rigamarole.

At dawn slow music would penetrate
The neighbors deciding to vacate.
Music to make them hesitate,   45

For it left out the rigamarole! For a moment omitted
  the rigamarole!

On Christmas week, when luck was good, they sold a
  song of adultery,
Or a hymn, or a part-Brahms melodee, to be played
  Slavically, crawlingly.
Then Vodka drank, on the thinning winnings.
Made free, made free,   50
Their neckties new, their morals loose, at a place of
  glee called
"The Pig and the Goose,"
And spoke with a rigamarole.

Once, when spring came in a day, each thought to bear
  one maid away,
A gold-haired Mehitable who could purr.   55
Two Slavically moaned to her of obstetrics, Russia,
  and the like,
Straight on to the Universal Strike.
Psaffonoff, scoundrel, had no plan. Hid with her behind
  the door.
Squeezed her just like some hired man.
Each Cossack thought himself engaged. She liked to
  see three Cossacks crawl.   60
But loved the electrician proud and tall! Wop who was
  bigger than a cop!
Married him that very week. Her flirting, sad to say,
  was very sneak.
(She hated rigamarole.)

Sorrow was their seneschal. Sorrow was their all.
Excuse me if I cry into my handkerchief.   65

Cock-robins under the skylight-glass!
There in the attic with moans ecstatic, three Cossacks
  moaned disclosures grave,
Each exposed himself her slave. Quiet, for once, in
  conversation,
Said softly, without telling the nation, that that
  bridegroom was a knave.
Yes, they were brave. Despite their ache, said "What's
  the use?"   70
Declared a truce, for Red Hair's sake, and gave the
  winner game good speed,
(The jokes were broad, the talk was loose)

At the place of glee called "The Pig and the Goose,"
And chatted in rigamarole.

Far off in Spokane Washington that wop electrician
   sells his wares.   75
Electric bulbs and stoves and mats. Blown-out fuses
   he repairs.
He turns on currents that would kill anyone but
   Mehitable.
Mehitable ties packages and brings about some
   wreckages,
Far from the rigamarole. Far from the rigamarole.

Three Slav musicians climb the stairs within their
   New York knightly hall,   80
Sorrow is their seneschal. Each man at the skylight
   glares.
Nothing to eat. No one to love. They sit in broken
   Morris chairs,
And leave out the rigamarole.

Sorrow is their all. Love brought about their fall.
Excuse me if I cry into my Ptchainkannnnnkerscheffffff,
   my Pscqnickjofffchkiff,   85
My Zkqechechookerchief, my handkerchief, my
   handkerchief.

The chicken-faced two, forgiving her, sing of her sweet
   former days
As Melisande, upon the wall, Rosamund within the
   maze.
Right classically,
Majestically! Monastically, Astringently,   90
To show thereby her fires were true, her brows were
   high.
They know not why they're losing style, and quitting
   rigamarole.
Psaffonoff, who was rough in play, the ape-faced one,
   writes classics grand,
That call her "Theda, White of Hand." Makes queer
   slow-time songs to show,
Her fires were high, her ways were low.   95
He knows not why he's losing style, and quitting
   rigamarole, quitting rigamarole.

Love brought about their fall. Yet not complete as yet.
   They play no blues at all.

Nor Mammy tunes nor saxophone at all, nor for The
   Vitaphone.
They have not played for the phonograph, nor the radio
   so rude,
Only the closest neighbors say—"These men intrude."   100
Goodby to rigamarole, Goodby to rigamarole.
They'll be Americans, yet, I'll bet,
They'll be Americans, yet, I'll bet,
Goodby to rigamarole, Goodby to rigamarole.

   1928

A SWAN IS LIKE A MOON TO ME
   (This is specially suggested as a poem-game.)

                                 I

A swan is like a moon to me,
A swan is like a moon to me,
The swan floats through the reeds and foam,
The swan floats through the reeds and foam.
The moon floats through the clouds and stars,   5
The moon floats through the clouds and stars.
White mysteries floating on toward home,
White mysteries floating on toward home.
Both are feathery—both are frail,
Both are feathery—both are frail.   10
Both are things that swoop and sail,
Both are things that swoop and sail;
And if they dance it is so slow,
And if they dance it is so slow,
And if they swoop it is so low,   15
And if they swoop it is so low,

They touch the bending, sleeping soul, . . .   *These two lines*
And by their touching make it whole. . . .   *spoken slowly.*

                                 II

Both born of sleep,
Both born of dream,   20
Twin birds of God these planets seem,   *With increasing*
Twin birds of God these planets seem,   *rapidity to the end.*
Twin birds of God these planets seem,

Twin birds of God these planets seem,
Twin birds of God these planets seem,   25
Twin moons of thought,
White flames
White flames
White flames
White flames of dream. . . .   30

    Spring, 1925

THE RIM ROCK OF SPOKANE

These two poems were the beginning of a series printed in The Spokane Chronicle, while I was the guest of Spokane.

I

Under Spokane's brocaded sun, and her deeply
    embroidered moon
I walk on the Rim Rock rampart put there by heaven's
    hand,
Long before the city came, before the ocean or the land.
This Rim Rock has one eastern notch for the river to
    run in
And the other notch is a water gate at first northwest;   5
Then south;
Grotesquely around, coils the rampart, like a
    hoop-snake
Tail in mouth.

Yet a sentinel, deep in the ages, a wall with a city to
    keep,
A city as young as a homesteader's farm,   10
As young as the chickens that cheep!
And a rampart mystery golden and green,
Black, watchful, stern and steep!
And there I walk with my father's soul, while the town
    is awake or asleep.

We walk to a music on the wind, a lost Kentucky tune,   15
Under the trees, green, yellow, and dim,
We march to that alien bluegrass hymn,
Under Spokane's brocaded sun, and her deeply
    embroidered moon.

II

We look out from the Rim Rock
  On the circuit of the earth.   20
  Not to the deep sky only,
    Where the golden stars have birth.

But day and night we vision
  The whole earth set in flowers,
    New cities acting our dramas,   25
    And chanting these young hours.

  (*A song, a song, a song, a song!*)

The whole earth for our victory
  When we build and carve and paint.
    The round globe our tomorrow,   30
    Columbus our old saint.

For we would sing the song we make
  Within these whispering walls
    So well the quivering aspens hear
    At the Rhone's upper falls —   35

  (*A song, a song, a song, a song!*)

So well the skylarks sing it back
  From Babylon's ruined halls;
    So well the sea round Fujisan
    Hears, and replies, and calls.   40

  (*A song, a song, a song, a song!*
  A lost Kentucky tune!
  An old Virginia tune!)

  Spring, 1928

BUTTERFLY PICTURE-WRITING
  (*Written for Ruth St. Denis to dance on the top of a*
  watch-crystal.)

Kind friend, see the word-signs
On the butterflies' wings!
Red Indian hieroglyphics

On the butterflies' wings!
The bee buzzes,   5
The orchard bird sings,
But
Read the picture-writing
On the butterflies' wings,
Read, read the long story   10
On the butterflies' wings!

    Fall, 1924

THE VOYAGE
    (*Written for Ted Shawn*)

See my mast, a pen!
What are my sails?
Many crescent moons.
What is my sea?
A bottle of ink.   5
Where do I go?
To heaven again.
What do I eat?
The Amaranth flower
While the winds through the jungles   10
Swing old tunes.
I eat that flower with ivory spoons.
While the winds through the jungles
Swing old tunes.
The songs the angels used to sing   15
When Heaven was not old autumn, but spring,
The old sweet songs of Heaven
And spring.

    Fall, 1924

WHAT THE BEACH HEN SAID WHEN
   THE TIDE CAME IN

Proud waves break into cocks' combs
When the sea is crowing.
The sea is a great rooster now
Green-eyed, and very knowing,
Strutting in the sunrise   5
With his feathers blowing,

With his big plumes foaming,
With his green eyes roaming,
With his long spurs glistening,
With his high neck bristling,   10
"Cock-a-doodle crowing, crowing, crowing!
Green-eyed, very knowing!"

    1924-1925?

WHEN THE SUN ROSE FROM THE
MARIPOSA LILY

(*This is suggested as a poem-game*)

When the sun rose from the mariposa lily in the sky,
It was first a feather, . . . then . . .
It was next a bird's wing, . . . then . . .
For the livelong day,
The fire-dove, the cloud-dove, of the sky, east and west.   5

And so again the days had come to pass,
When the sun rose from the lily,
And the moon rose from the moonflower,
And the stars rose,
The stars rose
From the grass.   10

    1927-1928?

QUITE ENCHANTED

On Spokane mountain I met a dragon fly;
He seemed a messenger of high adventures.
He said, "If you would be the world's explorer,
Let some dragon fly be pioneer,
All dragon flies are quite enchanted creatures."

    1927-1928?

ADDRESS TO A CANOE-BIRCH

Canoe-birch, Canoe-birch
What shall we do?
Shall we cut you down, my dear
And make a half-moon boat of you?

    1926?

THE RED INDIAN WITCH GIRL

The north wind barks on Gunsight Pass.
And the witch looks sly, and the old trees sigh,
As she chants her charms on the glacier grass.
The witch looks sly as the howl goes by,
The hound called the north wind, doomed to die.   5
The witch is the Manitou's daughter, so young
That she still is learning the Indian tongue.
Yet that young witch is so very old
That she knows the south wind soon grows bold
And spring comes in on the north wind's track.   10
The witch bends low. On her fairy back
She carries a burden triple and strange,
Across the sunset-gilded range,
Seeds for spring
In the spotted sack,   15
The cries of spring,
In the crimson sack,
And the dreams of the midnight chirping birds
Are hidden away in the sack so black,
And the witch looks sly as the howl goes by,   20
The howl of the north wind, doomed to die.

    1927-1928?

WHAT IS THE MOHAWK?

This I mean by ''The Mohawk'' —
There is a dragon-soul
In this land,
That lived here before Leif the lucky
Came with his Viking band.   5
There is a power in the soil
Deeper than oil wells or mines.
There is a soul of the mountains
Of the Appalachians and of the Rockies,
Higher than lumbermen's favorite pines.   10

This is The Mohawk: he is every Red Indian.
Every Red Indian is in him; and so, friend, are we,
If our hearts are still Western
Hard-riding
And noble and free.   15

    1928

THE MOHAWK IN THE SKY
   (*Being a Parable of the Sudden Appearance of the United States Ideas in World Affairs.*)

Beware,
Oh British Empire,
There's a Mohawk in the sky!
Beware,
Plotters of Servia,   5
There's a Mohawk in the sky!
Beware,
Oh Russian Red-Fire,
There's a Mohawk in the sky!
Beware,   10
Sages of India,
There will be war on high:
There's a Mohawk in the sky!

And beware,
Each Irish gnome,   15
There's a Mohawk in the sky!
Beware,
Ghosts on the Rhine,
There's a Mohawk in the sky!
Beware,   20
Ghosts of Rome,
There's a Mohawk in the sky!
A war of dreams on high!

Oh ghosts of dusty Egypt,
And dusty Palestine,   25
Awake your priests and prophets,
Fill them with battle wine;
Send them to war on high.
Beware,
Beware!   30
See there
In the roaring air,
There's a Mohawk in the sky!

   1928

BEHIND MOUNT SPOKANE, THE BEEHIVE MOUNTAIN

Comrades, behind the mountain
There are hiding

Honey-sweet plans that hum for our children to come.
The scamps have been but a few months on this planet
And now they hear their ancient beehive hum.   5
Bright bees! They hope for singing and honey-making
And robbing flowers for nectar for the crowd.
Stillness can be rest at the noonday nap time
And then they hear their mountain hum out loud.
Grown folks, who eat that honey, sooner or later   10
Will find United States visions in the sky
and hunt for more, till they are broken and footsore,
But hiking on with faces lifted high.
The faithful will see The Mighty Mohawk Dragon
Who ruled the wilds before the days of steam.   15
Then see in the sky The Locomotive Dream: —
The dragon that is father of locomotives;
All the United States dragon-fires a-stream,
The smoke screen dragons of the airplane squadrons,
And dragons driven by wireless, now unknown,   20
Climbing Aldebaran's porch and Saturn's throne.

     1927-1928?

THE VIRGINIANS ARE COMING AGAIN

Babbitt, your tribe is passing away.
This is the end of your infamous day.
The Virginians are coming again.

With your neat little safety-vault boxes,
With your faces like geese and foxes,   5
You
Short-legged, short-armed, short-minded men,
Your short-sighted days are over,
Your habits of strutting through clover,
Your movie-thugs, killing off souls and dreams,   10
Your magazines drying up healing streams,
Your newspapers, blasting truth and splendor,
Your shysters, ruining progress and glory,
Babbitt, your story is passing away.
The Virginians are coming again.   15

All set for the victory, calling the raid
I see them, the next generation,
Gentlemen, hard-riding, long-legged men,
With horse-whip, dog-whip, gauntlet and braid,
Mutineers, musketeers,   20

In command
Unafraid:
Great-grandsons of tide-water, and the bark-cabins
Bards of the Blue-ridge, in buckskin and boots,
Up from the proudest war-path we have known   25
The Virginians are coming again.

The sons of ward-heelers
Threw out the ward-heelers,
The sons of bartenders
Threw out the bartenders,   30
And made our streets trick-boxes all in a day,
Kicked out the old pests in a virtuous way.
The new tribe sold kerosene, gasoline, paraffine.
Babbitt sold Judas. Babbitt sold Christ.
Babbitt sold everything under the sun.   35
The Moon-Proud consider a trader a hog.
The Moon-Proud are coming again.

Bartenders were gnomes,
Foreigners, tyrants, hairy baboons.
But you are no better with saxophone tunes,   40
Phonograph tunes, radio tunes,
Water-power tunes, gasoline tunes, dynamo tunes,
And pitiful souls like your pitiful tunes
And crawling old insolence blocking the road,
So, Babbitt, your racket is passing away.   45
Your sons will be changelings, and burn down your
    world.
Fire-eaters, troubadours, conquistadors,
Your sons will be born, refusing your load,
Thin-skinned scholars, hard-riding men,
Poets unharnessed, the moon their abode,   50
With the stateman's code, the gentleman's code,
With Jefferson's code, Washington's code,
With Powhatan's code!
From your own loins, for your fearful defeat
The Virginians are coming again.   55

Our first Virginians were peasants' children
But the Power of Powhatan reddened their blood,
Up from the sod came splendor and flood.
Eating the maize made them more than men;
Potomac fountains made gods of men.   60
In your tottering age, not so long from you now,
The terror will blast, the armies will whirl,

Cavalier boy beside cavalier girl
In the glory of pride, not the pride of the rich,
In the glory of statesmanship, not of the ditch.   65
The old grand manner, lost no longer:
Exquisite art born with heart-bleeding song
Will make you die horribly, raving at wrong.
You will not know your sons who are true to this soil,
For Babbitt could never count much beyond ten,   70
For Babbitt could never quite comprehend men.
You will die in your shame, understanding not day,
Out of your loins, to your utmost confusion
The Virginians are coming again.

Do you think boys and girls that I pass on the street   75
More strong than their fathers, more fair than their
     fathers,
More clean than their fathers, more wild than their
     fathers,
More in love than their fathers, deep in thought not
     their fathers',
Are meat for your schemes diabolically neat?
Do you think that all youth is but grist to your mill   80
And what you dare plan for them, boys will fulfill?
The next generation is free. You are gone.
Out of your loins, to your utmost confusion
The Virginians are coming again.

Rouse the reader to read it right.   85
Find a good hill by the full-moon light,
Gather the boys and chant all night: —
"The Virginians are coming again."
Put in rhetoric, whisper, and hint;
Put in shadow, murmur, and glint;   90
Jingle and jangle this song like a spur.
Sweep over each tottering bridge with a whirr,
Clearer and faster up main street and pike
Till sparks flare up from the flints that strike.
Leap metrical ditches with bridle let loose.   95
This song is a war, with an iron-shod use.
Let no musician, with blotter and pad
Scribble his pot-hooks to make the song sad.
Find
Your own rhythms   100
When Robert E. Lee
Gallops once more to the plain from the sea.
Give the rebel yell every river they gain.

Hear Lee's light cavalry rhyme with rain.
In the star-proud, natural fury of men   105
The Virginians are coming again.

The foregoing poem was written as a poetic summary,
after I had published the prose book, "*The Litany of Washington Street.*"

Early 1928

THE LOCOMOTIVE DRAGON-HIPPOGRIFF
(*First printed in The Spokane Chronicle, while I was the guest of Spokane.*)

Now there is a track with white rails on its back
That goes straight on to the sky.
It starts at Sun Mountain close by a blue fountain,
And the long curve takes your eye.
The lines were surveyed; by white eagles were made,   5
When the Star Spangled Banner was young,
And the telegraph wires are connected star-fires,
And the trestles by lightnings hung.
And on Fourth of July routed through to the sky
Goes the engine for which it was made,   10
The Hippogriff—father of all the steam trains,
In bunting and silver arrayed.
He looks like a dragon and he is a big one,
You beheld him just once on your trail,
The first time you saw a steam engine go by,   15
When you were but three, and frail.
When you were but three and could fearfully see
The monster belching up flame,
As a four-footed creature, a midnight amazer,
Hobgoblin without a name.   20
You were nearer to reason than you are just now,
You are twelve and too smart and too wise,
So think of the engine, the first you encountered,
With terrified baby-eyes.

The Father of engines goes up the long railroad   25
On Fourth of July with a cry.
If you will believe me, implicitly trust me,
I will outline his thoughts on the fly.
Sung to the tune, the magical rune
Of that engine chug-chugging so high.   30

His mental adventures like stars without number,
Will take a large volume or two.
But watch the white track for the engine comes back
With a load of red apples for you.

1928

THE CLOCKS THAT I LIKE BEST

The clocks I like the best are these,
The rising sun, the setting sun.
I like clear days and endless time,
And things begun and then half done,
And then well and completely done,
Between the rising and the setting sun.

1927-1928?

THE MOON IS A FLOATING SEA-SHELL

The floating nautilus of the upper sea,
One of the boats that sweep above the sun,
Humming its sea-shell song, sailed down to me,
And bore my thought away—a white-winged one,
A proper little thought, a school-marm thing.   5
But the sky, that little teacher of mine,
That sharp-voiced old maid thought, will learn to sing,
Choiring with shell and sky and every iridescent thing,
With every pearl cloud on the wing.

1927-1928?

THE RANGER'S HOUND DOG

Guarding the shack from poacher and thug,
The hound dog sits on the bearskin rug.

March 1924

A HIGH-SCHOOL NATIONAL SONG

This is the song we would sing:
"Glory to this land,
Let glory be given

By every voice and hand.
We abhor   5
The cry of war,
The strut, the pride, the hate."
This is the song we sing:
"Let Beauty be the State,
Let Peace be the State,   10
Let Wisdom be the State,
Let the Wonder and the thunder of Great Music be
    the State."

Man marched west from Asia,
Hunting the world's soul
And we are near the end of the west,   15
Have almost touched the goal.
Let us find it here.
Let us build a nation
Where Wonder is the deep of it,
And Peace its best creation,   20
Wonder that comes from Labor,
Peace that comes from art.
Peace that comes from prayer,
While the Nation sets apart,
All its Youth for glory,   25
All its Youth for Beauty;
Counting the years
In trees kept green,
And girls and boys taught noble duty.
Counting the years by highways white,   30
And towers that magnify the night,
While skylark Youth,
All wings, uplifts its flight
Through dawns of new delight,
Singing and winging on and on: —   35
"Let Beauty be the State,
Let Peace be the State,
Let Wisdom be the State,
Let the Wonder and the thunder of Great Music be the
    State,
Let the Wonder and thunder of Great Singing be the
    State."   40

(*The above is not to be set to musical notation. If a group of
students read it carefully and expressively in chorus, they
will discover the natural chant of reading to which it is
already set.*)

    1928?

THREE RED INDIANS

Three Indians stood beside a creek,
In the Spokane valley-land,
Their medicine bows and arrows
Waved above the purple sand.
And they heard Chief Joseph's last retreat,   5
Red ghosts went by through the apples and the wheat.
And the stream turned to blood beneath their feet,
The Blood of Joseph's ancient band;
And one of them said,
"The stain will go   10
When rivers of battle never flow,
When every sea smokes the pipe of peace
And every captive finds release,
When only winds of friendship blow,
The stain will go   15
When the world is at rest,
The stain will go
When the world is at peace."

     1927-1928?

ON PORCUPINE RIDGE

I met a little porcupine,
He hardly made a sound,
He waddled down the muddy path,
And scornfully looked round.
I did not touch the porcupine,   5
I did not stroke his quills.
They say that if you do, you end
In fever and chills.
We slept in an old cabin,
We barred the windows and doors.   10
We tried to rest, we covered up,
Affecting sleeps and snores.
Yet all night long the beasts,
The moose, the grizzly bear,
The catamount, and such like, climbed   15
The roof and took the air.
One of them sawed a board and scared us
    most to fits,
Pushed the woodpile over,

Tore a bush to bits.
We peeped out in the morning,   20
Like Noah for a sign.
All the animals were gone,
But just one porcupine.
Do you suppose that all that noise
Was just that porcupine?   25

I rebuilt the fire next night,
To keep the beasts away.
We quivered in our sleeping bags
Until the dawn of day,
What was it gnawed the cans?   30
What was it climbed the tree?
What was it scratched the gravel?
What could it be?
My pard had a theory,
And of course I had mine.   35
But when the sun arose,
Once more that porcupine.

        1925-1926

THE CALICO CAT

Yes, he came
Through the storm
Without stain,
The Calico Cat, in the rain.

When the rainbow had come,   5
And gone,
He still had his best things on.

Sunset flamed,
And passed,
But the calico colors   10
Were fast.

1928

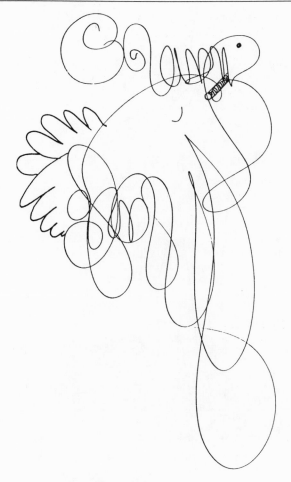

Rachel Lindsay 1928 ~

THE WICKED POUTER PIGEON

The wicked pouter pigeon
Puffed cigarettes,
On bets.

1928

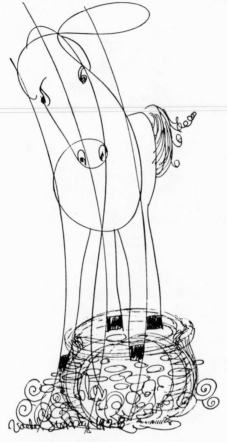

FRIEND FOREST-HORSE

Friend Forest-horse is bold,
Sagacious, and serene,
Walking through the rainbow,
And the gold,
And taking in the scene.

    1928

INTERLUDE: DO NOT STUFF THEM WITH CHILDREN'S SONGS

Do not stuff them with children's songs,
The neat and the pretty sugary words,

The cheap, the tawdry, the tinkling tunes.
Give knives and forks, as well as spoons;
Serve them, sometimes,   5
With grown-up runes.
Let them use, without much care,
The words with which you free the air.

Let those little men be gay,
Sparring, rioting, riding away.   10
Teach the little women to be
Squirrels, elves and girls of the sea,
Centaur's children, riding far,
Mature bright angels, on this star.
This planet has wings, is flying with joy.   15
And the songs fair Chatterton wrote as a boy
Excel the rhymes from a nurse-girl's lips,
And the tunes that cherub Mozart made
Are still tremendous ocean-ships
Where other babes sail on and on   20
To where their own best thoughts have gone,
To shores they have already reached,
Where their little Noah's arks have beached.
I'll not debar shrewd Mother Goose.
That sharp cartoonist still is good.   25
I'll not debar wise Edward Lear.
His rhythms bad, his drawings queer,
For even there, in the nursery air,
Twice-triple thoughts appear.

And in the midst of this, my book,   30
Plain mimickings of him you find,
And Thackeray, cartoonist kind,
Whose pictures in the "Rose and the Ring"
Started young thoughts voyaging.
Scribblers maybe, and yet they kept   35
Young birds upon the fledgling wing,
And made the nest-born fancy sing.

    Summer, 1927

"HOW" AND "HOW"
   (*A Poem-Game*)

A proud young parrot with a crest,
And a grandma parrot in a cap,

Sat in the hot West Indies,
And they heard a "tap, tap."
Great-grandma parrot, tapping,   5
A ghost upon the bough.

And the youngster said: — "Good Evening,"
And the youngster said: — "Good Evening,"
And the youngster said: — "Good Evening"
And the gray ghost said: — "How,"   10

And "How, How, How,"
And the youngster said: — "Good Evening"
And the gray ghost said "How"
And "How, How, How."
         And so on, ad infinitum.   15

      1927

IF YOU ARE A MOUSIE

Pack rats are fat,
They yip and they yap
On Yakinakak Creek.
They clack and they squeak
On Yakinakak Creek.   5
They skin their own kin
On Yakinakak Creek.
The pack rats are fat
On Yakinakak Creek.
If you are a mousie   10
Away from your housie
You will never come back
If once you get slack
On Yakinakak Creek.
They drive in a pack,   15
They will hurry and hack
And hunt you straight on
To the hot Hornet Creek.
Alas and alack,
You will never come back,   20
If you ever get slack
On Yakinakak Creek.

      1927-1928?

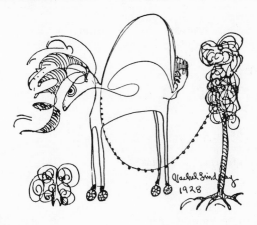

THE PET ELK

Peep
Through the curtain.

This scene
Reveals

The pet Elk,
On Wheels.

1928

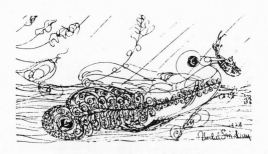

THE WILD FOREST DUCK

A wild forest duck,
A speckled, marauding duck,
Stole for his tail a peacock's feather,
But he had not the peacock's squawk-talk,
Nor the cityfied peacock's irritated air,
As though mere beauty were hard to bear.

5

He was too well suited, altogether,
Could not complain of the forest weather,
He found most any forest fair.

Did not sneer at the animals,   10
Did not stare.

Nor long to walk where peacocks walk,
Would not shriek nor peck in his talk,
Nor slander the animals, tear around,
Nor hump up feathers and glare.   15

As though mere beauty,
As though mere beauty,
As though mere beauty were hard to bear.

    1928

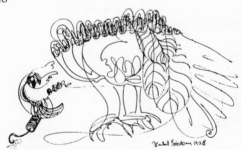

MIKE WHALER AND THE PARROT

Mike Whaler, a sailor, a whaler on the seven seas,
Found a parrot in a forest where volcanoes take their ease,
In between the mountains talking, squawking, and walking.

He took it back to his old home
Resolving never more to roam.   5

On Fourth of July just to make merry
He gave a giant, well-lighted fire-cracker
To humble the mussy, fussy old parrot and scare it.

And there was a riot when the cracker exploded,
The parrot knew not that the cracker was loaded.   10

Do not talk too much, you may get in dutch.

    1928

THE FUR-BACKED SKATE FISH

The fur-backed skate fish come and go
In the glaciers, dressed like the Esquimaux.
They swim and crawl
From Hudson Bay.
They are not caught with string and stick —   5
You must dive in and knife them quick.
You must be quick,
You must say "Boo!"
And scare them, too,
Or they'll bite you.   10

They keep quite warm in the glacial cracks,
But freeze to death on the horses' backs,

When we bring a catch to camp to fry —
They are frozen hard
On the Fourth of July.   15

    1928

THE BREAKFAST AND DINNER TREES

Stemming gooseberries, stringing beans, shelling peas,
And raking garden and yard are hard.
Weeding the garden and yard much harder,
And you feel like a sizzling skillet of lard.

Then dream   5
Of the breakfast and dinner trees
That bloom while the monkeys take their ease
In the Robinson Crusoe Islands overseas.

    1928

THE EAGLE HEN

Our valiant eagle hen
Who does her level best!
Who builds a brushwood nest near the mountain lion's den,
And nature takes her course and does the rest.

The eggs, in the sunshine,
Tumble and roll and hatch
And then the little eagles run and peck and scratch.

THE WHISTLING MARMOT

Queer is ambition,
Queer are the thwarted animals
To which ambition makes appeal!

The whistling marmot stood on his hind legs
And whistled to the bears
How his ambition
Was to be a nice trained seal.

1928

THE FERN CALLED: "THE GRASSHOPPER'S GRANDMA"

The fern called: "The Grasshopper's Grandma,"
Knitted six sox out of grass for her grandson,
Bracken Hop Green, her most favorite one.
She began in the morning:
By night they were done, every one.

1928

ROBINSON CRUSOE'S PARROTS

I saw in the smoke of the Hallowe'en bonfire
Leaping on high to the midnight sky,
In the smoke green as spinach,
Smoke green as green grapes for green-grape pie,
Smoke yellow as carrots,
Pictures that looked like Crusoe's parrots,
And the bonfire chattered like Crusoe's parrots.

1928

THE INFORMATION BUREAU

"The baby bears," the ranger said
To the little New York girl,
"Put up their hair in papers,
"To make it curl."

"This is the way," the cowboy said   5
"The baby bears are fed:
"The mamma bear
"Catches a fish;
"Then serves it raw,
"In a stone dish."   10

1928

THE THIRSTY PUPPY'S DREAM

Ralph's puppy dreamed on a day of drouth
Of a funny little dog-fish with a cup in his mouth.

Then dreamed of a mountain waterfall
That came from a hole in the wall.

1928

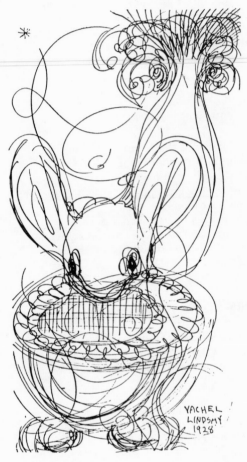

A SNAIL PARADE

And is anything else
Quite so stately and staid
As a snail parade?

And is anything else
In such whimsy arrayed
As a snail parade?

5

I saw on the rose-walk
While May winds played
A snail parade.

I saw in my lettuce   10
Spoiling my trade
A snail parade.

I saw in the woods
Where the Autumn winds bayed
A snail parade.   15

They looked so wise
Those bad snails made
Me feel afraid.

"We know a secret,"
Their air conveyed.   20
"All thoughts have weighed."

"We know the seasons.
And why the blade
Of winter is made.

"We hide in the sky   25
Till the frost is allayed.
Till the snail parade.

"By Hallowe'en bonfires
We rise unafraid
By the smoke conveyed."   30

And I saw in the smoke
Of a Hallowe'en bonfire
Up to the star-fire
Up to the moonfire
A gorgeous tremendous   35
Fire cavalcade,
A snail parade.

1928

THE WOOD-SQUEAK
(Chant this rapidly, with repetitions)

Deep in the park after dark
The wood-squeak troubled us more and more,
Till we nailed his skin to the old barn door.

1928

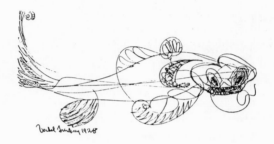

THE TREE-CLIMBING FISH

Down near Salton by the village of Alton
There was once a tree-climbing fish.
That fish, in haste and pain,
Left his buckhorn cactus tree
For the Salton Sea
When it threatened rain.

1928

MY TREE TOAD

My tree toad
Climbed
The Curly
Little Fern-leaf.

Then
Tumbled
Off,
And came to grief.

1928

THE WATERFALL THAT SINGS LIKE A BACCHANTE

The trail has the tracks of bears and of cubs and of deer,
Of wolves and of porcupines, half beaten out
By the merry horsemen who drove by with a shout
Only a little while ago; and here
Are everlasting flowers and reeds and bracken,   5
And strawberry leaves turned red in the late year.
We sit and listen to a waterfall
Far away in the deep woods to the south,
It sounds like a bird with a bacchante mouth.
And we look at the glaciers high above the wood,   10
And watch the waning day, and call it good.

        1927-1928?

THE POWERFUL SQUIRREL

In the monotonous forest where all the beasties whine,
How and why did the squirrel drive the porcupine?
He promised him a better place than home in which to dine.

        1928

THE WICKED OLD TREE

A wicked old tree at the top of the pass
Was so wicked his surface-roots blasted the grass.

        1928

HOW WE PAPOOSES PLANT FLOWERS

"Sometimes they take root in a week.
"Sometimes a loon plants a flower with his beak.

"Sapsuckers and flickers, jays and nutcrackers
"Are our heartiest backers.

"We have watched them at sunrise,   5
"When they were not looking,
"Gathering first and then scattering seed,
"Planting harebell and egg-plant and crimson fireweed,"
Said the flying papooses.

        1928?

THE WHALE WE SAW

In the Hallowe'en bonfire we saw a small whale,
The fire was his eye, the smoke was his tail,
His scales were new tin picnic pans and picnic palm-leaf
    fans.

1928

BEWARE OF THE SILVER GRIZZLY

There are bears in the woods around us,
There are bear-rugs on the floor,
There are bear skins on the wall
With the snow shoes and the flags,
There are bear-heads over the door,   5
Stuffed bears in the hall:
Terribly tall.

Bears are always perilous.
Bears are serious.

But the dangerous bear of all   10
Is that Silver Grizzly called the moon,
Above the waterfall.
Beware how you meet him in the trail.
Beware his deadly blow.   15
One touch of the Silver Grizzly
Will lay the best man low.

1928

MISTER CHIPMUNK
    (A Poem-Game)

In the thimbleberry, raspberry, huckleberry trail,
On the way to Indian Pass,
We heard the cheery, pert and leery, swift and eerie
Chipmunk's hail.
The chipmunk, the chipmunk,   5
The brisk and frisky chipmunk
Who will take a risky trail
To satisfy curiosity
And chatter, whisk and wail.
The chipmunk, the chipmunk,   10

The monkey of the squirrel tribe
Quivering with monkeyshines
Alert from ear to tail—
In the thimbleberry, raspberry, huckleberry trail.
In the thimbleberry, raspberry, huckleberry trail.   15
He is a rascal and a rip:
He carries moonshine on his hip.
The chipmunk, the chipmunk, the chipmunk, the chipmunk.
No butterfly is quite so drunk,
No butterfly is quite so drunk;   20
He haunts the tent,
He gnaws the pack,
Even before you turn your back
He steals a cough drop from the sack.
Even before you turn your back   25
He knocks the towel from the rack;
He licks the can that held the beans
And stores the label in his jeans,
The chipmunk, the chipmunk, the chipmunk, the chipmunk.
In the thimbleberry, raspberry, huckleberry trail,   30
In the thimbleberry, raspberry, huckleberry trail.
The chipmunk is a little chap
No bigger than a kindling scrap,
And yet he sits there like the boss—
An Injun chief no man should cross.   35
Preaching in Choctaw on a pail,
His paw he waves, his foot he stamps,
He twitters, sniffs and whirls and ramps,
Takes full possession of the camps.
No butterfly is quite so drunk   40
No butterfly is quite so drunk
In the thimbleberry, raspberry, huckleberry trail.
Oh he is full of ginger, oh he is full of sin,
Oh he is full of ginger, oh he is full of sin,
The original Tom Sawyer and Huckleberry Finn   45
The original Tom Sawyer and Huckleberry Finn,
In the thimbleberry, raspberry, huckleberry trail,
In the thimbleberry, raspberry, huckleberry trail.
The chipmunk,
The chipmunk,   50
The chipmunk,
The chipmunk.

1925-1926

THE SMOKE LION

Behold the mountain lion sometimes seen in the campfire
  flame,
"Kit Carson" is his name,
All smoke and gold and green.
And he is mean and game.
He is like a forest fire, hard to tame.

  1928

THE GLACIAL FLEA

Glacial fleas who are really nice
Are supposed to live upon weather and ice.
This glacial flea was a greedy brute,
This glacial flea bit the May-apple fruit.

  1928

THE CAULIFLOWER WORM

Bad worm!
He eats the cauliflower.
Yet dreams of higher things.
Listens to the meadow-lark!
And wonders how it sings!

  1928

ROBINSON CRUSOE'S MONKEY

Zip! flared the Hallowe'en bonfire,
Hip hip! called the boys as they rolled up a log,
And sat in the smoke and the firelight and fog.

They saw in the smoke of the Hallowe'en bonfire,
Smoke that wagged like a very small doggie,   5
Crusoe's monkey, the fog for a donkey.

Then it climbed up a sunflower higher and higher,
Up, up, up a sunflower,

Up a sunflower,

A sunflower fire.   10

    1928

CONCERNING A WESTERN MOUNTAIN
  SHAPED LIKE A WHALE
  (*Whale Butte Near Whale Creek*)

The whale tried in vain to swim from his pain,
When the hornet drew near and assaulted his face
Without grace.
The whale tried in vain to crawl from his pain,
Down the little Whale Creek, he grew fainty and week   5
And no longer could speak.
And was petrified there in whalish despair,
For the hornet drew near and again stung his face
Without grace.
Beware of the hornet, though silly and small,   10
Do not scorn him at all.
And if born a whale, stick to the ocean:
Beware of the perilous mountain emotion.

    1927-1928?

THE FLYING PAPOOSES ARE BOYS
  AND GIRLS WITH WINGS

Dressed in bead strings,
And the wings of butterflies and storms,
Of night owls and of day owls,

Of waterfalls from eagle mountains,
And all strange wide-winged, lovely, terrible things,   5
These beautiful brown flying birds
Burn our eyeballs dim.
There is no flaw from bonnet to toe,
Or in their Manitou hymn.

They fly above and sing new songs   10
Where the willow-tree combs its hair.
Swinging boughs by the cliffside, fog-white and fair,
Snow-white and fair,
Very tall and fair!

The willow sings to them, they sing to her,   15
And the little trout revelling there.

    1928?

    *And so we conclude our discussion of The Clowns of the
    Mountains, of the Deep Woods Clowns, and the funniest part
    of the Forest Menagerie.*

ON ENTERING A MORE SOLEMN FOREST

This is the place where learning sweeps upon us.
We are overwhelmed with things that we do not know:
The learning of the rocks, the beasts, the weather—
Into a million mysteries we go.

    1928

WHEN WE PLUNGE INTO THE WILDERNESS

When we plunge into the wilderness
My wife and babes and I,
We feel ourselves drawn in and in forever,
And we will serve the lost trails till we die.
When we march on into the wilderness   5
We know not how to dress
Nor where to sleep, nor how to keep the fire.
Yet we are drawn forever by desire,
Hunting the Eden of the Bible days,
Hunting the haunts of fays of nursery days,   10
Hunting the ways of our fathers, the pioneers,
Hunting the ancient world's lost lovely years.

When we plunge, plunge into the wilderness,
My wife and babes and I,
Drawing apart the veils of rain and weed,   15
Drawing apart the curtains of the bush,
Drawing apart the veils of snow and sun,
Drawing apart the curtains of the wind-cry and the hush
We find the silence of the hidden lake,
We find the sunlight of the reed and rush,   20
We find the reasons we would like to dress
Like hills, in sod,
Like cliffs, in mountain flowers;
And build our fires like Indian ghosts and powers,
And sleep like wild-cats, mountain sheep, and bears,   25
And learn the secrets the old Edens keep,
And untold secrets of the western lairs,
When we plunge, plunge into the wilderness,
On, on, into the wilderness,
My wife and babes and I.   30

    1928

MEETING OURSELVES

We met ourselves as we came back
As we hiked the trail from the north.
Our foot-prints mixed in the rainy path
Coming back and going forth.
The prints of my comrade's hob-nailed shoes   5
And my tramp shoes mixed in the rain.
We had climbed for days and days to the North
And this was the sum of our gain:
We met ourselves as we came back,
And were happy in mist and rain.   10
Our old souls and our new souls
Met to salute and explain—
That a day shall be as a thousand years,
And a thousand years as a day.
The powers of a thousand dreaming skies   15
As we shouted along the trail of surprise
Were gathered in our play:
The purple skies of the South and the North,
The crimson skies of the South and the North,
Of tomorrow and yesterday.   20

    1928

MY LADY, DANCER FOR THE UNIVERSE

I

THE CIRCUS CALLED "THE UNIVERSE"

My lady, dancer for the Universe,
Teaches our children to spread out small hands
Gesturing welcome to all beasts and lands.
My lady, hostess to the Universe,
Teaches the birds to open wide their homes,   5
Teaches all friends to open wide their homes,
Saying welcome to all golden tomes,
Saying welcome to all great devices
That bring us chariots of fire at wild-wood prices,
Saying welcome to each caravan   10
That comes with forest messages for man.

My lady, hostess to the Universe
Says to our little son: ''Peace, peace, my child,
And welcome to our pine-cone fire,
And to our candle-lighted table,   15
And a little crib by little sister,
And this world so wild.''

II

FOREST-MIRRORS

''For Christmas, you shall welcome in your time
Mirrors that flash from forests far away
Upon the spangles of the Christmas-tree —   20
Pictures that come from farther than Cathay.
Yes, television will be greater soon,
Bringing new wing-wrapped scenes from beyond the moon.
Television follows the air-mail arrow,
And wireless brings it, as spring brings the sparrow.   25
And what of the world-wide vitaphones that rise?
Will they be better than the butterflies
I see in my new Christmas baby's eyes?

''Will they bring songs too sweet for human ears?
None will be soft as your dear smiles and tears.   30
None will be wild, like the dear hope we hold
To keep you changeless with your hair of gold,
To keep your cheeks like fruit, your gestures bold.

No forest-mirror that queer day will bring
Reporting nightingales and flying men a-wing,   35
Reporting curious bees and talking swans a-wing,
Equals today's wherein we see your sister play and sing,
And make small faces, clap her hands on high,
Strutting through our cabin, curls and cap awry,
Preening with home-grown vanity sublime.   40
With this small strut my babes must conquer time.''

III

THE DRUID-HARP

''For Christmas you shall welcome in your day
The Harp that comes from this candle-flame with rhyme.
For when at Yule this cabin-candle burns,
The flame sings on, in forest shapes by turns.   45
Even the harp it makes is forest made,
And like a waterfall, its tunes, self-played.
It burns not down, but leaps like a tree-spire.
A Druid harp forms in the ancient fire.
It gives an old tune from an unseen hand   50
That reaches here from far-off fairyland.''

IV

THE DRUID CHRISTMAS

''For Christmas you shall welcome in your day
Moon-mistletoe that never knew the earth,
And Christmas-trees that are not grown from earth
But from this Druid candle-flame have birth,   55
And strawberries of winter, not July,
And Druid roses that go floating by.''

December 1927

THE SICK EAGLE

We found an old sick eagle in the path,
Too tired for soaring and too weak for wrath,
Drooping like a great old man gone down
Before his youngest rival in the town.
Too lost for fear, and dizzier by far   5
Than when he flew above the sun's hot car,

This eagle could not leap above the trail,
The weeds were far too high, his legs too frail;
And so he winged along ahead and sprawled,
Fluttered hard and crawled,   10
Like an old farmer trying not to be
A nuisance to the babes about his knee.
And then he found a root and clung in pride
Holding his place,
Holding his wings wide.   15
He was a brother to the birds you see
On state house domes above the cliff and hill,
Gilded, wide-winged, and still;
Brother of that great bird that screams and soars
For orators who shake the out of doors,   20
Disappearing in great freedom's sky
On Jefferson's birthday
And the Fourth of July.
And now my pal and I,
Hiking through Montana's most tremendous wood,   25
Stopped laughing—for there the eagle stood.

    1927-1928?

THE SONG OF MY FIFTIETH BIRTHDAY

I

THE RIM ROCK

(*Rapidly, to the oldest, best known of all kettle-drum
marches, the human heart-beat*)

When our four bright years of adventure began,
We paced on the Davenport Roof, Spokane;
On the very dawn when the dream was strong,
We traced where the river and Rim Rock ran.

And we saw the Wild Flower City, Spokane,   5
Like The Jade Flower gardens of Kubla Khan,

Then saw it swirling, cheering, parading,
Swaggering, swarming, careering, rampaging,
Through centuries climbing, glittering, teeming,
And we whistled and danced this song, this song.   10

In the light, Spokane,
In the light, Spokane,
In the light,
In the light,
In the light, Spokane.   15

Here, once, was a circular, crater-like bowl,
Lava that boiled like Niagara's soul.
But the Rim Rock is now like Nuremberg's wall,
A violoncello, an orchestra hall
That echoes with any man's free-hearted call.   20

With the Rim Rock august as the moon and the sun,
And dawns that are new while the zodiacs run,
We see the free city eternally one.

After long trips reconnoitering here
In a sky where genuine eagles are screaming,   25
A republic of news, and of dreams come true!
We saw *TEN PLAGUES* through the air disappear
Like the fumes of an assay, the breath of a steer,
As we paced on the Davenport Roof, Spokane,
And whistled and danced this song, this song.   30

No canned goods town! No mail order town!
And free from the boomer with drawing and plan!
A station gold-lacquered, its compasses span
Spheres too high for the faint-hearted few,
Curve over curve to the crystalline blue,   35
Where the Felts Field Flying men circle with pride,
Tip the moon aside,
With an uneven song, but a song.

II

THE TEN PLAGUES

The Ten Special Plagues who rule other towns
All over the nation with telegraphed frowns,   40
Rule nevermore here, nor shoot from afar,
Nor come in an overstuffed annual car.
The Grendels called: — "Trickster," "Slick," "Sneer,"
     and "Huff,"
The Grendels called: — "Leer," "Simper," "Liar,"
     and "Bluff,"
The Grendel called "Fixer," who seldom is rough,   45

The Grendel called "Letter," all collar and cuff,
With a ciphered, invisible code on his shirt,
Maneuvering, plausible, staring and curt,
Rule nevermore here, in this crystal sphere,
Nor in all-steel cars appear.   50

No wire-tappers, telephone-listeners, spies,
Their own hot suspiciousness blasting their eyes,
Are sweating their deputies, studying mail,
Till the Power Trust hijackers come over the rail.

In the dark, Spokane,   55
In the dark, Spokane,
In the dark,
In the dark,
In the dark, Spokane.

We have seen a few thwarted yes-men go by;   60
But a Terror is cracking the bones of the spy.
Perhaps Thomas Jefferson came to affright
While the night scenes whirled and the smoke-clouds
      curled,
And the scrolls of the future were there in the stars,
And the radios flashing from Sigma to Mars,   65
Perhaps Thomas Jefferson came in the night
And commanded to carry from Rim Rock to Mountain
The titanic Star Spangled Banner, unfurled.
They bend too low. They shrink, do not grow.
They groan with the burden. That flag-staff unseen   70
Is breaking their backs, while the dawn-winds clean
Destroy the capon, or shaman, or man
Who would rule or ruin reborn Spokane.

III

O'ER THE RAMPARTS WE WATCH

Sea-faring parrots, canaries from anywhere,
Robins from somewhere, larks from nowhere,   75
Down in the lobbies the rare birds sing
In cages of platinum, silver, and gold.
All the brave corridors rustle and ring
With a high-plumed genius, a tale untold.

We two, once again on the glittering roof,   80
Above the lobbies that all night zoom,

Above the marbles, the fountain room,
And the Phi Beta Kappas, Moose, Rosarians,
Lions, Optimists, Elks, Rotarians,
Above toy gardens of hide and seek, 85
Above Honolulu ferns and fronds,
Above the gold fish streams and ponds,
Above Northwestern Luxury Gods,
Above the pits where the stoker plods,
We are drinking frost-air, tiptoe on the roof, 90
And we put the whole Northwest to the proof.
While the Felts Field Vikings circle with pride,
Tip the moon aside,
With an uneven song, but a song.

On our way to Springfield's intimate gleaming, 95
On our way to that twilight town, grown bold
With religions and saints and shrines untold,
The home of our love, and of Lincoln's dreaming.
With hearts in our birth land, The Middle West,
Approving mountains in pine trees dressed, 100
And millennial forests with apple-flowers streaming,
And clouds coming over the Rim Rock edge
With ruby, jasper, and sardonyx blazing and beaming,
We whistle and dance this song, this song.
We proclaim from The Davenport Roof, Spokane:— 105
"This backwoods is good as a Samurai clan."

A Denver, born without brag or bloke,
A Pittsburgh born without slag or coke.
This tank-town will never see ox teams again,
This one night stand is making big men. 110

Where Washington cuts across Main, Spokane,
The streets have a sheen, like the past of Japan!
And Howard and Riverside, dizzy and fair!
Great Northern engines, hippogriffs whistling,
With jacinth and beryl bristling, preening, 115
And Spokane Falls, and the foam in the air
Make mating dragons, a crapulent pair.

Dawn breaks the chains, once more, for the world!
We hear the thrones down to darkness hurled.
O'er the ramparts we watch, from this roof and no other 120
With pearl and with jade and with chrysoprase beaming,
With blood and with snow and with azure gleaming,
The *DAWN* is a *WORD*, making heaven our brother,
Dawn is The Star Spangled Banner unfurled.

IV

THE SUN-UP DANCE

While the Grendels renounce us in far off fens,   125
Rule us no more with their fountain pens,
Quit pulping these forests, snouting these streams,
Choking these schools, wrecking these dreams,
This Inland Crater that prayed for rain
Has treasure tides like the Spanish Main;   130
This cow town, so far from the shore, sets free
Portents from deep in the Singapore sea.
This hick-town forgotten, this Indian Camp,
This Grubstake, has dug up Aladdin's lamp.

Are we self-deceived? We have long believed   135
Only the aged are self-deceived.
And we whistle and dance this song, this song.
The East is a flag with the flag-staff unseen,
The midnight storm has washed the world clean.
And we danced the United States language at dawn   140
And our thoughts in a storm follow on, follow on.

We race on The Davenport Roof, Spokane:
Like the free old west is our sun-up dance,
Covered Wagon thoughts emerge and advance.
We write on the air like bathers that fly,   145
We are super-flying machines high-raring,
Locomotive griffins taking the sky,
Dragons with buffalo heads roaring by,
Or Coeur d'Alene sachems with feathers on high.

V

THOMAS JEFFERSON RULES

No empires, flunkeys, or crowns began   150
When Jefferson's arm reached the river Spokane:
Jefferson saw it the River of Man.

While the heterodox Star Spangled Banner is streaming
We dance the red carmagnole of our seeking,
For the two are one in our patriot daring;   155
While the Felts Field Vikings circle with pride,
Tip the moon aside
With an uneven song, but a song.

We, passers-by, look the place in the eye.
Not in Jefferson's town are artists run out,   160
Actors run out, musicians run out,
Novelists out, architects out,
Philosophers, painters, and sculptors run out;
Gardeners, scholars, or poets run out,
Oftener starved by whisper than shout.   165

No boys are poisoned with lies like drugs
For not esteeming the bluffs and thugs.
No ten crowned cormorants sit on the nest.
Jefferson rules, northwest of the West.

VI

A PERILOUS WHISPER

Unabashed and obscene as boys of sixteen,   170
From high on the snow-line where all winds fan,
They march in rose-vision for you, Spokane!
Lumberjacks, knee-deep in creaming snow,
March on the world in a gaudy glow.
Lumberjacks, dollarless, singing and young,   175
Do their best with the words that our forefathers sung,
Lumberjack armies, whose meaning is plain,
Are shouting "Your empire, like Caesar's, is vain."
Take Washington Street in the name of the trees,
Main Street they know like the snows and the seas.   180

If one boy limps alone, his whisper can kill
All the ages devise of corruption and ill.
O lost Hamiltonians, far away,
The Tory party has seen its day!
O Doges of Wall Street, fallen and glum,   185
You knew a perilous whisper would come,
The Grendels were fools, were they fifty or ten:
One poet can laugh off a million old men.
One "Open Sesame" opens all caves,
Digs up your secrets from sacrosanct graves.   190

Not all of your star-chamber sessions could drown
One lumberjack marcher who questioned a crown,
Or send over Bridges of Sighs without trial
With charges unproved, with detectives most vile,
One Red Man, thinking, one dancer of light,   195
One twelve-year-old who would fight,

In a new town whose rim is like Nuremberg's wall
That echoes with any boy's free-hearted call,
One eaglet who screams "These are Liberty's hills,
"With dew and with snow and with daisies gleaming!"   200

VII

SACAJAWEA AND CHIEF JOSEPH

We hunt from the world all ridiculous scheming
Possessing the thought-giving roof of Spokane.
We two are the boomers with drawing and plan.
Hail, hail to the Jefferson country! He wrought
In this Ultima Thule for souls unbought,   205
Sent men like Lewis and Clark to find
These quenched volcanoes, these rivers kind.
And their new Pocahontas, the young forest mother,
The bird-woman guide, the scout through the dark,
Sacajawea, the world her brother,   210
Was more worth finding than all the wide park.

In the dark, Spokane,
In the dark, Spokane,
In the dark,
In the dark,   215
In the dark, Spokane.

And we dance her praises, in dawn-stars dressed,
Daisies, spangles, and wings like the lark.

Again a blood-red Indian we praise,
The Northwest-soul in its war-swept days: 220
By powers beyond dream or thought he stays,
Cloud-tearing Chief Joseph controls your ways,
That mountain, all granite, past master of fame,
When years are unsparing and time is a name.
In the light, Spokane,   225
In the light, Spokane.

Yes, this is adventurous Washington's west;
This is reckless Jefferson's west,
They would wipe from the earth every arrogant town,
Wipe from the earth every caste system town,   230
Every cabal-ruled town, every martinet town,
Every landlord town, every closed door town,
Every secret committee, Tory town,

And the Felts Field Vikings circle with pride,
Tip the moon aside   235
With an uneven song, but a song,
In the light, Spokane,
In the light, Spokane.

VIII

THE HEART-BEAT

(*Much more softly and slowly, to the same drums*)

Such is the power of one birdling or fawn,
Such is the spell of one whisper at dawn,   240
Unless Penitentiary Silence is here,
Absentee landlords are leprous and drear.

In this City, History is present as faith.
From Vikings to Red Men, the compasses span.
The Scout is no longer a desperate wraith;   245
And Poetry, Beauty, Talent, and Hope
Have learned that their whisper hangs hangman and rope.
In Spokane, where Glory and Talent and Fire
And God and Democracy have their desire: —

Their desire, that goes marching with each April breath   250
To the drum of heartbeats stronger than death,
In the light, Spokane,
In the light, Spokane,
In the light,
In the light,   255
In the light, Spokane.

So set not this dance to musical scales,
Nor to orchestra strings, but to Felts Field sails,
Arrogant striplings, there in the sky,
And the dawn-born Star Spangled Banner on high.   260

Let the wings of your heart beat low in your ears,
Set the lilt of this dance to your secret tears.

Hark to your breast with its quick broken drums
Before the floats gleam, or the band-wagon comes.

Hear the half-music the uneven heart makes   265
Deep in bright years, before it breaks.

In the light, Spokane,
In the light, Spokane,
In the light,
In the light,   270
In the light, Spokane.

        1928

TWENTY YEARS AGO

To the right Honorable The Earl of Chesterfield: —
    (When, upon some slight encouragement, I first visited
    your Lordship, I was overpowered, like the rest of mankind,
    by the enchantment of your address, etc. . . . but)

                                    I

You call me "a Troubadour,"
But I am an adventurer, in hieroglyphics, buildings,
    and designs.
When I was eight years old, I had two hundred building
    blocks,
Given to me by The Reverend Fred H. Wines.
And I gave them to his grandson, in due time afterward,   5
Remembering I had made out of them,
A Springfield built of silver blocks, and towers and
    vines and valentines,
And a paper doll with a paper diadem.
A Sangamon palace of the soul,
With the American flag upon a fishing pole.   10
And kite-lines rose to dizzy heights, and underneath
    were caves and mines and coal,
And those who came to view the sights paid five cornelian
    marbles for the toll.

                                    II

, With insulting volubility, eyebrow-lift and leer,
You label me a "Sonneteer," but still I claim my liberty,
Your advertisements weigh me not in chains.   15
I am going to be a painter like old William Morris,
I am going to put a strain on all your brains.
I choose to be a Mayor, like old Tom Johnson, if I have
    to run for
Mayor of Loami.

I choose to be an etcher studying James M. Whistler.   20
You say I am a rhymer, but who am I?
Your silly big-timer, to do a turn for you?
Your Tom Thumb in the side show to make talk?
I tell you, Lord Chesterfield, I'm no man's baby wonder.
I will go and harvest wheat in Kansas thunder,   25
I will go and feed the red corn to the stock.
Perhaps, Lord Chesterfield, the next time you meet me
You will find me building watches on Mount Blanc?
I claim the right to make the worst watches you can shake;
It is better than to die drowned in a tank   30
Of advertising ink, so thick no fish could think,
A grave that is no grave it is so rank.

III

I have loved, for instance, Whistler, and Jimmy's
    gentle book,
As an art student, years and years ago.
There are days when Whistler's dog-whip is the one
    lash in the world   35
There are days when his long cane is all I know.
Then all men are my enemies except my oldest enemies,
Who knew me in Springfield when a child.
They do not read my books, but O they have read me,
An egotist by no means mild,   40
Who would throw the seas away to have but one more day
Of his own whims and fantasy and pomp.
In Springfield this is better than the Pyramids to men
Who have learned how to scrap and to romp.
We were plain with each other, with Sangamon River calm;
    We laid on the lash long ago.   45
They are right. I am no poet, but they know my lifetime
    style,
And give me all the liberty I know.

IV

If I should land in Springfield, tomorrow morning early,
With blue-prints for a zebra farm and track,
Proposing zebra races, no Springfield Citizen   50
Would turn a hair, nor like you, turn his back.
If I came with Spanish books for the Illinois State Library
From Mexico City or Madrid,
They would not insult me as you have insulted me.
They would not insist the books be hid.   55

If I should come with cages of Spokane canaries
And hang them up in front of every store,
The Springfield Citizen would laugh and spit and swear,
But he would not take the birds down from the door.
He might yap and squint and blah blah, but would let me
    have my way,   60
Like old Samuel Johnson would stand pat.
You fill me full of food, you think you are not rude:
You will not let me have my way like that.
If I should print new drawings in The Illinois State
    Register,
They would not gabble "pen stroke," "swirl" or
    "passion."   65
They would merely grunt "Again?" like honest, blunt
    he-men,
Would not assume to call me not in fashion.
If I take old Springfield, after years of absence
With freight cars full of some new Burbank's breed,
Cyclops oak-trees that grow faster than Australian
    Eucalyptus,   70
Golden rain-trees that scatter honey-seed,
Trees hardy as the north-pole tabby cat;
If I should plant my gift, in circles round the city
Till they sheltered and shadowed every flat,
They would not cut down the trees. They would leave me
    at my ease.   75
You will not let me have my way like that.

V

I do not take on friends who tinker with my liberty,
No matter how they boot-lick or beguile.
O foolish Lord Chesterfield, you ask me for one drawing
With your tongue in your cheek all the while.   80
You would sweat me for one sonnet, then paste your
    label on it
Like a druggist who has standardized a drug,
My works are unstandardized, and not Peruna-advertised,
O sweat me not for trinkets with a shrug.

And I know you still are silent on those Springfield zebra
    races.   85
I hope you keep on sweating till you're flat.
With two Merchants of Cathay, brothers in roundelay,
I will put them on before you can say "scat,"
And you will fade all dazy if you find they're there to
    stay,

"You will not let me have my way like that?"   90
O you want a cutie epic, yet you want no naughty song,
It must be a sonnet—fourteen-count-'em long.
You want a poem operated on.
An end-page ornament, of the purest prig descent,
Not Venus-kissed, with reputation gone.   95
Therefore one Manhattan luncheon, one long afternoon
    of flattery,
Exhausting your word-battery.
And then I am to sit in my cell for seven years,
Till with seven cents and seven glycerine tears,
Your third assistant janitor appears.   100

VI

You call me a Troubadour,
But I am an adventurer, in hieroglyphics, buildings and
    designs.
When I was eight years old I had two hundred building
    blocks
Given to me by The Reverend Fred H. Wines.
And I gave them to his grandson, in due time afterward,   105
Remembering I had made out of them
A Springfield built of silver blocks, and towers and vines
    and valentines,
And kite-lines rose to dizzy heights, and underneath
    were caves and mines and coal,
And those who came to view the sights paid five cornelian
    marbles for the toll.

VII

The music of that iron word "Reconciliaton"   110
Calls me back to the Springfield voting-booth,
To the Springfield Elections, as funny as Mark Twain,
And sometimes free and beautiful as Youth.
We will elect a mayor, we will elect a president,
We did it twice, could do it any time.   115
And I say that this outshines your Main Street Magazine;
I reject your little market for a rhyme.

The music of that soul's word "Reconciliation,"
Will roll me back to Springfield after while,
And three or more will sit with me in the Leland music
    room,   120
And we will free Old Ireland in Style.

Yes, I will go back to that heartbreak that is home
And scrawl my work, if need be, on the fence
Of folks who are not worried if I do not fit their pattern,
Long reconciled to my born lack of sense.   125
In Springfield, that iron word "Reconciliation"
Will bring me back, will break my heart of stone,
And Protestant and Catholic, Jew and Unbeliever
Will bear me back to Love, and to my own.
And I will pray to Mary, and to the Sacred Heart   130
In "The Church of Peter and Paul"
And watch the aged saints do the stations of the cross
And hear the great saints of tomorrow call.

    1928

THE FIVE SEALS IN THE SKY

I

SUNRISE

The daybreak flames as a picture for the birds,
They feast in the grass, then fly with tiny words.
The sunrise girds and harnesses the herds,
And comes
A sky-picture   5
For men, for men.

For the first ray stays throughout the stormy day
Deep in the breast, though the bramble bushes flay,
To the sea, west-way, we walk the morning ray.
The dawn-path   10
Is a picture
For men, for men.

II

THE WAR-PATH

The spring-plumes flare, on the heads of bulls and birds.
They fight, they die, with ancient forest words.
The war-plumes come, up the road with gun and drum.
They come.
A sky-picture, 5
For men, for men.

For the soul makes war, when the head is bent and gray.
The gun-fights end, with glory or with pay.
No soul wars cease, though the body be at peace.
And plumes are 10
Sky-pictures
For men, for men.

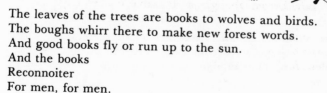

III

THE BOOK-PATH

The leaves of the trees are books to wolves and birds.
The boughs whirr there to make new forest words.
And good books fly or run up to the sun.
And the books
Reconnoiter
For men, for men. 5

For book-thoughts stay from May on round to May.
We read on high, though grizzlies block the way,
And The Doomsday Book opens up in Heaven's day.
The book-path
Is a picture
For men, for men.

IV

SUNSET

Into the sunset, moths or wild cranes fly.
On through the sunset all the highways lie.
The last light flares like a window on the stairs.
It comes
A sky-picture   5
For men, for men.

For the evenings stay through childhood's livelong day.
We sleep all night yet sing the sunset lay.
The west-way sun is the playwright of our play;
The Shakespeare   10
Of heaven
For men, for men.

V

THE MOON-PATH

When the moon hangs low, a crescent by a stream,
The waterfall sleeps, we dream a holy dream,
Moon-tides turn, night rainbows swirl and burn.
Sea-pictures
For land-birds,
For men, for men.

COMPLETE POEMS   731

For, in swift sea-wind, old voyages sweep by,
Our own sure ships are launching there on high.
One more marked way the feet of men obey.
The moon-path
Is a picture
For men, for men.

     1928

   *And so we conclude our discussion of The Deep Woods
Mysteries and the most solemn part of the Forest Menagerie,
and that Sawdust Ring which is in the deepest of the deep
woods.*

OTHER PUBLISHED POEMS

1905-1932

"Is there no refuge-house of song,
No home, no haven where songs belong?
O precious hymns that come and go!
You perish, and I love you so!"

From "In Praise of Songs That Die"
by Vachel Lindsay.

AT NOON ON EASTER-DAY

At noon on Easter-day a candle-spark,
My prayer, was carried by an Angel to the skies.
I would I were my prayer to bend beneath his sighs
Yea, pure enough to live before his ·eyes.

Early 1905

THE DANCE OF UNSKILLED LABOR

The music was coarse as the dancers,
Their lips were quivering less than mine,
The sounds were crashing and rasping;
But worn and clumsy hands were clasping
And tired eyes gleamed with a light divine.   5
Then I loved the dear warped women and men.
Oh Saviour mine, Saviour of Men,
Teach me to love such dancers again!

Bring me that music again:
Gritty as sand that goes into plaster: 10
Stern as the walls that such fathers of men
Build for the shelter of many a master.
Harsh as the dens where their children shall welter;
Greater than music bright palaces shelter:
Oh Saviour, Saviour of Men,   15
Teach me to love such music again!

September 1902

THE MOON IS COMPARED TO A CITY
What the Tired Reformer Said

The moon's a perfect city, with
Curved walls encompassed round;
With yellow palaces upreared
Upon a glittering ground.

Sometimes a disk, a planet dead;   5
But on this splendid night,
When all the sky is shining clear,
When my whole heart is light,

I think it is a place for friends.
My soul is there in mirth,   10
With golden-robed good-citizens,
Far from the dusty earth.

Hail to the perfect city then!
I love your doors and domes,
Your turrets and your palaces,   15
Your terraces, your homes.

1912-1913

THE MOON IS A KNIGHT IN ARMOR

What the Soldier Said

Oh, see the knight in armor,
Who keeps his visor down
And charges with a moon-beam spear
On hard hearts of the town;

Who makes the shabby fountain-square   5
A flowering, glimmering park,
Who pierces with a sharp-sweet dream
The crabbed minds and dark;

Who conquers those who see him not,
Their brooding heads bent down;   10
The knight whose scarcely-heeded strokes
Have cleansed and cleared the town!

1912-1913

THE RECREANT QUEENS

*To be tied to a pebble and thrown through a palace
window*

The moon's a mirror where dim shades
Of queens are doomed to peer,
The beauteous queens that loved not love
Or faith or godly fear.
The night-wind makes their mirror gray.   5
The breath of Autumn drear,

And many mists of time and change
Have clouded it apace,
In mercy veiled it lest each queen
Too clearly see her face,   10
With long-past sins deep written there,
And ghostly rags she now must wear,
While slain men o'er her shoulders glare,
Leering at her disgrace.

1912-1913

WHAT THE YOUNG RHYMER SAID

No poet spent with visions,
Bit by the City's teeth,
Laughing at fortune, seeking
Fame and the singer's wreath,
But must grow brave this evening,   5
Humming a wilder tune,
Armed against men and nations.
Why? He beholds the moon!

1912-1913

THE MOON IS A BOOK

The moon's a book of fairy-tales
    Writ in a magic tongue,
That tiniest children read untaught
    And even birds have sung.

The Sandman chants those happy rhymes   5
    At evening on his way:
Too delicate for day-light-time
    The things the moonbeams say —

Secrets, surprises, whispered whims!
    And though the book is old   10
New leaves keep turning all the year,
    New fairy-tales unfold.

1912-1913 .

THE CHANDELIER

Being a Discourse by a Blue-green Gnome

The night with all its shadowy tracts
    Is but our palace-room,
With music by the katydid
    And insects of the gloom.

We sleep by day in blue-bells deep.   5
    We dance until the dawn,
And print the green-gnomes' minuet
    On many a well-clipped lawn . . .

Everywhere, everywhere, dance and dance!
    The soft winds make good cheer   10
This earth is but a ball-room floor.
    The moon's the chandelier!

    1912-1913

WHAT THE MISER SAID

The moon is but a coin methinks,
    A penny in the sky,
That God has fastened there beyond
    The scamps that peep and spy.

I wish that all the coins were made   5
    One big coin for myself
And then could always be in sight
    Upon so safe a shelf.

    1912-1913

THE MOON IN FOREIGN COUNTRIES

(The Traveller in Nuremberg)

The moon in foreign countries
    Some say is just the same,
But even in this castled town
    I find it dull and tame.

The moon above the raw home place   5
   Where once I walked and dreamed
Above those brown church-steeples
   Far, far more holy seemed.

    1912-1913

GIRL, YOU SHALL MOCK NO LONGER

You shall not hide forever,
I shall your path discern;
I have the key to Heaven,
Key to the pits that burn.

Saved ones will help me, lost ones   5
Spy on your secret way—
Show me your flying footprints
On past your death-bed day.

If by your pride you stumble
Down to the demon-land,   10
I shall be there beside you,
Chained to your burning hand.

If, by your choice and pleasure,
You shall ascend the sky,
I, too, will mount that stairway,   15
You shall not put me by.

There, 'mid the holy people,
Healed of your blasting scorn,
Clasped in these arms that hunger,
Splendid with dreams reborn,   20

You shall be mastered, lady,
Knowing, at last, Desire—
Lifting your face for kisses—
Kisses of bitter fire.

    Winter, 1912-1913

MY MIDDLE NAME

My middle name rhymes not with satchel,
So please do not pronounce it "Vatchel."

My middle name rhymes not with rock hell,
So please do not pronounce it "Vock Hell."
My middle name rhymes not with hash hell,   5
So please do not pronounce it "Vash Hell."
My middle name rhymes not with bottle,
So please do not pronounce it "Vottle."
My name is just the same as Rachel,
With V for R;   10
Please call me Vachel.

    Summer, 1914

THE GOODLY, STRANGE LANTERNS

    (In praise of Edison's great invention, and in sorrow at
    the news that must be shown.)

No prophet, though mighty, forecasted
These lanterns of wisdom and mirth,
These innocent, stuffy, brief conclaves,
These shadow-tales, sweeping the earth.
    (What do the great reels show tonight?)   5
To see the films flashing a legion
Of freemen make haste to the show.
The wealthy are eager and early,
Their autos outside in a row.
The newsboys, the Sunday school children,   10
The preachers, the weavers of song,
The slum-dwellers, villagers, farmers,
The broken, the hopeful, the strong
Rejoice at these goodly, strange lanterns
Then pour forth to ponder or sleep.   15
These restless Kinetoscope vigils
Our proudest, best patriots keep.
    (What do the great reels show tonight?)
O films more beloved than red liquor,
White gates, wellnigh free as the park.   20
First doors, since mankind made the tavern,
To draw such tired feet, after dark.
O, lamps gilding gutters with beauty,
World-gossip, world-splendor and joy.
Equality's wide-flashing art-fire   25
And Edison's goodliest toy.
        But what do the great reels show tonight?
        Fairy tales for the heart's delight?
        Bits of science, made so plain

They stir the dull ditch-digger's brain?   30
What do the great reels show tonight?
A civic pageant brave and bright?
What do the great reels show?
    WAR, WAR,
Brother's hand against brother,   35
    WAR, WAR.

Summer, 1914

THE WOMAN-VOTER COMES

A Rhymed Editorial.

The woman-voter comes! Make room!
Democracy at last in bloom!
We celebrate, with pomp and state,
The mop, the dustpan, and the broom!

The apron flags parade today.   5
The sooty streets make holiday.
The washerwoman's cake of soap
Goes forth to scrub the shames away.

The tiredest farm-wife in the land
Brings blessings in her voting hand   10
To make our total life a flower
More fair than she can understand.

Our sibyls blossom more and more.
Lectures and study they adore.
Our woman's clubs are civic leagues   15
Where patriot larks and throstles soar.

These scholars men have proudly made,
Whose leisure they have bought in trade
On sidewalks crude, in markets rude:
These artists, making men afraid,   20

Will strike at once the civic note
The tired men hoped to learn by rote.
The marriage of man's dreams and deeds
Comes with this fluttering, singing vote.

The woman-voter comes. Make room   25
For silks upon the civic loom!
Bright, broom-swept cities from the dark!
Democracy from out the tomb!

        Summer, 1914

SATURDAY NIGHT IN THE PARK

    A chant to the ancient Egyptian tune, "There'll Be a
Hot Time in the Old Town Tonight," which the band is
supposed to be playing for all it is worth.

Now park bands play ragtime shrill and high,
Wanton, rank, the city's mating cry,
Dumb young things join hands, they know not why,
Except — it is Saturday night.

    (The band plays)
        Please, O please, do not let me fall.   5
        I love, I love you best of all.
        Be my man, or I'll have no man at all,
        There'll be a HOT time
            In the OLD town
                Tonight.   10

There beneath the dust-blurred city moon
Boys and girls in gangs take up the tune,
Love grows blind, far blinder than at noon
On reckless, flushed Saturday night.

    (The band plays)
        When you hear the bells go "jingle-jing,"   15
        We'll all join hands, and sweetly we will sing,
        Go downtown and get your sins forgiven
        There'll be a HOT time
            In the OLD town
                Tonight.   20

Who is there to say, "Boy, watch you well?"
No guide comes to break the music's spell.
Will he choose the wanton, miss the belle,
On shadowy Saturday night?

    (The band plays)
        Please, O please, do not let me fall, etc.   25

Who is there to warn the weary girl,
Save her here from fiend or flashy churl?
Who will match clean souls with souls of pearl
On mystical Saturday night?

(The band plays)
   When you hear those bells, etc.   30
(The chant becomes slower and fainter.)

No guide comes except the pale moon's smile,
Haunting, taunting, further to beguile
Youth unstrung, mad-wooing all the while
On fatal, sweet Saturday night.

(The band plays softly)
   Please, O please, do not let me fall, etc.   35

   Late 1912

THE ANGLO-SAXON LANGUAGE

   (What the Old Rhymer said to the Young Rhymer.)

The Anglo-Saxon language,
Like the endless salty ocean,
Washes every shore of earth
And lifts to meet the moon.
And every world-wide rain of talk   5
Upheaves the ravening breakers,
And every rat or cow or king
Takes ship there, late or soon.

Rouse, O little minstrel,
You walk not by a fishpond,   10
But skirt the waves of Saxon speech
Where far-brought seaweeds shine.
Now make your singing boat so stout
That it will ride like witchcraft
From evening land to morning cloud,   15
From Greenland to the line.

From Avalon to Thule,
From Elsinore to Xanadu,
No power forbids your boat to go
Except your silly hands,   20

That make a sail so flimsy
You could not cross the Wabash,
Much less launch forth on such wide floods
That sweep such granite lands.

Where is the mob-crowned Homer,   25
Whose silver songs establish
This foaming, weltering Saxon speech
In one great glory-tune?
A Charlemagne in chaos,
To bind colossal kingdoms,   30
A captain Noah on the sea
That lifts to meet the moon!

     April 1914

ST. FRANCIS

I saw St. Francis by a stream
Washing his wounds that bled.
The aspens quivered overhead,
The silver doves flew round.

Weeping and sore dismayed   5
"Peace, peace," St. Francis prayed.

But the soft doves quickly fled,
And carrion crows flew round,
An earthquake rocked the ground.
"War, war," the west wind said.   10

     Late Summer, 1914

THE MAGGOT, THE HYENA AND THE JACKAL

The Maggot, the Hyena and the Jackal
Are making war on the red human heart.
The Maggot calls himself "The Lord of War,"
The Jackal calls himself "The Christian Prince,"
The dull Hyena is the "Holy Czar."   5

The Maggot waves his sword and leads the van,
For he is something mightier than man.
The others follow close and quarrel with him,
Declare themselves at knightly war with him
For graveyard skulls and scalps, and eyeballs dim.   10

But Jackal and Maggot and Hyena
Are making war on the live human heart
And tear its quivering, singing strings apart.

Late Summer, 1914

BUDDHA WAS A PRINCE

Buddha was a Prince. We look today
Adown the lane of life to where he stands,
His palace left behind, the road his home,
The begging-bowl in his patrician hands.

Buddha was a Prince. But brotherhood   5
He sought with birds and beasts and all mankind;
A prince who touched the heart with love austere,
Who opened spirit eyes that once were blind.

And hatred left his path like April snow
Before the sun. The Golden Age drew nigh.   10
If this be royal, are the wide world's lords
True princes, ravening under this red sky?

Late Summer, 1914

THE CHRISTMAS SHIP

Behold the masthead light,
A star of rose and white,
That holy sky-born gem,
The Star of Bethlehem.
And right and left, behold   5
Forms in robes of gold,
Cherubs upon the air,
Seraphs crowned and fair,
Swinging censers bright
And singing in the night: 10
"The world must play again
And pray and love again.
Peace and good will to men."

Now why the voyage bold?
What cargo in the hold?   15
This barque to Europe brings
Toys and useful things:
Flannel petticoats,

Clockwork motorboats,
Boxes of children's shoes,   20
Hammers boys can use,
Blankets, shawls and wraps,
Scarfs and gloves and caps,
Wreaths and bright festoons,
Whistling balloons,   25
And Christmas candies fine,
All sent but as a sign
That love may still be found
In babes the world around.

Giraffes are down below,   30
Tin herds of buffalo,
Deers and bears and hens,
Wooden pigs and pens,
A sort of Noah's ark,
With beasties on a lark,   35
Woolly cats and dogs,
Rubber jumping frogs,
Elephants that caper
And dolls of colored paper.

Thus speaks a little sled   40
With body painted red:
"A Kansas German boy
This Christmas will enjoy,
So hope I will make glad
Some rosy Russian lad."   45
A staid New England child
A sawdust Santa mild
For a Prussian child's delight
Gives with words polite.
A Yankee-Belgian hopes   50
His hoops and jumping-ropes
Will be the whims that please
On Austrian Christmas trees.
A doll with smiling face
Sings with a lisping grace: 55
"From Halsted street I part
From a Servian Anna's heart;
I seek to find a sweet
Small German Marguerite."
And all the gifts are bold,   60
Sing to the storm and cold:
"We toys are silly things,
But we may conquer kings."

To orphans in the street
Whose hearts in terror beat,   65
To families on the march
Whom bloody heavens arch,
To peasant mothers bowed
In fields by cannon plowed,
This ship of filigree   70
Is crossing the iron sea,
This children's new crusade
Goes onward, unafraid.

And will the dear design
Achieve its Palestine?   75
Or like that one of old,
In wreck and loss untold,
Be turned to weed and spray
And rags of yesterday?
Who is the pilot then?   80
A chief of armored men?
And does he dress in braid,
In sword and stripes arrayed?

The Christ-child guides the wheel,
So let the wild world kneel.   85
Lovelier than the day
He steers the star-ship's way.
Oh, shining face, too fair,
Soft hands and wind-blown hair!
This babe should curl and rest   90
Against the Virgin's breast.
The little roses bound
His lily forehead round,
Have cut him with their briars
And the storm has blasting fires.   95
Thunders that make him reel,
That shake the mast and wheel.
But the Christ-child bravely steers
Through the blackness of the years,
Through the sadness of the seas,   100
With his dolls and tinsel trees
And his bales of useful things
And the angel chorus sings:
"The world must play again
And pray and love again.   105
Peace and good will to men."

Late Summer, 1914

WHAT THE BURRO SAID

The moon's a thistle-poppy.
    Men see naught but the flower.
I spy in the deep space behind
    Thorn-leaves I would devour.
If I could fly there like a crow
    I'd stand and chew and chew
Those long divine delicious thorns.
    Then eat the blossom, too.

        Summer, 1912

WHAT THE SAILOR SAID

The moon's the jade that leads the tides,
    A Jezebel in the skies.
The Oceans are in love with her.
    And wind and wave arise
Bemoaning and adoring,   5
    Pursuing round the zones
This painted gal fantastical: —
    Making them wild and sorrowful,
Weaving her wicked miracle: —
    By the house of Davy Jones.   10

        Summer, 1912

WHAT THE COURT JESTER SANG

"The moon's a wig for nuncle,"
    Sang the jester, with a grin.
"A charming wig for nuncle.
    He's grown so old and thin,
He is so bent and bald of head   5
    So toothless and so bad
A wig of Springtime innocence
    Should certainly be had.
We'll fit it close around his ears
    And nicely comb the gold   10
In cataracts upon his coat.
    He will not look so old,
And at the King's high levee
    Quit leaning on his cane,
And be the cock of all the walk,   15
    Poetical, and vain.

He may deceive some half-grown child,
  Some hoyden all untamed,
And we who comb the moon-wig
  Will praise him, unashamed.   20
For he has promised, ere he leaves
  This world of sinful men,
A million ducats if we bring
  One night of youth again!"

      Summer, 1912?

WHAT THE CLOCK-MAKER SAID

The moon's a madman's timepiece.
  It will not regulate.
Yet tells the time to travel,
  To poison, stab or mate.

With neither key nor pendulum,   5
  With neither bell nor hands,
It shows the hour most magical
  Throughout the teeming lands.

It tells the day for planting wheat,
  For battle, feast or fast,   10
To harvest home or Easter
  Guiding the race at last.

      Summer, 1912

OH WISDOM IN THE WINTER

Oh wisdom in the winter
But folly in the springtime
Remembering the ragged days
When the full heart overflowed.
Wisdom in the winter   5
But now for empty pockets
Hunger, dust and sunburn:
The road,
The road,
The road!   10

      Summer, 1914

WHY IS A MOUSE WHEN IT SPINS?
(*Or, The Temperamental Cat*)

All night the lean cat waited
    (A rat beneath his paw)
To catch a mouse with moonbeam eyes
    And starlight fur, he thought he saw.

The killed rat in his grasp   5
    He had gathered all in vain:
At last he dropped it down our well
    And caterwauled his pain.

Hungry, now, forever
    For a mouse he could not win,   10
In the bran-bin and the wheat-bin
    He saw it dance and spin.

Of course he ate his meals—
    But nobly sang and spoke
Of the mouse he saw, without a flaw,   15
    The night his lion-soul woke.

The night he learned to jump and sing
    And make the jungle proud—
When he saw that mouse pop down from Heaven
    From a wisp of purple cloud.   20

        Summer, 1922

I LIKE NANCY BOYD

I like Nancy Boyd.
I read her poem in *Vanity Fair*
For August, 1922, page 44.
It is the poem of a dear, sweet,
Angel-faced   5
Patriot.
Breathes there an American
With soul so dead
He would not like Nancy Boyd
When she praised her own good land   10
With such a game laugh?

My country, 'tis of thee.
Sweet land of Nancy Boyd.
Of thee I sing—

And of all good girls like Nancy Boyd   15
Who love their own.
Whatever the provocation to
Do something very else.
Who scorn not
Their own potato patch.   20
Their own redwood trees.
The pit whence they were digged.
The ladder by which they climbed.

Hell's bells for the birds
That foul their own nest   25
Piously, altruistically,
Incessantly and forever,
Hyphenates,
Cheap skates,
Expatriates   30
Who like everything under Heaven.
Even Thibetan cheese—
Who can give a thousand noble reasons
For an exclusive diet
Of mouldy Thibetan cheese   35
(Which is, no doubt, very good in its way)—
Who love, as I say,
Thibetan cheese and such
But hate their own
Corn pone   40
United States.

A hot psychological griddle
For the birds
That think the American eagle
Is an unrefined old buzzard.   45
Bad as he is, he is all
The eagle we've got.

God bless the little birds like Nancy,
The homesick little birds
Way off there in France,   50
With their heads on one side coquetishly,
That can sing of their
Native delicious apple trees.
God bless the little birds
Who can view the American eagle   55
But still admire him—
An act of faith, I admit—
Who can sing sweet songs

To that damned old eagle
And look away a moment   60
When he spills food on his vest.
God bless the little birds
That, far from Columbia,
The gem of the ocean,
Can still see she is something more   65
Than a phonograph record.

I have not cried at the theatre for years
And Armistice Day
Was a grand day all over the lot,
But no tears, no weeps;   70
But your little song
On European versus American housekeeping
In that scandalous August *Vanity Fair*
Made me weep
Little weeps of patriotism.   75
That's me all over, Nancy,
And so I, who abhor free verse
And think that every line
Should contain seven rhymes
And scan like a game of checkers   80
(Except in the case of Carl Sandburg)
Do find your cadences in my mind
With exquisite pleasure,
Do write you, in my haste,
My first free-verse poem,   85
Possibly my last.
I declare, within the limits
Of my power to declare
That your poem is an honor
To John Randolph of Roanoke, Andrew Jackson,   90
    Daniel Boone, Pocahontas, Sitting Bull,
    Dwight L. Moody, Stephen Collins Foster,
    Frances E. Willard, Old John Brown, Benjamin
    F. Butler, Abraham Lincoln, Robert E. Lee,
    Lillian Russell,   95
My sacred Kentucky ancestors,
Your sacred Kentucky ancestors—
I declare your poem is an honor
To John C. Calhoun, Booker T. Washington, Edna
    St. Vincent Millay, Ralph Waldo Emerson,   100
    David Wark Griffith, Mary Pickford, Willa
    Sibert Cather, William Allen White, and all
    the rest of us, living and dead. We don't

know just where we're going, but we certainly
are on our way.

Summer, 1922

THE NAVY AND MARINE MEMORIAL

(Inspired by the Navy and Marine Memorial movement,
which plans erecting a national shrine to those who have
been lost at sea.)

Where is the ruddy adventurer
Who went where ships could go?
Where is the rainbow soul that sailed
Wherever
Salt sprays   5
Blow?

Where is the fine marine we knew
Who loved
Every harbor
And sea?   10
Let us sing on the shore of our land.
    He comes
Through the night
To you,
To me.   15

The sailor that drowns with the drowning stars
Lives with the stars of the sky.
The broken marine goes down,
Grows dim,
Yet his proud wings flame on high.   20

Star souls that break in the breaking waves
Are reborn in the bay that clears.
Then look to the sky.
They are there on high
Outsailing the storms   25
And years,
My dears,
Outsailing the storms
And years.

Early 1925

THE RHINOCEROS AND THE BUTTERFLY

"Who shall find a valiant woman? far and from the
uttermost coasts is the price of her." — Proverbs, 31:10.

Once a rhinoceros went quite wild
He mixed his metaphors all day long,
He was deeply in love with a butterfly child.

The rhinoceros said to the butterfly,
Filling the skies with his metaphor-song,   5
"You are like a sky-writing flying machine:
You write great stories in front of my eye,
You write new names for love in the air,
As you hurry by toward the wild rose bloom,
Drunk with honeysuckle perfume,   10
Wild with the thought of your silk-thread tomb.

"You stormed your way from the death-bed room,
To the light, to the air, to the palm, to the moss.

"I like the way you are turning and burning,
The way you handspring and jump and toss,   15
Refusing to keep good time with your wings,
Though the nightingale (with the mudlark) sings.

"While you write great stories in front of my eye,
Write new names for desire as you please —
I will stand by this river ten thousand years   20
Reading the writing, taking my ease."

        Winter, 1924-1925

THE DOVE OF NEW SNOW

I give you a house of snow,
I give you the flag of the wind above it,
I give you snow-bushes
In a long row,
I give you a snow dove,   5
And ask you
To love it.

The snow dove flies in
At the snow-house window,

He is a ghost   10
And he casts no shadow.
His cry is the cry of love
From the meadow,
The meadow of snow where we walked in a glow,
The glittering, the angelic meadow.   15

    Winter, 1925-1926

WE WILL SAIL IN HENDRIK HUDSON'S
HALF-MOON FOR SINGAPORE

Dear Heart, when you and I
Are on that boat
For Singapore, —
For Singapore
The mad and old,   5
For Singapore
The green glass flower,
For Singapore
The devil's dreamland door . . .

We will find within us   10
Once, once more,
All the tales
That ever filled a throat with song,
Or spread old Hendrik Hudson's sails
Magellan's or Marco Polo's sails,   15
Hunting for Singapore,
Hunting for Singapore . . .

Dear Heart,
When you and I
Are on   20
That boat for Singapore,
It will be
But walking down
This village street
For one time more.   25
With hearts awake
For happiness,
In every sight from left to right,
From bookshops
To stray cats;   30
With hearts

That make discoveries
Of newspapers
And hats,
We find in Greenwich Village   35
All of Marco Polo's lore,
Or Hendrik Hudson's lore,
Kissing under the awnings,
On the ship to Singapore.

Late 1925

WHEN LINCOLN CAME TO SPRINGFIELD

When Lincoln came to Springfield,
In the ancient days,
Queer were the streets and sketchy,
And he was in a maze.

Leaving log cabins behind him,   5
For the mud streets of this place,
Sorrow for Anne Rutledge
Burned in his face.

He threw his muddy saddle bags
On Joshua Speed's floor,   10
He took off his old hat,
He looked around the store.

He shook the long hair
On his bison-head,
He sat down on the counter,   15
"Speed, I've moved," he said.

1926-1927

MANHATTAN, 1927

There's a new king in Babylon
Every hour,
There's a new queen in Babylon
Every year,
And the kings   5
Go down,
Then the queens
Go down
With a heartbreak,
And a terrible cry of fear.   10

1927?

WHERE MY LADY SLEEPS

Where my lady sleeps,
Is home.
Where my lady rests,
Is laughter.
What my lady hopes,
Is my hereafter.

1925

RETURNING TO SPRINGFIELD

Oh, you I am adoring,
When we go exploring
Bewailing or admiring
In the oldest streets of Springfield,
We will go on and on   5
Till passing many a cornfield,
We will find a haunted house
With a porch where the steps are gone.

Nothing but weeds and lilacs!
Where were lilacs and a lawn!

If we scramble onto the porch,
If we push the loose door open,
We will see a lighted torch,
We will hear a queer word spoken.
Some boy in a "wide awake" rig,   15
A boy for the Lincoln parade,
Starting out for the evening,
To join the campaign brigade.

A ghost of 1860
Going the way he went,   20
When the sons of the abolitionists
Made their president.

We will not know the ghost.
Their torches now are rust,
And they sleep in a green tent,   25
And their houses are haunted,
And their bones are dust.

Winter, 1925-1926

BLOWING UP HELL-GATE

While I wait for you to dress,
I sit and drink my coffee straight,
And think up what we yet may do,
Toward blowing up Hell-Gate.

The little harbor Hell-Gate here,   5
Was blown up by electric wires,
That led to pits of dynamite,
And small machines adjusted right
For giving Hell-Gate dynamite.

But in the harbor of all souls   10
Where we would blow up Hell-Gate reef,
We must dive much deeper down,
We must place more marvelous wires,
Or all our tricks will come to grief.

Yet we have hoped to blow up Hell   15
And give mankind relief.

        Late 1925

A REMARKABLE STORY FROM KOKOMO, INDIANA

Once upon a time—long, long ago,
There was a golden house in Kokomo,
Cherished by a family most polite,
In Indiana was a tower of light,
Underneath it   5
Roofs of alabaster,
With lightning rods to keep off all disaster.

Lightning rod agents in the long ago
Used to tell brave stories of their wares.

With lightning rods they hoped in that small place   10
To keep that house serene in power and grace.
A glory before the whole world's face,
A place that cured all pilgrims of all cares,
A symbol of the preacher's heavenly stairs.

And yet that fair house fell, not in the rain,   15
But turned to ashes, to cinders black and vain,

Purple and sad, and anything but white,
Burned by a phoenix-wing on a clear night,

The Phoenix made a night's nest of the roof,
Then burned the place, calling with delight,   20
"Beware of lightning on the clearest night."

December 1925

THE FREER GALLERY, WASHINGTON, D.C.

Whistler, Whitman, and Poe are named together,
Americans, all three, great in their way.
When we walked the Freer Gallery of Whistler's paintings,

We found it empty,
All devotees away.   5

And when we speak of Whitman's songs of Lincoln,
The Republican Party stares, the Democrats
Follow their fashion,
With disdainful airs.

When we speak of Poe,   10
The cheerful sages
Show that they have never turned his pages.

In the peacock room that Freer gave the nation,
They keep the peacocks hid from observation.

Freer brought that room across the ocean;   15
It is made void to please some trustee's notion.
Fat guards are trained in snobbery to hide
Whistler's supreme peacocks, and his pride.

Thus, genius has its dry-as-dust deep tomb;
You are shown all but the peacocks in that room.   20

Late 1925

THREE ROOSTERS

There is a wonderful crowing rooster,
A trumpet on the shed,
Another wonderful rooster,
Crowing in my head.

There's a bigger blazinger rooster   5
On the top of the tallest tree,
On the edge of the Sangamon River,
And these three crow to me.

Each rooster's wings are purple,
Each rooster's comb is red,   10
And there is a sunrise round each one,
Sharp beams around each head.

What do they say as they crow?
What do they sing?
Indeed a simple thing,   15
"In our souls, twice-born and crowing,
Our every month is spring."

　　　　Late 1925

WILD CATS

Here, as it were, in the heart of roaring Rome,
Here as far as men may get from the soil,
Here where political lords
Are proud of oil,
Oil in their skins,   5
Oil in their robber wells,
Where money and stone and orations are combined,
Here in Washington, D. C.,
Here where sins are refined and over-refined,
Here where they ape the very walls of Rome,   10
The temples and pillars of Imperial Rome,
We think of the time the wild cats kept awake
Our little camp, and filled our hearts with fright,
When porcupine and bear-cub stirred the brake,
And the friendliest wind seemed cold and impolite.   15
We think of our terror through the campfire night,
Of how we hoped to kiss the earth aright,
In spite of fear, and hoped not all in vain,
Of how we hoped for wild days, clean with power,
Of how we sought the fine log-cabin hour,   20
Of how we thought to rule
By leading men to a lone log-cabin school,
We think of our pioneer American pride,
Our high defiance that has not yet died.
Here, as it were, in the heart of roaring Rome,   25

In Washington, D. C.,
Where they ape the very walls of Rome.

November 1925

OUR LITTLE NEW CAVE-MAN

The only son
Of the only son
May yet be hard to break,
So many Lindsays
Long ago   5
Fought onward
For his sake,
So many Cave-men
Long ago,
So many Indians   10
Long ago,
Fought onward
Through the shadow
For his sake.

The only Lindsay cub I know   15
Born in captivity
May yet be very hard to tame.
His Mother is an Irish child,
Poet, bard and prophetess.
"Elizabeth Darling" is   20
Her name,
And "Nicholas Cave"
His name.
"Elizabeth Darling" is
Her name.   25
And "Nicholas Cave"
His name.

   To be hummed to the tune the wind makes as it blows
through the northwestern aspens.

September 1927

THE TALL FIFTH MONARCHY MAN

This was a parable told
By a sibyl in Baltimore,
Cobwebs over her windows,
Torn books over the floor: —

"I saw, in a dream unstable,   5
A vision, all gone wrong;
Yet it leaves in my sky a cathedral,
And in my house, a song.

"The lofty Charles was beheaded,
His armies wrecked and wild.   10
Old England, who hated the living man
Cried like a slave, or a child.
His palace was empty as Pharo's tomb
Robbed of mummy and crown,
Was ghostly and tense as the Forum air   15
When Caesar laid him down.
The palace was mouldy and hollow
Like a sea-cave of toadstool stone.
And into the hall clanged Cromwell
Toward the terrible, empty throne.   20

"The one guard of the regicide
Was a gaunt fifth monarchy man,
A saint from the ranks who was seven feet tall;
The blood from his broadsword ran.
Cromwell's dagger was bloody;   25
New wounds on his strong, brown throat.
'The Lord Protector' in his own blood
On the marble table he wrote.

"Wounded by Charles' last friends
They had cut their way past the gate   30
Six corpses outside, in the ditch,
Of fops who would tamper with fate!
The victors clanged bolts and bars,
And stood in the center of pride,
Cromwell bleeding like Brutus,   35
His Casca close to his side.

"Only two lamps to light them
On the terrible throne-steps flared,
And the throne was domed like Hell's dark arch,

And Oliver's throat was bared.   40
Bloody and muddy his jackboots,
And his heels made the pavement red,
But he would not heed, nor staunch his wounds
Nor lie in the King's lace-bed.
With his dagger in hand, held warily,   45
His eyes by power made drunk,
He thought with a laugh, the protestant guard
Had a face like a fasting monk.

"Fifth monarchy man from the ranks!
O Ironside, seven feet high,   50
With the pointed assassin's face
And a restless fanatical eye!
Cromwell read him, and knew.
But was born with a lion's mind.
And every fifth monarchy man   55
Cromwell could loose, or bind.

"So, he turned with a preaching whisper
To his ironside comrade in pride: —
'Why does the wind blow, always,
Tell me, my pastor and guide?   60
Does the inner light still come to you?
Tell me, now we are alone,
Does the still small voice say this is my house?
Is this my horse, and my throne?'

"The faithful one answered him nothing.   65
Studied his texts, and stood
Bible in hand, sword in hand
Under the throne's sad hood: —
Gems from the book of Samuel,
Praying his chief might find   70
In the doom of Saul and his pestilent crown
A sermon to warn his mind.

"And when Oliver sank at last on the throne
His friend grew alert and straight,
Thinking: — 'Is this the end?   75
A despot inside the gate?'

"Then Cromwell read him more deeply down,
Defying that face of stone,
And sighed: 'Must I get my discipline
From Lucifer's lonely throne?   80

Am I sent of God to take this seat?
And would you kneel to me?'
(And Cromwell laughed with a lion's mind: —)
'Should I knight you cunningly?
Or will you come but one step more   85
And cut me down this hour?
I own I have King Saul's black heart
But Saul's anointed power.

"'I have watched you inching towards me, friend,
Since your murdering thought began.   90
Now leave all vengeance to your God.
Put back your blade, strong man.'

"Suddenly, from a far-off room
The organ began to play:
Popish tunes from the Vatican   95
And Psalms of Charles' high day.

"Instantly unified for God
An army of two, once more,
They thought of the six dead royalists
In the ditch, outside the door.   100

"They dreaded no ghostly thing.
But this was a power, apart,
And the private soldier found a mind,
And the regicide found a heart.

"The tall fifth monarchy man   105
Surrendered his sword, and stood
Like an oak that burns not down
In the brush of a burning wood.

"Saluting, he peered at his chief,
And his hawk-face wryly smiled.   110
Like sentinel bronzes they held their lights,
By a new fear reconciled.

"'Has Lucifer risen?' breathed Cromwell,
'Why come his tunes again?
I had thought to drive the music of Baal   115
From the haunts of honest men.'

"The soldiers lifted their golden lamps
And marched to the organ throne.

Who was it, playing with changing tunes
To those roundheads, harsh and alone?   120

"He seemed like a boy, all splendor,
With his long, curled, golden hair.
His grace at the organ, Italian,
His hands too supple and fair.
They did not know that he played alone   125
Because of the pride of his mind.
They did not know that he played in the dark
Because he was well-nigh blind.
Higher they lifted the wavering lamps
To see his shadowed face,   130
While the roof, to listening Cromwell
Was a smoke-wrapped battle-place.

"Who was the lone musician,
His cheeks all lily and rose,
Stone boned, and battle-drunk   135
Yet dressed like the ironsides' foes?
Ah, he was bold as Charles at the block!
He fixed on Cromwell a glare
Like the tiger of far-off Bengal,
And his tunes made wheels in the air.   140

"Like David, with Saul, after battle,
Harping all night in the tent,
As strong as a son of Anak,
As hot for his tunes, unspent.
Then he turned his back on the roundheads,   145
And they stood, in the prison of night;
Too proud to give in to their terrible wounds,
They bled till their cheeks were white;
While the Master of Music builded the doors
Of Heaven, and Chaos, and Hell,   150
And lifted the swaying roof till it arched
Like a bower over asphodel.
And the soldiers saw the great wings of the Dove
Of the Spirit spread and weave;
And the lawns of paradise,   155
And the marvelous birth of Eve
To God's great Bridal Tune;
Then Adam, with Eve, on the midnight moon;
Then thrones in England, thrones in Rome,
And rainbows rolling high,   160
Thrones, thrones in the deep of the uttermost deep,
Thrones, thrones in the awful sky.

" 'Who is this Cavalier?'
Whispered great Oliver, then,
'His ruffles are long, his curls are long.   165
Was he one of Prince Rupert's men?'
'The seraph of Christ's College,'
Said the man, with his heart laid bare.
'Lucifer's enemy, Milton,
John Milton, God's holy Scholar.   170
His soul is the dayspring air.'
And Cromwell thought the fifth monarchy man
Had the face of a King at prayer.

"And Milton played through the dying storm,
His long, gold hair tossed round,   175
Apollo's air! King David crowned!
And little for listeners could he care.
He saw not till the sunrise came
That they bled like soldiers there."

       1929

THE EZEKIEL CHANT

    Ezekiel Chapter One

            I. Ezekiel's Vision

Ezekiel saw the skies unroll,
    All wings and wheels and beasts of flame.
He spoke, and set his tribes afire;
    The chants no king could kill or tame.

Ezekiel spoke his scorching words,   5
    Then words too sweet for human ears.
Therefore, today, the wise grow strong
    And many a mourner dries his tears.

Long after, from his book of dust,
    The flames break out in lonely souls.   10
The scholar sees his heavenly kin:
    Ten thousand tribes with aureoles.

While wings of flame, new beasts and wheels,
    In New York subways, towers and skies
Are portents to prophetic hearts   15
    Shaken with terror and surmise.

On, on, the fearful skies unroll.
    Only the wise can breathe the blast.
Tried as by fire, corrupted hearts
    Into the pits of terror cast,   20

Know not our towns go back in time
    To where Ezekiel prayed with power;
Know not how Heaven unbinds, unwinds,
    Till God brings forth His perfect hour.

Strike on, town beasts! Sing on, town wings!   25
    Weird wheels in wheels complete your tour
On to the light beyond the suns —
    The road is cleared, the goal is sure.

II. Hiram's Classic Hill

Now on this hill apart, we watch
    The future through the stars astream;   30
Far from the towns we therefore see,
    In special forms, Ezekiel's dream.

We see the colors of his mind
    In maple sugar groves turned red;
In autumn winds through chestnut boughs   35
    Hear special words the prophet said.

And when high thoughts have caught the hill
    The student orators, made great
By youth's applause, and Heaven's applause,
    Unlock the far millennial gate.   40

Away from New York mobs and towers,
    As far from old Ezekiel's throng,
Over this hill some wings appear,
    From his old scroll comes this new song.

III. All the Hills of Vision

Race on, all beasts! Sing on, all wings!   45
    Weird wheels in wheels complete your tour
On to the light beyond the stars;
    The road is cleared, the goal is sure.

1930

THE DUNCE-CAP ON THE GHOST

For a brag, for a scandalous boast,
I put a dunce-cap on a ghost,
Because he did not know
That he was wasting his free hour
A-haunting of me so.   5

For I have looked on Pride grown tame,
And Friendship turned to hate,
And Patriot fervor now gone lame,
Martyrdom out of date,
And Beauty turned to bait,   10
Unselfishness, to lust,
And vows to dust.
While these keep me a-shiver,
What is a shabby ghost or two,
Or a dead man from the river?   15

    1930?

POP SPINK AND THE MICE HAVE A CHRISTMAS

1

Susan and Nickey were two white mice,
Who lived on an acre of wheat.
Their friends were the bumblebees fuzzy and nice
Who fed them on honeycomb sweet.

2

When the mice were afraid of the rabbits so nimble   5
They hid in a hole in a log
Not very much bigger than mother's gold thimble.
And the rabbits ran by on the jog.

3

Soon Susan and Nick from the knot-hole would peep.
Then phone to their friend Mister Spink.   10
Mister Spink was most often away or asleep,
Or deafened from trying to think.

4

But sometimes he answered the grape-vine phone.
And then he would come to the party.
He was three times as big as a nice corn-pone,   15
And was always too hungry and hearty.

5

They fed him on honey and wheat-roots and pears;
And asked him the news of the Spinks.
But he answered with jokes about hollow-tree bears,
And tried to explain his new thinks.   20

6

On Christmas they ran all the way to his home,
(White mice would not show on the snow)
But the bumblebees stayed in their beds in the comb,
For cold makes them sleepy and slow.

7

Pop Spink had a home where the mice liked to come.   25
Oh his corn tassel beard! and peaked hat!
With pants like George Washington! coat like Methusalem!
And a Japanese sash for cravat!

8

Mister Spink and the mice ate their Christmas together
By his hearth in the cave by the creek.   30
It was banked up with sod to keep out the bad weather.
They feasted a day and a week,

9

Consuming the turkey, plum-pudding, cranberries,
Popcorn, and bits of green moss.
And they slept between meals guarded over by fairies   35
Of whom Santa Claus is the boss.

10

At the end of the feast not a scrap was in sight.
But Spink was quite eager to please.

And he gave "Happy New Year" to them, and "Good
   night,"
With two fat big pieces of cheese.   40

      October 1930

THE JAZZ AGE

   (To be read and chanted, quite aloud, by an open hearth-
fire, with the radio turned off. Reading time: 4 minutes 3
seconds.)

Good-by, Jazz Age, I'm going Home, and fish in the
   minnow crick,
With any old twine, a good bent pin, and a worm, and a
   hickory stick.

Good-by, Jazz Age. The Wagon Bridge, broken, finds the
   Broken Bridge Farm.
A sign on the rail warns motors away, so stray lambs
   meet no harm;

And so scarab beetles take to the trail, unterrified
   gypsies again;   5
Swans cross the lane: — Greek ladies of old! And roosters
   are Robin Hood's men!

Good-by, Jazz Age. I'm going Home. The tottering bridge
   will stand
If you take it afoot, whistle a charm, a witch-hazel wand
   in your hand.

The minnow crick shines! Curves on the grass! The path
   by the bank finds the yard,
A blue iron deer, a green iron dog, and a live pup that
   barks at you hard.   10

He bites only those who are togged out for golf, wear
   movie clothes or puttees.
Oh, you must be dressed like Josh Billings at best, to
   put the quaint hound at his ease.

We will never come back from the Broken Bridge Farm.
   Home-logs uphold every shack.
We eat what we raise, and raise what we eat, and spare
   any stranger a snack.

On the mantel are dream-books. They came in oak
bureaus in Cumberland Gap wagon-trains.   15
The novelty volumes are Riley and Nye, and the Jumping
Frog yarn, Mark Twain's.

Good-by, Jazz Age. I'm going Home, where Artemus
Ward is still hot,
And Falstaff is quoted when pigs are in clover, and
Burns, when the weasel is shot.

The Biglow Papers are cutting up capers, the whiplash
of Gulliver stings,
And Widow Bedott is a friend to the fancy, and
Tennyson's Camelot sings.   20

When the sun's on the field, the jigs of Dan Tucker will
make us young yokels again;
When the rain's on the pane, the poems of Poe transform
us to musical men.

Good-by, Jazz Age, I'm going Home, to a parlor with
wax flowers and candles,
Spinning wheels, snuffers, Washington's picture,
chromos of saints wearing sandals.

We will eat what we raise, and raise what we eat, and
will not be shattered by noise;   25
Will dress like the pictures in dog-eared McGuffey: —
Third Reader sweethearts and boys.

As Emerson sang: — "Good-by, proud world." The hill
of sun-burned Uncle Sam
Is a citadel set for ten thousand years yet, far from the
scramble and cram.

His homestead the State, the Hearth, the Hope, The Star
Spangled Banner of Power.
Good-by, Jazz Age. I'm going Home. "The Clock on the
Stair" strikes the hour.   30

Fall, 1930

BALLAD OF THE ARIZONA SHERIFF

The Arizona Sheriff of the days long ago
Took a more decisive stand,
And died with his boots on,
Gun in hand.

The afternoon they swore him in   5
Began the din.
Less than a day to live, he knew!
He grinned because the moment flew.

Trick lawyers did not stay to fight,
Thirteen skedaddled overnight.   10
The slick claim-jumpers left the land.
Sheep-stealers, underhand and bland,
Were instantaneous in their flight,
One horsethief tried in vain to stand,
Despite their diamonds, starch and crust,   15
Three dressy gamblers' shirts were mussed.
The one bad redskin bit the dust.

Less than a day to live, he knew!
He grinned because the moment flew.
And his best work was done with rope.   20
There upon the lava-slope
The gallows tree was high and grand,
Heavy with bullies as he planned,
Before the desert sun went down.
And he had cleaned the little town   25
A branded thug, a hissing fake,
A big-spurred greaser, on the make,
Whose eye was clear, whose gun could rake.
That greaser shot the Sheriff dead.
Before the Sheriff's gun was cold,   30
Before the evening bats could fly
The greaser ceased to raid the fold,
The boys had hung him, kicking high.
Yea, crows were pecking at the head
Of the skunk who shot the Sheriff dead   35
Before the evening star was old.

Oh hill of pinyon, pine and bone
Helping the sagebrush clumps intone
A glory cry, a glory moan!
I wish that I could hum that tune   40

You taught to the meandering moon.
Over his grave, so proud and lone
Men scratched upon the lava-stone:
"He died with his boots on,
Gun in hand."   45

Four hours past sundown
All was done
Then honor for the matchless one.
The Sheriff's torchlight funeral
Saw all the crooks four hours in Hell.   50

Your funerals were not polite
Oh public foes, who stayed to fight!
No sweet, grand opera floral bowers
For scorpions spoiling golden hours.
There upon the lava-slope   55
Your funeral wreaths were hempen rope.
There, on the air, you had to stand.
But local learned sages said
The Sheriff joined the Spartan Dead.
And plain men with approval read: 60
"He died with his boots on,
Gun in hand."

Oh, his were simple days indeed!
"Death to the deadly" was his creed.
He knew the she-wolf from the owl.   65
(Each one had a different howl).
He knew the cactus from the reed,
The buzzard from the barnyard fowl,
Coyote from the new-born calf,
Tarantula from horned toad,   70
He knew the wheat, he knew the chaff,
Could tell the rabbit from the rat,
The Maltese from the panther-cat,
The rosebud from the loco-weed,
A proud horse from the locoed steed,   75
An oath of office from an ode.
He knew his road, and took his road,
He could drill clean, and he could laugh.

Go, stranger, and at Flagstaff tell
Obedient to her law he fell.   80
"He died with his boots on,
Gun in hand."

December 1930

BALLAD ON HOW TO WRITE A POEM

"Listen to the Mocking Bird," with Stoddard and other
     noble Kings.
Act the Mikado, Pinafore. Sing in the limber, classic
     things.
Read Ben Jonson, sing Ben Bolt. Listen when the church
     bell rings.
Read St. Paul, Ezekiel. Fly like Ezekiel's beasts with wings.
Listen when Tornadoes laugh and Lear's frail jester kneels
     and sings.   5
Then listen to the groans of Man,
And write your poem, if you can.

For style and vogue in deathless mode, get Herrick's
     Julia perfectly.
For suppleness and sharp-eyed wit, read the light rhymes
     of Thackeray.
For whips more keen than press-rooms guess, read all
     the "Colyumns" merrily.   10
"Colyumns" are hot with lightning-play, magnates are
     missing every day.
Listen, while syndicated swine mistake brag for posterity;
Listen, while the radio squalls with that kind of flattery.
Then walk your soul at Walden Pond with Thoreau and
     Philosophy.
With Bret Harte at the Golden Gate, meet the slick
     "Forty-Nine" Chinee.   15
Then hunt the Jabberwock and Snark. Get Mother Goose
     mightily.
With Alice "Through the Looking Glass," brush up on
     Relativity.
Then listen when your babies shout, spying the mouse and
     bumblebee.
Then praise the berries, curse the weeds, and sail with
     Masefield through the sea.
Then listen to the Sangamon, and Oak Ridge, mourning
     musically.   20
Then listen to the groans of Man,
And write your poem, if you can.

Think of Wodin, think of Thor, think of bold berserk
     Ericson
Cutting westward through the ice to find the vineland's
     benison,

Think of the Northwest states today, ruled by Hans
    Christian Anderson.   25
Think of Columbus, Spanish Trails, and Santa Fe, so
    Mexican.
Then Daniel Boone, Kit Carson, and Lewis and Clark and
    Jefferson.
Then Sandburg, Lindbergh, Admiral Byrd, Edwin
    Markham, Edison.
Laugh with all these pioneers who keep our hopes so
    bright with fun,
Like long white covered wagon trains, like long lines to the
    setting sun,   30
Roll your rhymes, slow wagon-wheels, across the plains
    to Oregon.
Where California sea-shells gleam, hold to your ear the
    singing one.
Then listen to the groans of Man,
And write your poem, if you can.

Oh! Humanists unmetrical, snarled with the "Classics"
    in their prime,   35
You cannot prose like Henry James with poetry, and make
    it chime.
Listen while the flat-wheeled car, the Pullman
    masterpiece, keeps time,
Clickety-thump, thumpety click, but plan a less insistent
    rhyme.
Go to a Punch and Judy show. Now there you find the
    "Classic" mime.
Then listen while the "Talkie" queens howl like
    Glumdalclitch in the slime.   40
In the Grand Central Depot sit, for hours, and note the
    grunting grime.
Then buy a movie magazine. Then at a dime store, spend
    a dime.
Doctor your democratic soul with new devices, dry
    as lime; —
At some slick-trick amusement park watch well the
    innocence and crime.
Listen in the State House halls, hyenas laughing
    overtime.   45
Go down a mine. Watch them dig. Watch the mine
    elevator climb,
Giving birth to steel and coke, to Pittsburgh and its
    groan sublime.
Go to the County Hospital. Join the doctors' silent clan.

Hear Woman giving birth to Man,
And write your poem, if you can.   50

Listen when your dear love reads Emily Dickinson,
    saint of dreams.
Listen when real patriots sigh, the eagle genuinely
    screams.
Listen when young poets come — whispering High School
    Bards, in streams;
Armies of little Homers born: defeated where the taxi
    teems.
Listen when the great rains talk, shaking some old log-
    cabin's beams.   55
Listen to one, listen to all, for rhymes, and far Millennial
    Themes.
Sit on a mountain top alone, under the sky-wind's flurry
    and fan,
Remembering still the groans of Man,
Write the song American,
Write your poem, if you can.   60

        Winter, 1930-1931

FASHION PLATES FROM WHIMSYLAND

Fashion plates from Whimsyland
Are never out of mode.
From Mother Goose till now they take
The middle of the road.

        1930

THE TEENSEY WHALE

Said the scorn-fish to the baby whale,
"Go back, young tadpole, to your mud.
Go home, young nothing, to your pool."
And the teensey whale at once turned tail.
He knew not he was born to rule
And the scorn-fish was a fool.

        1930

THE MAGNANIMOUS SUN

The Sun
   Rises.
The Sun
   Sets.
The Sun sees a lot
   He
Kindly
   Forgets!

1930

THE PHILOSOPHER

THE SUN IS AN INVENTOR

Beginning the preamble of my walk with hill and sky,
   I sing of mud, and dust.
Above this tree I love so well, the birds are beating
   high. Only the cities rust.
The sun may wreck the overborne, and blind the
   sweating eye. But I am a still pool.
And buzz his queer derision, when business captains
   cry. But I am wild, and cool.
The sun's the gadfly of the town, the ox-like hides to
   sting. My soul is looking wide.   5
The sun's a young inventor, who will rectify the thing
   he does with cruel pride.
Hurrah for the cold seas, the young trees, the bumblebees!

THE SUN IS AN ENGINEER

The city street, one hell of heat, seems to solidify. How
   will he make the place
The powerhouse of his ice plant, and teach men to
   comply with Christmas moods, and grace?
Oh, he is heaven's engineer, will make the summer
   cool, will boil good brains, down there,   10
Where city towers are incubi, inventors play the fool,
   then fight toward frozen air.
Always the sun has goaded man, with his schoolmaster
   stare. Much schooling still remains.
Some *dry-ice fan-and-wheel device*, cheap as an
   armchair, will come from sun-cooked brains.
Hurrah for the cold seas, the young trees, the bumblebees!

THE SUN INVENTS NATURE

Under some weird attic roof, the cold air, pouring down
  (next Christmas, it may be)   15
Will help some deep brain think it out, glorify the town,
  and set the winter free
Through summers that come after! Remembering at
  last (equipped to think it through)
The source of winter lives with spring, and neither
  holds men fast, if they will hope anew!
Meanwhile my sun *invents* outdoors, and is my best
  ally. Our house is the cool grass.
My sun's the epic-maker, and spills the sunset-dye.
  Who cares if chances pass?   20
Hurrah for the cold seas, the young trees, the bumblebees!

NORTHWARD, ALONG THE SEACOAST

Now I will take a seacoast hike, north, to the teeming
  farms, to finish this long year.
And rise against the army of my city-bred alarms, and
  lose the factory fear.
Every poet goes with me, and writes upon the sky. I
  cannot feel the rain.
Oh, tree-born cloud-compellers, and Yankee Samurai!
  Rain makes us grow like grain.   25
The gleemen help the sun invent, and glorify, the deep,
  help it splash and reel.
The League of Young Inventors, who have the town
  to keep, do not so well, with steel.
Hurrah for the cold seas, the young trees, the bumblebees!

THE NEW TIME-CLOCK

My *HEART-BEAT* is my time-clock. It is not a feeble
  thing. There's a devil in my feet.
I may fumble, fry, and stumble, but I have a tune to
  sing. My war has no retreat.   30
No longer will I hide behind the time-clock, and the
  bench. The sun ticks off my days.
This bench of rock will satisfy. I watch the shadows
  blench. I watch the sunflower blaze.
Now I will be a bumblebee, a bard of bright July;
  corn-tops my folderols!
Renounce all year my boarding house, for farm-wife's
  apple-pie! The scare-crows are my dolls.
Hurrah for the cold seas, the young trees, the
  bumblebees!   35

THE HIKER WELL-STARTED

Unfolding hillsides amplify, fern vistas now complete,
and make my soul more bold;
Teaching my wild feet to obey the deer-path still and
neat. I strip for inlets cold.
Land-winds, now, crumple up the smoke, clear the
sky's blue eye. My brain skips like a lamb.
Sea winds, now, tear the clouds apart, and start an
eagle-cry. Who knows the thing I am?
Friends! I will amble, with the tides, and qualify no
more; and find things *now* well made.   40
Defy myself, supply myself with staples, from God's
store, and, with the orchard, trade.
Hurrah for the cold seas, the young trees, the bumblebees!

THE BLUE-PRINTS

My books on Ford and Edison I'll read behind the hay,
and guy such men, sometimes.
And then I'll read friend Bill Benét, and prance to Jade
Cathay, knowing the whole world rhymes.
I will hear the threshers mumble, and watch the windrows
go. I may be asked to farm.   45
And find the key to some good things the sweating
farmhands know, some neolithic charm.
And I will study blue-prints the years make on the sky,
of better plans for streets,
When *all* four seasons fill each town, December, and
July, and *all* years are heart-beats.
Hurrah for the cold seas, the young trees, the bumblebees!

THE SUN IS AN ELECTRICIAN

Some day I will go back to town, and watch men satisfy
Schoolmaster-Sun, *and* school,   50
Returning well in time, to see sky blue-prints amplify,
of cities April-cool.
The sun, an electrician, will teach how to invent all
seasons and great years.
He is full of quaint devices. His strength is never spent.
He cures, when he appears.
Each newborn Jeremiah, each crying Malachi, turned
to a wild thrush, then,
Will change town-songs to hillside-songs, while vast
dreams verify, and men are kind to men.   55
Hurrah for the cold seas, the young trees, the bumblebees!

WILD HONEY

The sky's a cornfield of the Lord. He cuts deep with
  his plough. And all my troubles sleep.
The sun's the bumblebee of God, and makes wild honey
  now. And I must sow and reap.

     Summer, 1931

MENTOR GRAHAM, SCHOOL-MASTER ONE HUNDRED AND ONE YEARS AGO

Wondering if his training was a waste,
And if the prairie laughed his thought to scorn,
Thus muttered Graham to his Plutarch book,
With none to shepherd, though a teacher born: —

"I light my tallow dip again tonight   5
And say: — 'PERHAPS A MODERN BOY GOES BY,'
Hurried past door-ways where the watch-dogs growl —
The hearths the stranger dares not come too nigh.

"They sit in stolid circle at the table,
And never a son or daughter tells a tale.   10
The faithful mothers find no cheer at all.
No pretty baby's crow can much avail.

"New Salem now grows dull with homes unstirred.
The preachers prate in too-familiar words.
Whittlers loaf with wooden eyes, to talk   15
Of weeds and fences, barns and flocks and herds.

"Perhaps, tonight, through sorrow, snow and rain
Some storm-blown boy moves on, that we should keep
To bring us laughter round the Franklin Stove.
To show us why we dream and plough and reap.   20

"Perhaps, tonight, a conqueror comes on,
Ruler of weariness and fate and pain,
Within his pockets, note books of his youth,
Within his soul, great passions held in rein.

"No doubt, tonight, some wild boy passes by   25
Bearing wise sayings from the LAW BOOKS grim,
Or, it may be, a better light than mine,
More like Aladdin's, not, like this one, dim.

"All it will need—The oil, and wick, and flame,
And schoolhouse room, to keep the wind away,   30
I can provide. Ah, if a lamp he brings,
It shall be trimmed and burnished every day."

Thus, Mentor Graham thought, on New Year's night.
And 1830 died, with lonely wing.
But 1831 came in with pride.   35
Abe Lincoln found that schoolhouse in the spring.

    1910-1911, 1931

EPITAPH FOR HENRY FORD

We cannot conquer Time. Sit down. Breathe slowly.
Muse a little, since old Time is king.
The moth and rust will do their destined work
Upon us, though we polish everything.

And all our quaint attempts to beat the clock,   5
To ride Time down to death with hurrying wheel
Shall slowly end. We will build high his house,
And count his everlasting bondage real.

The moth, the rust, the ivy, and the rain,
The hail and snow, even today wear down   10
Each car that speaks of newness all too well,
Each pompous factory with its glittering crown.

The moth, the rust, the ivy, and the rain,
The hail, and snow, and wind, will, at the last
Enter the thinking heart of this, our race,   15
Until we love no future like the past.

    1910-1912, 1931

IS WISDOM SUCH A THING?

Now let no man or woman, good or great,
Plan to divide me from my deepest dream
Won through blood and tears and watching years,
And stop the budding thoughts, the songs astream.

Let them not think it Wisdom, Friendship, Faith,   5
To lead the feet I kiss away from me,
To drive me from the cabin of my heart,
Or break me there, the while I bow the knee.

What is this Wisdom that will vaunt itself,
Stab at my ribs with cutting pride of mind,   10
With hot irons touch my eyes till they are blind?
Is Wisdom such a thing, and so designed?

    1930-1931?

TO A GIRL IN A SUN SUIT

What was the veil of Eve?
The mist before sunrise.
What was the veil of Eve?
The mist before rain.
What was the veil of Eve?   5
The shower in June.

What was the veil of our mother?
The mist in the stars' eyes;
The tall wild grain
Ripening soon;   10
The dawn from the seas;
Hanging moss from the trees;
Then the shimmering, open,
Sea-beach noon;
Then the mist of the evening,   15
A green place entwining,
While the wind in the vine gave a tune.

What was the veil of Eve
That made the twilight complete?
The mist in her eyes   20
And the tears in the eyes of her lover,
Tall Adam, our young father,
Who fell on the ground
And held her dancing feet.

    1929-1931?

WHEN I GAVE MY LADY A DOUBLE ROSEBUD

If you are not as double as these are,
At least a picture floats somewhere near you—
It is a part in Heaven's name of yourself.
To you and your twin soul I must be true.

Oh, when you frown, no world remains at all   5
Except the sea-foam and the gray sea-wall!

Nothing defeats me if I keep my eyes
Close on that portrait near your laughing face.
There is the lamp outshining earthly light,
A portrait so invested with your grace   10
That it reflects but one thing in the world—
Your beauty's majesty unfurled.
The prophet-angels, flying at your side
Guide through the air that mirror winged and free
Made of clear agates from the Crystal Sea.   15

Therefore I give this double rose—one furled,
The other, half-uncurled.
The furled one for your love-lit earthly soul,
The other for your saintly aureole.

   1924-1925?

THE POET IN THE ORCHARD OF ART

Where many a silvery treacherous thing abides,
Today through the garden of art he runs and glides,
Where is rest from pride, but is no rest from gleaming,
Where he sees the trees of silver and diamond beaming,
Drooped over walls, with boughs and petals streaming.   5

On to the orchard of civilized fruits he goes,
Singing this rhyme to the tune of a tame brook humming.
But over the top of the walls the artist knows
He must climb the rose-vine
And run to the uttermost wild,   10
If he would know and paint as a prophet divining—
A prophet of red men's thoughts since he was a child,
And given to catamount hunting, to nugget mining.

   1929-1931?

IN MEMORY

Frances Frazee Hamilton

The valors of an ancient race,
The rigors of an inbred clan,
The forest lights of human grace,
The cornfield flowers where spring began:

These were the making of her soul,   5
These made the power beneath her pride;
And so she danced to reach her goal,
And with this strength she lived and died.

1930-1931?

EPITAPH FOR JEB STUART

Let peacocks sing round this, my grave,
Even if they shriek and squawk;
Old dragons hunt and find this grave,
Even if they have to walk;
Red roosters crow above this grave,   5
Even if historians rave, calm professors misbehave,
Furies come forth from the cave.

Let white swans preen themselves and fly
In circles round this cemetery,
Or eagles quarrel above these lawns   10
Even if they swoop to kill
The peacocks and the dragon brave,
The roosters and the swans.
For sinful pride shall lift my head,
Up from this wild and well-watched bed,   15
After ten thousand dawns.

1930-1931?

UNPUBLISHED POEMS

and

Juvenilia

1890-1931

Reproduced Exactly from Lindsay's Manuscripts.

COME

He that is weary come, be refreshed,
He that is thirsty come and drink,
"I," says the savior "I am he
I am that fountain clear and free.

Come sinner, Come, why longer delay?   5
Hear what the Master has to say:
I have been crucified for thee.
Why not come? now come to me.

You may not live through the coming night,
Why do you waver this battle to fight?   10
The Master calls you with pitying voice;
You'll choose Heaven, or Hell, which is your choice?

If you obey his voice and follow him today,
Then with a joyfull heart he will say:
Come blessed servant, come to me,   15
Inherit the kingdom prepared for thee.

        1890

    THE EASTER-PRAYER OF A WHITE ROSE
        TO AN EASTER LILY

"Oh thou with shining crown—
Hope that is holiest under the skies
Lily, whiter than Angel's wings
Thy glory never dies.
Thy days shall know the worship   5
Of ten thousand butterflies—
Bright fairies pray when they pass thy feet
With fervent songs and anthems meet
For the Goddess of the flowers.
Thy purity, thy royalty in a holy halo shine   10
Thy glory, tall White Lily,
Is a glory all divine."

        Spring, 1897

THE NONSENSE TREE
  Dedicated to A. P. W.

The nonsense sea
Is smooth and green
The sunset tide
All golden sheen
And who is there   5
To see and know
That whining winds
Have ceased to blow?
Where the sea grows murky
Brown and dank   10
The lava-rock
With the wave-worn bank
Breaks the endless
Shimmer-sheen
Of the sunset tide   15
All golden green.
The nonsense tree
Through the lava stone
Has writhed its roots
And sturdy grown.   20
The tree is fair
As a promise fleet
The bloom is fair
As the nightshade sweet.
The leaves are fair   25
As the waves would be
If ever a storm
Should strike the sea
A wind of folly
From afar   30
From the nonsense sun
In his nonsense car.
Oh nonsense tree
What a thing to be
On a nonsense rock   35
By a nonsense sea
Oh senseless, illogical
Nonsense tree!

    1898

ASTARTE

You are holy in your glory, bright lady of the skies—
As I move beneath your presence, half-whisperings
    arise—
The murmured prayers of blossoms that nod and close
    their eyes.

As I muse with wayward wending, far friend, thy charm
    is wrought.
Deep I drink the potent potion my haggard soul has
    sought—   5
My weary brain is kneeling, pale peace confounds my
    thought.

Thy meek madness is a mercy in hearts all torn with toil—
A wildness sweet with grandure, dream-sheening on the
    soil—
Cool-flooding restless longings that seethe and burn and
    boil.

See, the little clouds with homage will leave your path
    apart—   10
The stars are dim before you, full lovingly they part
With half their gold in tribute and you pour it in my heart.

    August 1898

WHEN LIFE GREETS LIFE

Ah the blood is warm
When the blood is young
Then life greets life
With a reckless tongue
All sighs are vain   5
All songs are dumb
And the stars bow down
And the stars bow down
When the thundering heart
Bids the wild words come   10
When life greets life
When the wild words come!

    Summer, 1900

SONG OF THE MICHIGAN WAVES

I.

Oh Castles rising in the West good hero-hearts you hold,
They man your thousand watch-towers, they guard your
   goods and gold.
And Hunger and Fear defend you and Love and Fate
   extend you,
They will bind for you the Oceans yet, they will hide the
   earth in your iron net
Before our song is old.   5

II.

Oh rampart-crags of stone and steel, within your ribbed
   recesses
The pleasure-shrines and treasure-shrines of liberty
   that blesses
Shrines of Art and holiness, gateways crammed with
   Zeal;
Tomorrow—Temples of the world, where all the nations
   kneel!

III.

Oh Laughter's dreaming Capital: oh barracks stern of
   Truth!   10
Soon—darling daughter of the Lake you rule the tribes
   uncouth:
Your dauntless soul shall see the day when London
   Moscow Mandalay
Shall tremble their temple-stones and fanes of Art and
   Traffic-thrones
Shall fall before you. Great is Youth!

IV.

We spread your power for Love's sweet sake. Proud,
   generous to undertake;   15
The Spirit of the Continent: Chicago, good and bold!
We serve the Queen of Youth-unspent, tender, mad,
   magnificent,
      The Queen of Love and Labor,
      The Queen of Love and Gold!

   1901

THE GREAT SUPPER

Come feast for God, then die in fight,
Ere pleasure palls, while song enthralls—
Ironsides of the Dawning, revellers tonight!

Our captains are in Avalon
Nor shall they soon awake;   5
There Lincoln, Cromwell, Arthur sleep—
While the sin-sick earth must groan and weep
And all their deeds unmake.
But burning in our hearts we keep
Their memories. We take   10
The sword of Cromwell and the Lord
To smite again the hosts abhorred
With foolish hot delight!
To scorn what every age has said,
To rally round our holy dead   15
To charge where angels fear to tread
And set this old world right!

     Fall, 1901

FAREWELL TO CHRISTMAS

New Years has past.
And the holly is dry
And the carpet crackles
Where the crisp leaves lie.

As I step to the window where the frost-
   weeds shine   5
I wish that Christmas again were mine—
And I take the holly wreaths
Dingy and dry
And I feed them to the grate-fire.
Christmas—good-by!   10

     February 1902

THE IDOL AND THE GHOSTS

We, fairy hopes, that once were lovely:
Ghosts of his dreaming days gone by . . . .

Here we weep for his foolish failure
And cry to thee with our hands held high.

　　Thy throne is way above the dark   5
　　Queen Hope, that loved us not.
　　Oh woman idol, unforgotten
　　By ghosts she well forgot:

Who are we, to beg thy pity?
Who are we, to pray?   10
We are things that gibber for the light . . .
For Life, and yesterday.

　　April 1902

THE MYRAPOSA LILY

Oh myraposa with the stately stem
Leaning upon the young stream's hem—
You are a stream already and a sea
With green jade leaves like ripples and like waves
And white jade petals smooth as foam can be—   5
So loose your roots and trust the tiny creek—
So seek you the Atlantic in his caves
And Sea shall marry Sea
And yearning shall be done
As on the night when the Shulamite   10
Wedded David's son.

　　November 1902

THE SONG OF THE TEMPLE SPARROWS
　　AFTER THE TEMPLE FELL

Gone are the roofs and the eaves of Jehova.
There no longer the sparrow fledges.
Let us go, Let us sing in the Highways and Hedges.
For the Priests are dead. There is naught to find
But dogs of the street—all starved, unkind: 5
They eat the burnt flesh of the martyr's cold bones.
And the night mists that rise from the overthrown stones
Poison the birds from the highways and hedges.

Oh Sparrows dear, and swallows kind
Let us play in the dust with the halt and the blind,   10
Beside their paths there are crumbs to find,
And the Lord lives yet in the roots of the grass
That are soft to the foot through the Autumn hours
And warm to the taste while the blown snows pass.
And the Lord lives yet in the Summer flowers —   15
Yea, the Lord comes down in Springtime showers,
Let us live content in the Highways and Hedges.

    January 1903

TO MARY OF BETHANY

Tomorrow come and haunt me, tomorrow come and
    haunt me,
Tomorrow come and haunt me, oh brown sweet girl
    of Bethany
Borne upon the bosom of the Gleaming Garden of Art!
Bring no barren fig tree nor olive of Gethsemane
Nor any breaking heart —   5
Bring only boughs of Bethany
And he who wooed in Bethany
Christ the first of Chivalry —

And I will bring a prayerful maid
And lovers dear we four will be   10
And preach all holy revelry
To one another merrily —
Tomorrow, tomorrow
In the Gleaming Garden of Art!

We are cumbered with much serving —   15
Oh teach us Mary, you have learned
To choose the better part!
And we are undeserving
But teach us rest and laughter fast
Till quickly we are pure of heart —   20
And meekness we might learn at last
Within the Garden of Art!
There is peace from pride, rest from pride, genial rest
    in the Garden of Art,
Yellow Garden, Holy Garden, Gleaming Gleaming
    Garden of Art!

    January 1903

SONS OF THE MIDDLE WEST

Where, after all, is the soul of the nation?
Why do we turn to the East with yearning
When our fathers come to the West with yearning
Generation on Generation?
Live in the West! There is no returning   5
From the soil where buried breasts are burning.

Maybe buried after Lincoln
They lived through Freedom's second dawn.
Maybe pierced with Indian arrows
By cabins rude as the nests of sparrows   10
Or wagons wandering to the Sunset
On strange old plains in the days long gone
Or swept with prairie fires or floods
They died with their toiling all undone
Near the Gray Ohio or Black Missouri   15
Or Wan and Haunted Sangamon.

Say not—"That wild land is no more.
Whose voice was in the voice of Lincoln!"
Yea, Lincoln—how he haunteth us!
And unseen fires from buried breasts   20
Rise into the living hearts of us.
No other soil is haunted thus.
What has the East for us?

        February 1903

THE SOUL OF LINCOLN

Who had Freedom for a bride?
Angels cannot tell.
Some whisper it was Lucifer
Aeons ere he fell.
Leagues from angel town   5
Are Freedom's mistlands wrought
Of the wreck of ancient battle
Where sighing angels fought.

Fifty years ago
A wingéd censer came   10
And set the Widowed heart
Of Freedom all aflame.

Yea, that winged censer
Fell at Freedom's feet,
And cast a brilliant light   15
On her three children sweet.
We know not whence it came
Who gave it life or why.
"From Hell it soared" the angels say
"To terrify the sky."   20

Too bright for all but Her
Were lines of light that came
From ashes in the censer,
The mists were set aflame.
With Freedom's sad consent   25
Her strongest eldest child
Hurled with fierce disdain
Down down the censer wild.
Her tender daughters kissed
Freedom the forlorn   30
When the Plague that left their house
In our helpless earth was born.

It reached the earth unseen,
A mystic spirit-light
And gave a second soul   35
To a weary man of might.
Lincoln from that hour
Led us till he fell.
Our hearts, burnt out, are gleaming still
With fires from Heaven and Hell.   40
Oh foolish love of Freedom!
She dwelleth far away,
Beyond the fires of Heaven or Hell,
Beyond the Judgement Day.

Where is Lincoln now?   45
I see him humbly stand,
Hot ashes in his heart,
In the Gate of Heaven's land.
While hosts of sanctified
Go by with gay disdain.   50
(Their harps are chained to them
By many a jewelled chain.)
No balm or alms for him
Who burns for Liberty!
A choking, ashen heart   55
Shall be his penalty.

Far off are Freedom's mistlands.
Lincoln dreams them fair.
What profit is the dream
Of their wild and bitter air?   60
Yea, who shall be the bridegroom
Of Ancient Liberty?

Her children keep her hid
Jealous bitterly.
Only to dream of her—   65
That is Victory!

    1903

LET US RISE AND SING

Rise, sing of the Eagle crowned
While all the nations stare!
The while our Spangled Banner
A hundred stars shall wear:
Fit canopy to shelter   5
The Coronation chair
When Haughty South America
Shall bring her tribute there!

Sing of the Love of the Eagle
For his brown unwilling bride   10
That ragged South America
And her ragged Spanish pride:
Sing of the Bridal day
And the Golden chains of the Bride!

Maybe we will doubt our song,   15
Maybe we will grieve,
Maybe we will sing until
We joyfully believe!

    1 January 1904

MIDNIGHT ALLEYS
  (or The Alley Witch)

Witch's little daughter—
With the face that peers

Down the dumb dark alleys—
Why these trembling fears?

"I fear, because the Shadows   5
Prophesy, though dumb.
They show by signs our town shall die
And oaken forests come.
I smile, because I see
A forest as it blooms.   10
I weep. The forest-shadows
Are camped on broken Tombs.

"Yet trees that day shall hear
A Prophet-Shadow say
'Men will build a city.   15
Our power shall pass away!
Again in silent alleys
We shall nod and creep
And witches wandering by
Shall laugh at us and weep!'"   20

January 1904

THE FIVE DRAGONS

I dreamed I was a Laundryman last night,
I dreamed I sat entranced with open eye—
And five bright Dragons squirmed from out the stove
And round among the shirts began to fly.

First Dragon:

Quack-Quack—I'm the Dragon Mock-Duck   5
My Bill is a Laundry Bill
My Tongue is a Joss Stick
My Crown is a Flat Iron
My Eye is an Opium Pill.

Second Dragon:

From foam in the harbors of Frisco   10
I Dragon Chop-Suey was made:
By an Old Buddhist Priest
As a Sightseer's feast
For the Strictly American Trade.

Third Dragon:

Beware—I'm the Opium Fish   15
At first you will find me a friend,
But I eat up your clothes
And I eat up your house
And I eat you alive in the end.

Fourth Dragon:

Fear me not, I'm the Dragon named Work—   20
Though ugly and hard on the eye
Though I flop round the floor till my feathers are sore
And never able to fly
I'll be making you sigh by and by.

Fifth Dragon:

Beware—I'm the Fire-Cracker-King   25
Perpetually coughing up smoke.
When I speak, I explode:
Get out of the road—
And just as he spoke—I awoke.

    1909

PARENTS

My mother loves geraniums.
She pets them winter long.
When spring is here she plants them out
In spring I turn to song.

She hates the dandelion and   5
She digs it from the soil.
I sit quite still and write about
The worth of "honest toil."

My father works without a stop.
He scarcely goes to bed,   10
With potent drugs he wakes the world
That thinks that it is dead.

I rise quite late and write how all
The "Idle rich" are vile.

For six long languid hours I write,   15
Then sit around awhile.

     Summer, 1911

I TURNED MY HEAD AWAY

I turned my head away,
Reviling not the man,
And I forgave him soon.
I walked in happiness all afternoon.
I slept that night   5
A sleep like death
And killed him in my dream.

I turned my head away.
I loved my neighbor's wife.
Looking not again   10
I bade that love good-by.
Forgot her shining eye.
Most pious of young men.
I slept that night
A sleep like death   15
And killed her in my dream.

I turned my head away.
I would not curse my God.
Or look upon the crime
That made me doubt his name,   20
And very holy fame.
I loved my God, and sang
Throughout the afternoon.
Sang with all my life and breath.
Till I saw the stars agleam.   25
I slept that night
A sleep like death
And cursed God in my dream.

     c. 1920?

WRITTEN FOR THE EUCALYPTUS TREES

And now I look to the Eucalyptus trees
Across the road from this place,
And wonder at their classic power,

Their aspiration and their plumes and grace.
And I say that they will lead the souls   5
Of all who live beside them, in true prayer
Up toward the heavenly air: —
That they will make all worthy singers
Who know them, into such aspiring men
That the proud Plutarch hearts will come again,   10
Or rather come for the first time, because we know
That Plutarch dreamed those men.
It is not so —
They walked this earth below.
They rather walked the proud roads of his mind   15
High dreams of humankind —
The pattern, not the substance. But they come
Such men of pillared power, such souls no longer dumb;
When, after many days
California centuries beat the drum —   20
Where, in a thousand years, these Eucalyptus trees
Make a finished temple of these hills for birds and bees,
Make a greater classic than the nations ever knew
Of the California women,
And men,   25
And flowers, and towers,
And bread and honey-dew.

    Spring, 1920

THE MASSACRE

Death to desire.
Death to desire.
St. Michael draw your sword and slay.
Right and left
Clear the path   5
Of cupids that
Ensnare my way.

They weave across
From hedge to hedge
The cobwebs of   10
What seems but naught,
Yet they become
A barb-wire snare,
And feet and hands
And life are caught.   15

Death to desire.
Death to desire.
At least, good Michael
Bring to me
A sword, new edged,   20
On the whirling moon,
On that grindstone good
The new full moon,
That I may cut
My bound feet free.   25
But if you will
With a mortal ride,
Oh Michael guard
My weak left side.

The bones and skulls   30
Of cupids slain
Will strew this hedge path
All year through,
To testify,
And certify   35
To what a deadly spring
They knew.

So down the road
My saint and I
Will bravely smite   40
A great love waits
Far at the end
Of this hedge path,
Behind the waiting
Bamboo gates.   45

A sibyl sleeps
On the cold ledge,
Beside the window
In the court.
God make me   50
Her eternal guest.
She is my soul
She is my quest,
Worth all the cupids
And their sport.   55

Her name is
Springfield magical,

Although she sleeps so far away.
Her name is Avanel the good.
Her name is Our Millennial day.   60
Yet she will spread kind mundane wings,
And live here fairy-human wife,
In Springfield in the purple years
Of laughing and eternal life.

    c. 1921-1922

GOING TO THE SUN. WATERFALLS,
   REMEMBERED LONG AFTER

There vision, whim and sermon alternate,
Sometimes the flowers preach, sometimes debate.
And he who drinks those Waterfalls of fate,
May be possessed
Of words for which all burning and deserving
   lovers wait.   5

Yet so inconsequent
Nonsense by some Waterfalls is sent.
It takes a long time afterward to know
Which was the soul's glow,
Which was gigantic mountain laughter's flow,   10
Which was the soul's gigantic glow.

The sermon spoils the song, and then the song
Helps the sermon, helps to make it strong.
The whim destroys the Hieroglyph
And then   15
The Hieroglyph returns to form again,
I make no apology my friend,
The heaviest sermon is at the Book's far end.

    c. 1922

"NOW COMES A CARTOON LETTER"

Now comes a cartoon letter sent
To bold George Bellows and Rockwell Kent,
Earl Brewster and George Mather Richards.
I say to Rockwell Kent, "I guess
I too have scrambled in the Wilderness."   5

I say to Bellows, "I have seen fights
Between the rains and the glacial heights."
I say to him "This boxing bout
I draw is between the bleeding lout
The Memory of The City and   10
The Sunlight on an untouched land."
I say to both, "The only praise
I ever sought in all my days
That meant so very much to me,
Was from men like you." We drew together   15
When Henri made it springtime weather,
There on fifty-seventh street
When Chase was still alive and fleet,
When he stood on his tip-toes to glower,
And praised great Whistler by the hour,   20
And told us just the way to draw,
And all the wonders that he saw
In painting fishes in a plate.
But Chase was kind and great of soul
And great of pride, and put strong fight   25
In the harried students, braced them right,
Bought their pictures first, nor waited
To have the real ones long debated.
But Chase was old, and soon to go
To help the angels paint the sun,   30
But Henri was the dashing one,
The hero of young students then,
The raider of each pirate's den,
He was a catamount for fight,
He caught the student, put him right.   35
Would argue with the dullest boy,
And fill his breast with curious joy
For though he made the youngster weep,
He spoke the truth, and it cut deep.
The city now is full of whims.   40
The Greenwich Village Follies rims
The edge of new Olympus; now
Only the brave are low of brow.
Hysteria and elegance
And Sophomoric promise dance,   45
In that Bohemia that came
In the wake of Henri's fight and fame.
They see him as we saw Chase then,
A Nestor of the fighting men,
And do not know their glorious force   50
Came from his pioneering course.

He dragged sick dreamers from their pen
And made them Andrew Jackson men,
The ribbon of their waiting days
Was Henri's overwhelming praise.   55
And so I bring these squibs to you,
For my first public art review
As I used to pin them on the line
And wait to hear you come to mine
In the school on fifty-seventh street,   60
When Chase was still alive and fleet
When we drew and rowed together
And Henri made it springtime weather.

I here present some picture writing
Some Hieroglyphics you are sighting.   65
The United States Hieroglyphic
Is like the Egyptian, quite terrific,
One of them is the Paine Sky rocket,
A nuisance lighted in your pocket,
It's like a thought within the breast   70
That will not keep its smothering nest.

        1922

AVANEL BOONE FLIES FROM THE HEARTHFIRE WITH
AN ESCORT OF FLYING, FLAMING BOOKS

The cat was astonished, yes indeed,
Turn to the picture, re-read,
The drawing upside down spells cat,
And sideways it spells mouse,
Writing and drawing, close together   5
In this humorous toy-house!
I do not think that drawings should be puns, except
    to point
A special tale or give a limber joke a limber joint.
But still this helps an argument.
I think pen drawing should be sent   10
Along the road the high priests went
In Egypt the magnificent.
Their lion cats still led them on
To where the writing god had gone.
Thoth, the god of writing, reigned   15
Until the power of Egypt waned
For every scribe and artist

Writing and drawing were as one,
Each scroll and illustrated sun,
Each wall for imagists alone.   20
Picture and writing on the stone
Were hewn as one. There was no change
Wherever Thoth, the scribe, had range,
To write or draw about the mice
They used precisely one device.   25
To write or draw a lion Sphinx
They used the same good pens and inks,
And if they spelled the lion's name
As we would do, yet all the same
They drew him on the margin there,   30
He marched around, and took the air.
I know Whistler's words by heart,
We shouted for his flying start
When he shook Europe off its feet,
That book of his, I found it sweet   35
When we were twenty and twenty-three,
He set my heart with courage free
His art of making enemies
Would fill me with rhapsodies.
But because it is the commentary   40
Of all his works, he's literary,
His epigrams still fill the air,
His little book is open there
Quoted with a special tang
Wherever his gray pictures hang.   45
His arrangements are made literary,
By his own funny commentary.
I think the Hieroglyphics stand
The substance of the human hand
The basis of all art, and still   50
Songs and pictures work their will
Blended with each other so
Their separate ways they hardly know.

And here my song ends with a girl
Whost breast gives light and sparks awhirl,   55
From the rays of light go out
Daisies festooned round her head
Daisies round her throat and waist,
That drip with fire; and books make haste,
Flying, to follow her   60
Out of a hearthfire; and they stir
Like autumn leaves about the floor

Near the hearth, then up they soar
Following their lady on,
To the sunset and the dawn,   65
Following a Hieroglyphic girl
With unbound hair and arms awhirl,
The Lady Avanel of Dreams,
Maiden of wonders and of schemes,
Who flies from the earth to heaven, but comes   70
At the sound of patriotic drums
To build the Hieroglyphic towns
Of all this big United States
That for her restless spirit waits.

      1922

THE SUN IS A SPHINX

      (Maspero and other Egyptologists tell us that the Sphinx
is a statue of the God Ra Harmakhis, or the rising and
setting sun.)

The riddle of the stone is but the riddle overhead.
"Our Lord the Sun is a great Sphinx," the priests of
      Egypt said.

Woe to those men who cannot find a strangeness in the light;
Woe to those men who have no fear, until the black of night;
Who feel no awe at dawn, and see only a bright light there
When Ra is rising in his might, a lion from the lair!

      c. 1922-1923

THE PEACOCK'S DAUGHTER

Now are there wall-flowers in this place,
Leaning against the sea-washed wall,
Too proud to dance beneath hot stars
Or hear the ocean boil and call?
Step out upon the pine-boards, friends,   5
They're neatly laid, and smell of wine,
Magnolia flowers and turpentine.
This girl will lead you in the chase,
With straightened back outstrut you all.
She does not care if she is plain,   10

Or that her brain is rather small.
She lives in secrets well to know,
The open secrets, learned in light,
When Juno's birds trod amorous snow,
And clouds, on one Olympian height.   15
She trusts her breed, that glittering line —
Since pride first wrecked or ruled the world.
So, little wall-flower by my hand,
Now let your glory be unfurled.
The kindness in your ardent heart   20
Is better than the peacock tread,
So she may dance the steps of old,
But love will live, when fowls are dead.

     1923-1924

THE STARS FOR CHANDELIERS

Put out the lanterns now and see
These southern stars are chandeliers.
Now are the breasts as cool as snow,
Paler the sunburnt cavaliers.
Softer the music on the floor,   5
Louder the wind in surf and trees,
Be proud indeed, young beauties, now,
And bring your rascals to their knees.
Make them swear everything, forsooth,
That you want sworn and pledged and sealed.   10
What is a mere man, anyway?
Now let your iron souls be revealed.
Make them abandon every plan
That represents a lifetime hope,
For beauties have far stranger plans   15
And beauties have another scope.

If these boys be honorable,
Reserve your power for better hours,
And plan to help them in their race
With Time that still pursues, devours,   20
Respecting neither men nor flowers.

It is not dark, for now your eyes
Accustomed to the night so sweet
See colors, forms and lights no eye
Can spy at noonday on the street.   25

If now your boys seem grown up men
The stars have told the truth, my dears,
The stars are more than ball-room lights,
The stars are more than chandeliers.

    1923-1924

MY BITTER RIVALS

Plenty of other egoists will come to wipe me out
From the hearts of all the neighbors I love best,
They will come from my own gang,
From my deepest, closest kin,
But you, my dear, will love me without rest.   5

You, my dear, when the world-storm is over
Will hold me in some mountain, there in Mars,
Against your holy side,
Always my budding bride,
While we look down at the spluttering earth,   10
And the high-riding stars,
(Old Milton's battle-cars,)
Spluttering comet-sparks
And trying to impress us while we climb and laugh in Mars.

    1923-1924

"I AM TRAVELLING TOO FAST TO VOTE"

   (An Autobiographical Fragment)

I am travelling too fast to vote —
To comfort the old man in his grave
I would vote the Democratic ticket —
I want to help to make the world behave —
I will use the Initiative and the referendum —   5
I will vote for free judges and not be a slave —
I will vote for free schools and not be a slave —
But when it comes to a President
To comfort the old man in hisgrave —
I will never turn my coat. I will vote, I will vote,   10
I will vote the Democratic ticket.

My father, half blind and raging,
Told me of Kentucky overrun —

Of the old old home destroyed by soldier and gun—
Robbed of every horse, every acre, every slave—   15
The family scattered, Grandfather going blind,
Everything destroyed but the pride of the mind—
My father Vachel told me over and over
And I think of all the silent kin under every stone—
And to comfort the old man in his grave,   20
My father Vachel, my Grandfather Nicholas,
My great grandfather—Nicholas Lindsay—
To comfort my own in the grave
I will vote the Democratic ticket.

I remember my Grandfather ordering my curls   25
Cut from my head to make me a man—
Grim Vachel Lindsay blind, poor and old—
But he still had his vanities in his way—
An old silk hat and a gold headed cane—
I remember him there an old King in a dream,   30
In a tiny cottage by a waterfall stream.
Grandmother busy there, with still-Indian eyes—
Eyes deep and black—Indian's eyes—
Eyes like Old Kentucky—a Mammoth-Cave of dream
Waiting on my Grandfather passionately, faithfully—   35
He kept telling his sons to stand together
To stand by the clan through the desperate weather
And to comfort the strange old man in his grave
I will vote, I will vote the Democratic ticket.

I remember daguerreotypes, daguerreotypes,
    daguerreotypes—   40
One of my great Grandfather Nicholas Vachel Lindsay—
With an Andrew Jackson air and an old Virginia style,
With an old Virginia style and not a * * * * *

    1924?

YOUNG DAUGHTER OF THE ANCIENT SUN

Young daughter of the Ancient Sun,
Ambassador from Nikko's shrine,
Bushido rules obedient hearts
Wherever you may dance or dine.
I see a circle on the floor   5
Of cherry-flowers, when you hold court,
And from great Jimmu Tenno's sky
You bring to us a new report.

"The codes of Old Japan are dim,"
Some men have said. It is not so.   10
Any Iyeyasu stands to guard
Wherever girls like you may go.
Once I was young, and then I heard
Only of Athens, and Japan.
Once I was young, and wise men taught   15
All art bowed down to Fuji San.
In the name of this my youth, that still
Studies in art schools now long gone,
My youth that I must still obey
Though new arts put new trappings on,   20
To Utamaro still I cry
To Hiroshige give my praise,
And Hokusai great Whistler loved,
In golden days, in hero days.

I can but bow to you and draw   25
With scrawling hand my whimsy here,
But Jimmu Tenno shakes the sky
And all his islands still are dear.

          1924-1925

BEFORE THE ORATION

While we wait
Let us kneel, in soul,
Before the Gate
Of Milton's Paradise—

Let us watch the aureole   5
Of the guardian angels
That control old
Milton's Paradise.

Let us dream of
Innocence—   10
White as polar ice
Hot as the sun's heart
That leaves the spirit whole.
Let us dream of grandeurs
That give us self-control,   15
Let us dream of tenderness—
Upon a violet bedded knoll—
In Milton's Paradise.

Let us be just eight years old—
Making antiquity our goal   20
The days of holy nakedness,
And kissing twice and thrice
And Milton's Paradise.

Let us feel the aching
Wonderful, heart-breaking,   25
That comes when hearts are yielded whole
As innocent as leaping fawns
Yet paying the whole price,
Without one breath held back
With eyes that blend like stars and dawns   30
In Milton's Paradise.

Let us stand at Eden's gate
Stand and knock and pay the toll
That lets us in forever
The toll of perfect Innocence—   35
In Milton's Paradise.

Let us take there deep delight
Eating apples red and white
Giving each other sweet advice—
A rose leaf with each apple there   40
Eaten to keep us strong and fair—
Eaten to keep us proud and pure
In Milton's Paradise.

Oh there are rose-leaves in a heap
Oh there is solitude so deep   45
We hear the furthest rivers creep
So let us pay the price—
We hear the butterfly's white soul
We hear the little lilies ring—
The lilies of the valley toll and sing—   50
We hear the rainbow's
Breathing prayer—
It's cheap at any price
To hear the rainbow's
Breathing prayer,   55
To hear the glow-worm do and dare—
To hear the littlest shadows leap,
To be like fairies there.
Oh there is solitude so deep—
We sing each other there to sleep—   60

By breathing—half-asleep a prayer—twice and thrice
Naked and warm and stripped of care
In Milton's Paradise.

   5 November 1925

TODAY THERE IS A MARKET FOR PINK BUBBLES

   (For the Bulletin of the Author's League of America.)

"Blow pink bubbles,
Trembling slave,"
Said the tyrant, Monday morning.
I blew a bubble,
And a rainbow found it.   5
"Today there is a market for pink bubbles,"
Said the tyrant.
I blew a bubble. Then.........................
A rainbow ....
Bound it.   10

"Blow red bubbles,
Trembling slave,"
Said the tyrant, Tuesday morning.
"Blow green bubbles,
Trembling slave,"   15
Said the tyrant, Wednesday morning.
"Blow white bubbles,
Trembling slave,"
Said the tyrant, Thursday morning.
I blew a bubble   20
And a rainbow...................................
Crowned it.

"Blow black bubbles,
Trembling slave,"
Said the tyrant, Friday morning;   25
"Today there is a market for black bubbles,"
Said the tyrant.
I blew a bubble ....
And a rainbow...................................
Wound it.   30

So kicked the soapsuds over,
And he took my pipe away.
But still I blow my bubbles,

With a wheat straw,
Every day.   35
I blow a bubble ....
With a rainbow ....
Round it.

    28 January 1926

NEW FASHIONS

The bonnets of love, my lady,
Are made in new fashions, each day.
Each pretty milliner goes to her work
With sunbeams stitching away.

The bonnets of love, my lady,   5
Are made of tall roses and plumes,
Petals and thorns,
Deep grasses and morns,
Blue pansies, and bleeding-heart blooms.

    1930

IN PRAISE OF WIT

"And the night shall be filled with music,
"And the cares that invest the day,
"Shall fold their tents like the Arabs,
"And silently steal away."

      *   *   *   *   *   *

When I have been on Pullman cars
For three hard days (accursed thing)
I wear my carpet slippers out
At home, and read from Stoddard King.
For two long witty days I read,   5
And more than once I give a shout:
For Stoddard in his subtle way,
Has pointed all my troubles out,
And given all the world-old cures,
Sanity, sacred or profane,   10
Has pointed up the laughs and lures,
And shown my ravings are inane.

When I have quarreled with honest friends
And known that I was in the wrong,
He prompts me to apologize   15
By letter, book, or dulcet song.

When I have read the roaring blades
Who roast the universe or fair
I read this man, and he agrees;
But recommends a change of air.   20
Some universe across the street,
Some gentle throng a mile away;
Where wit will conquer gods and men
And make some tragedies half gay.

Realist, Idealist, exact in phrase, exact in rhyme, 25
Proteus, chameleon, and disappearing rainbowman,
He tells the truth so well, we grin.
Catch him at kicking, if you can!

What is your list of scorns and scars?
He lists in plainest words the lot.   30
And gives no quarter to your foes,
His words are plain: they get him not.

They think him highbrow and obscure:
The sure defense of all good men,
Because our bullies understand   35
Only the wolf-growl from the den!
The plainest talk is lost on those
Who think their foes must growl or grunt,
To laugh with Aristophanes
Is but a harmless highbrow stunt!   40

If they were tyrant Greeks of old,
That conquering laugh would get the hook,
But since our lords for fifty years
Will be the men who scorn a book,
But since the next bright fifty years   45
Such men will read but stock reports,
And all their valor, all their pride
Is tackling immigrants in court,
A man of plain American speech
Who writes the good word, because he must,   50
Is lost upon their feckless brains,
They never know they take his dust!

They think a poet proud and high
Is provender for Women's Clubs:
The business men who buy a book 55
Are dangerous idiots and dubs.

They do not know in fifty years
Laughter itself will shake them down;
They do not know this very hour
That wit, not business, rules the town. 60

They do not know, since time began,
An honest laugh could wreck the pride
Of autocrats and royal rats
And set their glittering crowns aside.

Villon outlives the lords of France 65
With not a word against their deeds:
Merely by honest rhyme and word:
His sons prevail, and they are weeds.

For wit can shake the heavens down,
Laughing the half gods from their throne, 70
For wit can make the great sky clear,
Leaving the true gods high and lone.

    c. 1930

REMARKS BY THE CAPTAIN OF A TRAMP STEAMER

Through long years of tremendous adventure,
  Comes the whisper of whispering days,
Through long years of heartbreaking adventure,
  I look back on glory and haze,
Through long years of too noisy adventure, 5
  I look back on delicate brows,
Through long years of unstinted adventure
  On fruits and intimate flowers.
"But these tremendous adventures
  Describe them for me," says the youth. 10
All I remember is further back,
  In the days of Green April and truth.

    1930-1931

MY NEW SINGER, SACAJAWEA

Red witch of wisdom, with this land set right
You will laugh loud with our American day.
And every sour-face shall droop low her head,
Her grove of shadows made your house of play.

Therefore, my Wildwood, laugh indeed, grow wise   5
With summoning shoutings of the wilderness.
Masquerade the more as cub or fawn
Sunburned and swift in that soft buckskin dress.

Sing loud the rhymes where thickset boughs are books.
My Indian clears all twilight when she roams,   10
Her voice comes down from where a red cloud foams,
Laughter, like starlight, finds ten million homes.

Now I shall be the prisoner of my song
Written to you, from my own cut heart's core—
And prisoner of your spell that keeps me strong   15
Rhymes you write from the old redskin lore.
And I shall be the prisoner of your song,
The voice of you, from the Pacific shore,
Vast memories at every wigwam door.

But you shall make, and sing alone and long   20
New lyrics, far from mine, I will adore.
Lay on my grave your whip, leave there a thong,
I shall live briefly, you shall blossom long.
And you shall not be prisoner of my song
But free as any redbird, shore to shore.   25

    April 1931

TIME GIVES ME STRENGTH EACH HOUR

Last night I heard the locust lift a funny song of love,
    I watched the first leaves fall.
I heard the tree-toad ratify the whippoorwill above,
    I saw a ghost-moon crawl.
Gilt butterflies in sun-suits near Dog Dugan lie;   5
    We laugh at no man's grief.
Here little spites have gone for good, and tiny worries
    die;
    We watch the aspen leaf.

All little blossoms sigh today, and no heart is awry;
    I cannot fight for power.   10
They sigh for true-love blue-grass tops, and ivy, bending
    nigh.
    Time gives me strength each hour!
Hurrah for the cold seas, the young trees, the bumblebees!

    Summer, 1931

/811.52L749P>C1>V2/

DATE DUE